THE SUPERPOWERS AND THEIR
SPHERES OF INFLUENCE

TABLES

INTRODUCTION

In any classification of the world, we usually find such typologies as the 'haves' and the 'have-nots', the 'developed' or the 'developing' countries. Between the 'Free' and the 'Communist' world, between 'East' and 'West', we generally speak of another category, the 'Third World' or *Tiers Monde,* a term that encompasses the continents of Africa, Asia and Latin America. Furthermore, when assessing the international system, attention is usually focused on the major powers and the non-aligned countries of the 'Third World. However, little notice is paid to Latin America and Eastern Europe in the analysis of world politics. Most studies dealing with these regions have treated them as isolated phenomena. One of the reasons might well be the relatively unimportant role of these two subsystems in the international arena. It is the aim of this work to analyse the position of Latin America and Eastern Europe, showing how they are bound by the restrictive policies of the superpowers. The intention is to give a brief descriptive outline of historical developments leading to the present situation, and to present a comparative analysis of the relationships between the superpowers, their ability to influence and the degree of their penetration into the two subsystems. The purpose is to establish general principles of behaviour formalised into an hypothesis which should contribute to the clarification of an important phenomenon of the international system, involving nearly a quarter of the members of the world community of nations.

The book is concerned with the analysis of the role of two units or subsystems in the world system. Subsystems (often called subordinate systems) are usually delineated geographically, proximity being the important element; however, another factor is also important: functional elements. Functional elements are based primarily on the points of interaction between states, and their importance varies with the intensity of the interactions; therefore, one needs to take into account such components as the social, economic, political, military and cultural relations of a system. One can find cases where countries belong geographically to a specific region, but as a result of the pattern and intensity of the relations of that country, are identified as belonging to an alternative subsystem, and may in fact be relatively isolated, in terms of interaction, from the subsystem to which they should belong on geographical criteria.

Eastern Europe and Latin America will be considered as the dependent subsystems of the USSR and the USA respectively. Almost instinctively the term 'sphere of influence' comes to mind and its definition in the historical context of a century ago still proves useful. A classic approach would be to consider them as 'regions as to which nations have agreed that one or more of them shall have exclusive liberty of action'.[1] Or, in terms more applicable to the bipolar reality of today: 'The term sphere of influence implies an engagement between two states that one of them will abstain from interfering or exercising influences within certain territories which as between the contracting parties are reserved for the operation of the other'.[2]

In the practical cases to which the term was applied (China, Ethiopa), the powers sought for absolute control for all practical purposes but without any formal claim for suzerainty. Their political relation with the local authorities was legally an equal partnership, and the control was even less institutionalised than in the cases of protectorates. Commercial, industrial or strategic interests were the major driving forces behind the concept. At a later stage of colonisation, when most of the geographic areas of the world were already distributed, the approach towards non-European areas with independent rulers was to introduce 'spheres of influence' granted by a more *de facto* recognition than in other previous cases. Furthermore, the new doctrines of the 'nation-state' and 'self-determination' were becoming widespread, and the United States particularly, as a former emancipated colony, could not but disapprove of the more *de jure* types of foreign domination.

In the post-war situation it is possible to retain for analysis of the two subsystems which concern us, the three basic elements which characterised a 'sphere of influence': (1) declared interest of a power to achieve such a dominating status; (2) recognition of this claim by other important members of the world community; (3) acquiescence of the local regimes or their resignation to a condition of dependency. Still, the present significance of such a term as 'sphere of influence' in a very different international system requires a slight change in the wording; therefore the adoption of the term 'sphere of direct influence' is suggested, as this implies an acknowledgement of the relevant differences, for the superpowers' influence is felt today in almost every part of the world. In addition, while the term 'sphere of influence' suggested that a place was *less* subjected to the powers than other types of more formal domination (colonies, protectorates), with the process of emancipation, we find today that the 'spheres of direct influence' of the superpowers have become characterised by a *higher* dependence on them than other regions. The use of the word 'direct' also implies geographical proximity; states that are not detached from the power, as in the case of the two spheres of this study. Finally, although the 'spheres of direct influence' are one per superpower and an eventual change from a bipolar to a different total international system could be accompanied by a proportional increase in the number of 'spheres', the present particularities should be kept in mind.

A 'sphere of direct influence' can be best described then, as a geographic region characterised by the high penetration of one superpower to the exclusion of other powers and particularly of the rival superpower. The subject as a phenomenon has developed chiefly since the end of the Second World War, but the conclusions are more valid if limited to the period of 'peaceful coexistence' (from the Twentieth Communist Party Congress in the Soviet Union, 1956 to the present). The beginnings of the cold war as a basis for international balance, along with the accompanying tensions, made it difficult to establish a stabler general model for the relations between East and West. These were defined in the period of peaceful coexistence as the politics that

> could facilitate the establishment of certain international guarantees that would greatly diminish the danger of war; and it also implied the *mutual recognition* [emphasis added] that each side had certain claims, interests and privileges that the other would respect and that if these were not respected, the injured party would bring down the curtain of peaceful coexistence.[3]

In the spirit of *detente,* the principle of peaceful coexistence has been further developed. A normalisation of relations and an acceptance of agreed rules of action brings about a wider recognition by both superpowers of the benefits of the *status quo* and this is extremely significant for the safeguarding and maintenance of 'spheres of direct influence'. Short-term processes often seem to point out trends which contradict the specific description of Eastern Europe and Latin America as 'spheres of direct influence' of the superpowers. However, in a broader historical perspective, these fluctuations do not change the basic 'prison' condition of the greater number of countries in these two regions.

This study is presented in two parts: the first part attempts to provide several explanations for the behaviour of the states in the spheres of direct influence. Its explanatory and often descriptive character aims at elucidating the characteristics that make countries in the two areas different from others in the rest of the world. The second part deals with the options facing superpower behaviour towards these two regions and is an evaluation of their long-term policy.

In the first part, the analysis is conducted on three levels: the international system, the subsystems and the individual states. The behaviour of the countries in Eastern Europe and Latin America is explained according to a number of variables. First, there are the characteristics of the international system, stressing the role played by the two major powers dominant in those areas. The varying levels of dominance are investigated; differences are acknowledged but similarities are close enough to make the comparison relevant. In this context, it is important to study the extent to which their penetration is accepted, not only by the rival superpower, but by other powers and subsystems, e.g. Western Europe, China, Japan or the Neutralist bloc.

Second, there are particular attributes of the spheres of direct influence as subsystems. A preliminary argument discusses the plausibility of considering them as separate and single units in the international system. In other words, the intrinsic relationships of the countries in each region classify them as cohesive units. The characteristics of both subsystems can be better understood by drawing parallels and noting the differences between the internal structure of the Eastern European and Latin American regions, and by discovering the differences between subsystems which are often considered to be closely related, i.e. Latin America with Afro-Asia and Eastern Europe with Western Europe. This will ultimately show the internal validity of the comparative operational framework of this research on a regional level, underlined by the external differentiation from other subsystems.

On a third level, we shall take as a basis for analysis (using a macroanalytic approach), the foreign policies of the individual countries, dealing with the vulnerability of small countries to intervention or domination by great powers. The analysis concentrates on explaining the independence of countries in the sphere of influence that project themselves as apparent exceptions, i.e. the cases of Cuba and Peru in Latin America, and Yugoslavia, Albania and Romania in Eastern Europe. Allende's Chile will be briefly mentioned as a *post mortem* case showing the impermanence of such exceptions. Countries in both areas are regarded as victims of the direct control of the superpowers. The emphasis given to the influence of the external setting on the foreign policy formulation of Latin American or East European countries does not deny the relative importance of domestic variables; the existence of exceptions to the rule of total dependence on the superpowers shows the significance of the internal political setting. What greatly restricts the freedom of action of the decision-making elite is not necessarily their weakness in the internal setting, but the absence of external opposition to the superpowers' hegemony. Thus macro-analysis is largely justified because in most cases external variables are of first importance in explaining the role of individual countries in the spheres of direct influence.[4] The few exceptional states, in both subsystems, with a non-conformist attitude towards the superpower are all incorporated in this study, in an attempt to provide statements on the common underlying principles.

The second part of the book is aimed at providing a more coherent and integrated picture. It evaluates superpowers' policies over long periods of time, considering the major possible alternative approaches towards the spheres of direct influence as well as the resulting choice and policy implementation. On a comparative basis, two sets of options are discussed: the superpowers' policy in their own sphere of influence (United States in Latin America and Soviet Union in Eastern Europe), and their policy in the rival's sphere (United States in Eastern Europe and Soviet Union in Latin America).

Major research questions arose from the formulation of the main theme: is there any relationship between the modality of superpower behaviour and the characteristics of the sphere of direct influence? What is the effect of the internal political structure of the superpower and the type of control it exercises on the countries located in the sphere of direct influence? To what extent is there an acquiescence or acceptance by the rival superpower and other powers of the *de facto* existence of a sphere of direct influence? What effect does political multipolarity produce on the superpowers sphere of direct influence? What conditions encourage member countries of a sphere of direct influence to become more independent of superpower rule than other states in the same region? How far can differences in the internal structure of the spheres of direct influence determine the attitude of the countries of the region towards the dominating superpower? What is the effect of *detente* on the attitude of the superpowers towards both their own and their rival's spheres of direct influence?

This study suggests some of the answers to those questions. In each chapter, working hypotheses accompany the elaboration of the subject. Some of the answers can already be listed as follows:

1. Countries with similar power elements will differ in position in the international system according to their location in different subsystems. Countries in spheres of direct influence tend generally to be at a lower power level in the international system than similar countries in other subsystems.
2. The attitude of the superpower towards a country in its sphere tends generally to be more rigid than its attitude toward countries outside this region.
3. The different behaviour of superpowers in their respective spheres is related to their internal political structure and ideology.
4. The effects of political multipolarity are less felt in the spheres of direct influence of the superpower than in other parts of the world.
5. External variables are generally more powerful than domestic variables in explaining the foreign policy behaviour of a country in a sphere of direct influence.

Briefly, the concluding chapter enumerates the propositions which can be substantially supported. It also discusses possible effects of an evolving international system on the concept of spheres of direct influence. Other regions could become spheres of influence of future superpowers, and the external validity of the characteristics defined in the analysis of the existing two spheres has to be investigated.

This book is based on a series of articles which dealt with the subject in more general terms.[5] In this work, I hope to present a systematic enquiry into the role and position of Latin America and Eastern Europe in the world system. But one serious obstacle to such a study is that most policy-makers of both superpowers would reject, from a normative angle, the possiblity of such a comparison. Indeed, few Communists or 'free world' supporters would tolerate any analogy between the foreign policies of two such ideologically opposed systems. Extreme partisans of both camps reach the point of absurdity by denying the possibility of a comparison, on the grounds that the policies of the superpowers are not *identical* and are therefore incomparable. In any comparison different units can be measured by the same scale, as the component elements are similar, but in different proportions or degrees of intensity. In this way two states can be compared, especially two states of more or less the same magnitude such as the Soviet Union and the United States. It can be shown that their foreign policies present a number of similarities and differences, and it is these which are being examined in the present work. It will refer not only to the 'objective' reality as appraised by the author, but also as perceived by the protagonists themselves in the two regions.

In this respect, it would also be fair to mention the difficulties experienced in maintaining an affective neutrality towards the subject of investigation. I have long been preoccupied with the superpower domination in their spheres of influence and considered drawing some sort of parallel. On my visits to Latin America and Eastern Europe, I encountered criticism of the paramount superpower yet very little awareness of the restrictions imposed by the rival superpower in other regions. It is to these perceptive critics in Latin America and Eastern Europe to whom I would like to dedicate this book.

The major task undertaken here is focusing on the analysis of the interaction of the two regions and the superpowers. The present enquiry mainly draws upon secondary sources to make inferences about foreign policy behaviour. Primary sources are used to supplement secondary sources or when directly relevant to the proposed hypothesis.

Finally, although the development of the subject follows the lines of theory building, it is hoped that the language employed will combine clarity and precise terminology with the avoidance of repetition. I wish to express my gratitude to all those who have helped me in the preparation of the present text, especially Mr Louis Mercier Vega, a notable expert in Latin American affairs, Professor Raymond Tanter of The University of Michigan, for his advice and critical evaluation, Dr Galia Golan of the Hebrew University, Professor Janice Stein of McGill University, my friend and assistant Gaby Heichal, for her devotion in the search of more and more data and to the Central Research Fund of the Hebrew University which generous grants made this study possible.

NOTES

1. *Encyclopaedia Britannica*, vol. XXV/2, 11th edn (Cambridge University Press, Cambridge, 1910-1911), p. 648.
2. Ibid., (quoting Ilbert, Governor of India, p. 376).
3. J.F. Brown, *The New Eastern Europe*, Praeger, New York 1966, p. 21.
4. In the Eastern European context, only in cases of absence of a clear and resolute Soviet stand: 'domestic demands in the form of economic performance goals, historical inhibitions, threats to political legitimacy, and commitment to foreign policy principles may interact with third party initiatives to produce a measure of Eastern European foreign policy autonomy better characterised as promotive or preservative than acquiescent.'
   ' William Clark Potter, *Continuity and Change in the Foreign Relations of the Warsaw Pact States, 1948-1973: A Study of National Adaptation to Internal and External Demands*, (dissertation, University of Michigan, 1976), p. 235.
5. Edy Kaufman, 'A Comparative Analysis of the Foreign Policies of the

United States and the Soviet Union in Latin America and Eastern Europe',
Co-existence, vol. VIII (MacLehose, Glasgow, 1971), pp. 123-38; 'America
Latina en el Juego Internacional', *Aportes,* No. 24, (Paris, April 1972),
pp. 137-62, and 'Amerika Halatinit Bamaarechet Habeinleumit' (in Hebrew),
International Problems, vol. X, No. 1-2(9), June 1970, pp. 7-18.

1 EXTERNAL VARIABLES: THE INTERNATIONAL SYSTEM AND THE SUPERPOWERS

1 Analysis of the International System

In analysing the relative strength of the two superpowers, it is necessary to discuss the power balance. It is convenient to begin with two polarised views on the subject.

George Liska[1] maintains that a *Pax Americana* exists — a position justified by the following points, which include Liska's own arguments:

1. The US has a nuclear superiority over the USSR. This is not just a theoretical evaluation, but is validated to a certain extent by Soviet efforts to avoid a confrontation with the US, once during the Cuban Missile Crisis, and later during the October 1973 Middle East War.
2. In spite of Soviet expansionist ambitions, with the exception of Cuba, not a single non-contiguous country has affiliated itself politically with the Communist Bloc since the beginning of the cold war.
3. The Communist Bloc has not progressed toward its 'inevitable' world domination. In fact, as a result of the Chinese opposition to Soviet hegemony, the Kremlin's supremacy in the Communist Bloc has been weakened, reducing the Soviet position in the international arena.
4. In potential conflict situations between East and West in which conventional military force has been used, the Soviet Union has refrained from directly using its own forces outside the East European region. The United States, on the other hand, did not place such a limitation upon itself in any continent. Furthermore, with the maintenance of bases in over 40 countries, the military power of the United States is clearly superior.
5. The geo-political position of the United States is more favourable than that of the Soviet Union, as a result of its geographical separation from its adversaries and competitors. The Soviet Union does not enjoy such a situation; it is faced by countries who are members of a potentially hostile alliance, and by China (a potential competitor within its own sphere — the Communist Bloc).
6. The level of American economic development permits the US to

maintain both a high standard of living for its inhabitants and a wide range of foreign aid programmes. Furthermore, even the Soviet Union and the Communist Bloc have found themselves dependent on the need for transactions with the United States.

7. The totalitarian governmental system has not succeeded in creating a wide consensus within the USSR. On the contrary, the lack of popularity of the government limits its scope of action in such fields as foreign policy; and in the long run could weaken it and cause a change in regime.

8. The influence of 'American culture' can be found all over the world even in countries under Communist rule. English is the most widely spoken language and the 'American Way of Life' is imitated and regarded as a symbol of development.

The theory of the absolute primacy of the USA is not widely supported and some foresee a continual relative increase in Soviet power. This is a dynamic process, and can be seen as a transition from *Pax Americana* to *Pax Sovietica*:[2]

1. The rate of growth of Soviet potential and real power indicates that it will eventually surpass US levels in certain fields, and the ultimate achievement of this change in power levels is only a matter of time.

2. This process is particularly important in the field of nuclear technology, as Pentagon sources have forecast that within ten years the USSR could attain a clear nuclear superiority.[3]

3. With the passing of time the US is becoming increasingly isolated in the international arena, as can be witnessed at the UN. The situation in the 1970s has radically changed from that of the 1950s. Today Washington cannot guarantee a majority on any subject, irrespective of how important it is to her interests.

4. An increasing number of Third World countries support the Communist Bloc on international issues, and are adopting a form of socialism. Today one can refer to Arab socialism' in Iraq and Syria, and 'African socialism' in Mali and Guinea, for example.

5. In spite of all the internal differences within the Communist Bloc, not one of those countries has defected to the capitalist system. They still maintain a common base and basic unity — with the major enemy remaining without exception the capitalist system.

6. The centralised system of the Soviet Union increases flexibility and scope in decision-making, allowing the USSR to take risks in both foreign policy formulation and action. The United States is limited

by the formal division of power, with diffuse groupings of organs and interests limiting and influencing foreign policy. This results in a hesitant and less effective policy, usually the result of a process of compromise.

7. Imperialism as a political system is epitomised by, and developed as a result of, capitalism. The contradictions between the various capitalist powers and the internal class struggle, intensified by the inherent faults of the exploitive system, will lead to the collapse of the US as a world power.

Many of these arguments are undoubtedly biased, and in some cases their extremism cancels them out; yet by combining the two opposing views and the points put forward, one reaches the conclusion that in reality neither superpower possesses significant 'power supremacy' over the other. The US may have, in absolute terms, a certain power advantage, but when one takes into account modern nuclear weapon systems and their destructive capabilities, such a small advantage is of negligible importance.

However, having a relative power advantage over the USSR places the US in a position of responsibility; the need to maintain a policy of restraint and moderation, and to protect itself from any 'irrational' action, or from provoking the other side into such a course. The Cuban Missile Crisis was an example of such a policy by the USA, when they defused the explosive situation by reverting to traditional and conventional means, i.e. naval blockade.

Henry A. Kissinger defined the present system as one with a military bipolarity but showing a political multipolarity.[4] Kissinger considers that the basis of this is the excess strength of the superpowers rather than their nuclear supremacy. The basic strategy of both is one of deterrence, restricting the use of nuclear weapons; and this mutual impotency enables the secondary powers to compete at a more general level of international politics.

In the world as a whole, the vacuum left by the retreating colonial powers, i.e. France, Britain, Belgium, Holland, etc. have paved the way for a new policy of neo-colonialism by the same countries, with the added presence and penetration of the superpowers: the United States, the Soviet Union and China. Today this is the situation for most of Afro-Asia, with the exception of those areas still under direct colonial rule — phenomenon disappearing with the independence of former Portuguese colonies in Africa. It is in this area of the world that secondary powers play a political role as important as that of the

superpowers: France in some Francophone African countries; Great
Britain in some of the Commonwealth countries, particularly Australia,
New Zealand and the ex-protectorates; China in Vietnam and North
Korea, etc. This new multipolar reality also allows smaller and developing countries to exercise a manipulative policy that enables them to
benefit from the competition of the major powers. However, this
would not be the case in the countries in the two areas adjacent to the
superpowers. No direct impact from evolving world politics has been
noted nor any radical alteration in their status. The possibilities of
change in both internal regime and/or international policy orientation
are far greater in Afro-Asian countries than in Eastern Europe or Latin
America (e.g. the sudden shifts of power in Ghana, Sudan, Cambodia,
Indonesia, Uganda, etc.). In other words, the contemporary international system bears a striking resemblance to what Kaplan describes
as a 'very loose bipolar system',[5] categorised by the uncommitted Third
World nations playing an important and noticeably independent role in
world politics. However, the Eastern European and Latin American
countries have not yet reached such a stage and remain far from liber-
ating themselves from a 'tight bipolar system'.[6]

It is this bipolar framework that we will analyse: the parallelism
between the policies of the USA and the USSR in the two subsystems.
There is also the possibility of considering the international system as a
tripolar one, in which Communist China is the third superpower. However, most experts in this field consider it premature to classify China
as a superpower; and as in the geographical area in which we are concerned the Chinese presence is minimal, the tripolar theory is as yet of
little relevance. The role of Peking in Eastern Europe and Latin
America will be investigated at a later stage.

2 Bipolar Legitimation

A most striking illustration of the validity of the bipolar classification
and an indication of the rigour with which it can still be applied is the
relative ease with which military intervention is carried out within the
spheres of influence. The aid extended by the United States to the
invasions against the leftist regimes in Guatemala in 1954 and Cuba in
1961 did not provoke a strong reaction from the USSR. The exceptional Soviet political advanture introducing missiles to Cuba in 1962,
ended with their removal and shame-faced return to the *status quo*. Yet
when the United States invaded Santo Domingo in 1965, with troops
under the American flag, the Kremlin restricted itself to a verbal protest. Considering the strong reaction of many Latin American states,

she could not but join the demand for a condemnation of the US action
in the Security Council of the UN, which could be considered as one of
the weakest possible responses available to the Soviet Union.

It is still premature to predict with any certainty whether there is a
trend at present to avoid provocative matters connected with the control of the spheres of influence of the rival superpower. The relative
passivity with which the United States reacted to the invasion of
Czechoslovakia in 1968 should be noted here: the 1956 invasion to
Hungary provoked a greater US response reflected in an attempt to obtain international condemnation at the UN. On the other hand, the
Soviet reaction to the issue of American intervention in Allende's Chile
was extremely mild. Interestingly in both the Santo Domingo and
Prague crises, in spite of the accusations against them, the overthrown
regimes showed no signs of a complete rebellion against their respective
systems, seeming concerned only with attempts of reform; but the
adjacent superpowers reacted in an extreme way, and without fear of
outside involvement.

A reluctance to challenge in deeds these acts of the rival superpower
differs totally from the extreme verbal condemnation, both making
similar demands for the abolition of the subjugated status of the
opposing dependent countries. The Congress of the United States, for
example, adopted the 'Resolution of Captive Nations', in which the
'imperialist policy of Communist Russia' was condemned; it listed the
countries considered to be victims of Soviet aggression, suffering from
the deprivation of national independence: 'Poland, Hungary, Lithuania,
Ukraine, Czechoslovakia, Latvia, Estonia, White Ruthenia, Romania,
East Germany, Bulgaria, Mainland China, Armenia, Azerbaijan, Georgia,
North Korea, Albania, Idel-Ural, Cossackia, Turkestan, North Vietnam
and others.' The Soviet Union, on its side, denounced American imperialism and 'Yankee exploitation' of the 20 Latin American countries:

> Our relations with Latin American countries have likewise made
> progress in the period under review, despite the barriers artificially
> raised by internal reactions and the US imperialists. The heroic
> people of Cuba, who have broken down those barriers, are estab-
> lishing co-operation on an equal footing with other countries. And
> even though the US imperialists stop at nothing – not even at over-
> throwing lawful governments – to prevent Latin American countries
> from pursuing an independent policy, events will nevertheless take
> their own course.[7]

We may, however, find a *de facto* recognition by each of the superiority of its rival in the respective sphere of influence, with both foregoing the fulfilment of declared aims of freeing the 'captive' regimes in order to maintain world peace. This was expressed by the then Secretary of State Dean Rusk when he said:

> Our capacity to influence events and trends within the Communist world is very limited. But, it is *our policy to do what we can* [italics added] to encourage evolution in the Communist world towards national independence and open societies.[8]

Helmut Sonnenfeld, Dr Kissinger's adviser on Communist affairs, provides an updated version based on the same principle, which straightforwardness provoked controversy among American politicians. The argument considers that the Soviet Union's dominance in Eastern Europe is due mainly to its military power. Sooner or later more 'popular democracies' would try to escape such a suffocating embrace.

> This inorganic, unnatural relationship is a far greater danger to world peace than the conflict between East and West . . . So our policy must be a policy of responding to the clearly visible aspirations in Eastern Europe for a more autonomous existence within the context of a strong Soviet geo-political influence.[9]

The Soviet Union, on its side says that 'the peoples fighting for their liberation from the imperialist colonial yoke have to be supported and helped.' The peoples who have already won their political independence but are economically dependent (which would include Latin America) have to be assisted so that they may gain strength, and firmly carry out a policy of promoting peace.

> All this implies that we must expose the ulcers of imperialism, its vices, still more vigorously. To prevent a war, including a local one because it may develop into a world war, every people should in its own country bring pressure to bear on the government and make it observe the principles of the peaceful coexistence of countries with different social systems.[10]

This shows to what extent the two superpowers are willing to sacrifice the realisation of their respective subordinate goals — the liberation of countries oppressed by their ideological opponent — for the mainten-

ance of world peace. It is perceived by the policy-makers of both superpowers as being in their national interest to avoid an inbalance in the
global system that might endanger world peace, and this places limits on
their mutual ambitions. In nearly all cases of potential conflict since
the Second World War between the United States and the Soviet Union,
they have both had to satisfy themselves with a compromise solution;
in many cases, after a confrontation at the level of conventional weapons; in others after skirmishes; and in others only after a period of
high tension in their diplomatic relations. In chronic conflicts persisting
for years, e.g. the Middle East, there seems to be a mutual agreement to
prevent an escalation of the situation to a stage that might result in the
direct involvement of American or Soviet military forces.

The relationship of the superpowers towards each other's area of
direct influence undoubtedly represents the most salient case of acceptance of the *status quo*. Both the spheres have gone quite a long way
towards nuclear disarmament, with the compliance of the superpowers.
Excluding the 'adventurist' incident of the Russian misiles in Cuba, no
nuclear weapons are normally attached to these regions. In Latin
America, a Treaty for the Prohibition of Nuclear Weapons for the continent was signed in 1967. Although three major countries, including
Argentina and Brazil, have announced their intention to detonate
'peaceful' nuclear explosives, 'nevertheless, twenty Latin American
states have formally renounced nuclear weapons and consequently
enjoy the pledge of four of the five nuclear weapon states "not to use
or threaten to use" nuclear weapons against their territory'.[11]

Within Eastern Europe there is no nuclear strategic danger — a product of the attitude of the Eastern European countries themselves, as
shown by their criticism of the French nuclear plans, by the Rapacki
proposals for neutralisation of nuclear weapons from Central Europe
and by Soviet reluctance to introduce such weaponry into that zone.

It is hard to establish that a mutual agreement does exist reciprocally
legitimising the rule of the rival superpowers in their respective sphere
of influence. However, it seems most probable that an understanding
does exist to a certain degree. Needless to say, no official documentary
evidence can be provided, but from a juridical point of view it could be
argued that when the Soviet Union joined the League of Nations and
accepted without reservation the basic principles embodied in its
Charter, it implicitly accepted the Monroe Doctrine as a 'regional
understanding'. The meaning of this 'understanding' should have been
perfectly clear at that time to the Soviet Union, as the Doctrine had
been used so often by North America to justify military intervention in

the Central American countries.[12]

Western recognition of the Soviet hegemony in Eastern Europe was forthcoming, as was later shown in the post-war meetings between the Soviet, American and British leaders. This legitimation has been further endorsed by the participation of the United States in the Helsinki European Summit Meeting of 1975, and its acceptance of the clause concerning the inviolability of the frontiers of all European States. The boundaries imposed in Eastern Europe and the Baltic nations by the Soviet Union were thereby confirmed. The pragmatic attitude of Secretary of State Kissinger in accepting the inviolability clause was considered by Senator Henry M. Jackson to be a 'retreat from a crucial point of principle, the right of self-determination of the Baltic and Eastern European States'.[13] Another fact that confirmed this view was the United States' acquiescence in the acceptance of two Russian states — Belorussia and Ukrania — into the UN as full members in order to counterbalance the dominating weight of the 'Western bloc' in the organisation.[14] This 'gentlemen's agreement' included a clause that the Soviet Union would select the country to represent Eastern Europe in the Security Council. Soviet delegate Vyshinsky bitterly opposed the election of Yugoslavia as a Security Council member in 1949 — the year of the fierce Stalin-Tito controversy — claiming that the United States had violated the agreement.[15]

While no text exists confirming official recognition of spheres of influence, we can identify the existing areas of agreement through an eliminative process. In recent years, at the Soviet-American Summit Conferences, emphasis has been placed on certain areas of agreement, i.e. the limitation of nuclear weapon systems, the Non-proliferation Treaty, technological and trade relations, etc. In areas where disagreement continues to exist and both sides for a variety of reasons are interested in publicising it (for clients, public opinion, internal or other reasons), wide publicity is received because the topic has been discussed without agreement (i.e. Vietnam, the Middle East). There are also those subjects that are apparently not discussed at all, or at least not reported as being discussed, because they rank lower in the superpowers' list of priorities. Our subject belongs in this category — neither Latin America nor Eastern Europe are brought up on the agendas. While other problems are regarded by the superpowers as being crucial and are discussed, the lot of the 'satellites' and periphery countries is left untouched. This legitimation by omission, by tacit acceptance, or by indirect compliance with the rigid doctrines of the superpowers' right to protect their spheres of direct influence, is a primary requirement for the maintenance of quasi-absolute rule and also discourages many secondary powers from adopting a challenging attitude – as we shall see in the following chapters.

3 The Soviet Union and the United States in Latin America and Eastern Europe: Similarities, Differences and Margins of Political Security

Similarities

In the other regions of the world, the declared foreign policy of either superpower is basically aimed at preventing the region from falling under the influence and control of the rival power: in Latin America and Eastern Europe the superpowers' aim is to maintain direct control of those regions to the exclusion of all other powers.

The interest of the two giants in their neighbouring territories has historical precedents. Tsarist Russia's special interest in the Balkans was indicated particularly by her need for an outlet to the Mediterranean Sea. This interest was demonstrated by Russia's continuous rivalry with the Austro-Hungarian Empire during the second half of the nineteenth century, for hegemony over Bulgaria, Serbia and Romania. Russia was also involved in several wars as a result of her ambitions in regard to Poland and her western border. Motives such as pan-Slavism were used by the Tsar as a justification for such an expansionist policy.

At the beginning of the nineteenth century the United States was voicing a growing interest in Latin America. Jefferson wrote, in 1823, 'I frankly confess that I have been of the opinion that Cuba would be the most interesting addition to be made to our system of the States.'[16] President Grant proposed to the Senate in 1870 the annexation of the Dominican Republic; his proposal was dismissed due to the excessive cost of the acquisition.[17]

> In the late nineteenth and early twentieth centuries, like today, the United States did not usually exercise direct political control over Latin America (particularly Central America) but rather exercised considerable political influence. It intervened militarily often enough to establish that it would and could take control if the weaker countries did not go along with major U.S. desires, but it did not find direct political control necessary for any length of time.[18]

Tsarist Russia aspired, less successfully, to achieve a similar status in Eastern Europe. The United States and the Soviet Union eventually achieved more absolute dominance over their respective zones of influence in different historical periods, following the collapse of the former powers in the respective areas, i.e. Spain and Portugal in the Western Hemisphere, and Germany in Europe. 'As the power of one state increases (relative to the power of other states) it tends to attract to itself those weaker states that were formerly "drawn" to other Powers.'[19] Obviously, in both cases the USA and the USSR could not afford to create outright colonies, not only because the process of decolonisation was already started, but since it was unacceptable to their respective ideological beliefs. The attitude of the superpowers towards the countries under their control is described by Nelson Rockefeller[20] as being, in the case of the USA and Latin America, one of a 'special' relationship. Vague as the term may be, it establishes that such countries are not treated in the same way as the rest of the world. In a way, the fact that they are the last world powers to develop an expansionist capability has meant that the countries of Latin America escaped the status of colonies, but have had to submit to being spheres of influence of the superpowers. Traditionally, the basic reasons for superpower interest in neighbouring countries were economic and geo-political. Economically these areas were sources for raw materials, with the contiguous superpower becoming the major economic trading partner. Since these possessions are relatively secure, greater effort is displayed to promote the superpower's economic presence in other continents.

In the ten years up to 1961, the United States granted Yugoslavia, two billion dollars, more than the total amount granted to all of Latin America during the same period. The Soviet Union has even pressured its East European satellites to become suppliers and conveyors of economic, military and technical aid to the countries of the Third World, and thereby part of its exploitation is getting them to pay for Soviet expansion elsewhere. After such traumatic crises as the Cuban Revolution and the 'Spring' revolt in Prague, 1968, the superpowers decided to increase their aid to the satellite countries in order to forestall similar situations arising from dissatisfaction over economic exploitation by the superpower. According to Walters, total Soviet economic aid to Communist countries in Eastern Europe from 1945 to 1966 amounts to $4.1 billion, but this cipher should be viewed in the light of an estimated fifteen to twenty billion extracted from those countries in the decade following World War II.[21] An even greater disproportion between foreign aid and economic exploitation is to be found in the relationship between the United States and Latin America.[22]

Recently, the United States has been encouraging the more devel-

oped countries of Latin America to provide technical aid to the less
developed ones — Brazil and Mexico in particular have provided such
aid. Ecuador — a nationalist military regime, recently in conflict with
the US — continued to receive aid indirectly via other Latin American
countries, while direct assistance was frozen for political reasons. This
was done so that Ecuador would not seek aid from another power. The
Soviet Union carried out a similar exercise on breaking off relations
with Albania in 1961, when it permitted its 'satellites' to continue trade
relations.

There is a diminishing strategic importance attached to control of
vast territories, as a result of the nuclear capabilities of the new ICBM;
nevertheless it remains a basic principle for both the USA and the
USSR to maintain direct control over their respective areas.[23] In
reality, the 'balance of terror', a consequence of the over-kill capabilities of nuclear weapons, has justified the retention of large conventional
forces, well equipped and spread over as wide an area as possible. This
is demonstrated by the fact that both superpowers maintain a widely
spread network of military bases and forces on foreign soil. Eastern
Europe and Latin America both represent a sort of a buffer zone for
removing any war far from the superpower frontiers. On the other
hand, the stationing of troops in adjacent countries, and/or the maintaining of control over the armed forces of those countries, is a method
of guaranteeing the continuity of governments and regimes loyal to the
superpower. The geo-political importance to the superpowers of maintaining control, for strategic reasons, of adjacent areas can be demonstrated by the US reaction to the vulnerability of its missiles in Cuba.
The US has always been more liable to intervene in Central America
than in South America on strategic grounds; and the Caribbean Sea is
considered more *mare nostrum* than the South Atlantic.[24] Similarly,
the Soviet Union is more sensitive to the three neighbouring states in
the north-east European zone (Poland, East Germany and Czechoslovakia), than to the Southern Balkans, with Hungary occupying an
intermediary position.[25]

The traditional policy, which always took into consideration the geo-
political aspects, is today expanded to include the necessity of blocs
containing 'satellites' or 'allied' countries: it is the existence of a periphery in the blocs which brings into prominence the leadership role and
the central status of the superpowers. In both cases, the almost automatic support of the line taken by the USSR or the US emphasises the
existence of two blocs in international politics; the East and the West.
Furthermore, it was always a condition of acceptance as a world power,

that one maintained a position of supremacy in one's own region of the world, and this is a further inducement to the superpowers to subjugate their nearest subsystems. All the countries located in the two spheres of influence have suffered from penetration by the superpowers to varying degrees. In some cases, the intervention has been permanent with annexation being the final solution. The Soviet Union annexed the Baltic Republics, while the US did the same in Puerto Rico and Panama's Canal Zone.[26] In other instances only a partial annexation of territories resulted, as when parts of Mexico were added to the USA, and similarly when Rumanian and Polish territories were taken by the USSR. Sometimes, military intervention is only of a temporary character. Haiti, Cuba, Dominican Republic, Nicaragua and Panama were occupied for varying periods of time by North American troops, nearly all of Eastern Europe was occupied by the Red Army when World War II ended.

After the popular democracies were established in Eastern Europe the USSR tried, in all cases, to justify intervention on ideological grounds; that is, the necessity to prevent a 'reactionary counterplot' (as in Hungary and Czechoslovakia), or because of the danger of 'an imperialist penetration' within the Socialist countries. Lately, it has attempted to make such acts appear as a joint enterprise by all the socialist countries, and not as unilateral aggression perpetrated by Soviet forces. Thereby the USSR justifies its actions on ideological grounds, actions which are normally recognised as being a violation of the independence of a sovereign state.

American intervention during the time preceding the cold war had had a more open character. Military intervention in Latin America took place without feeling any need to provide arguments to convince the world or other Latin American countries of the rightness of the action. In the spirit of this era, expansion being legitimate, it was mostly considered sufficient to be 'safeguarding American property', or 'protecting the lives of American citizens' living in a specific country or just simply 'to bring order to the chaos resulting from the inability of the authorities to govern'.

With the political evolution following the Second World War, and with the rapid increase in the number of new states, traditional imperialistic methods and policy were now being attacked. As a result, the United States was forced to produce justifications for its intervention in Latin America. Since 1954, year of the Guatemalan invasion by a Guatemalan military contingent backed by the USA, the 'menace of communism' became a dependable argument on which to fall back. The condemnation of international communism as a 'subversive and foreign doctrine' was supported at that time by the majority of Latin American governments. This was achieved through the application of diplomatic pressure from Washington which aroused in the ruling elite the fear of possible popular rebellion, or the undermining of 'deviationist' regimes.

Washington too attempted to avoid its military actions appearing as organised and instigated exclusively by the US. During the Dominican crisis, in 1965, the idea of an 'inter-American peace force' to replace the American 'marines' was evolved. As in the invasion of Czechoslovakia in 1968, the role of the satellites remains largely symbolic, the bulk of military intervention being left to the superpower. On other occasions the superpowers did not limit themselves to straightforward condemnation of the opposing extreme (left or right) — in order to show themselves as 'moderates' they also criticised other extremes. Thus President Kennedy justified American policy towards revolutionary Cuba in terms of a struggle against all totalitarianism, whether of the right or the left, and in support of this position suspended all aid to Papa Doc's regime in Haiti. At the same time, Brezhnev included among the conspiratory groups within Czechoslovakia not only the 'Zionist' elements from the right, but also 'Trotskyists' of the extreme left.

Military intervention, by both sides, is usually followed by an appeal for unity amongst the allies of the intervening power. On most occasions the intervention is also followed by an ideological explanation, i.e. 'proletarian internationalism', 'the common struggle for socialism', 'the example given by the Western hemisphere through its liberty and democracy' or 'in defense of the Free World'. The great powers also use linguistic, cultural, historical and economic arguments, or geographical ties for their propaganda. Pan-slavic lines, typical of the tsarist period, have been further employed by the Soviets, particularly during the war against Nazi Germany. On the other hand, President Nixon said in reference to the relations with Latin America: 'This unique relationship is rooted in geography, in a common Western heritage and in a shared historical experience of independence born through revolution.'[27] The 'Brezhnev Doctrine' (called by Ulam the 'Soviet Monroe Doctrine'[28]), as applied to Czechoslovakia in 1968, was previously given wider legitimacy by the 'Sovereignty and International Duties of Socialist Countries'.[29] Similarly, the 'Johnson Doctrine' was ratified by the US Congress 'Selden Resolution' in 1965, reaffirming the decision of the President to intervene militarily in the Dominican Republic.[30] A further example of the similarity of behaviour between the superpowers was expressed by President Ford with remarkable frankness.[31]

The so-called 'Brezhnev' and 'Johnson' doctrines have certain common features. According to Brezhnev,

> ... when external and internal forces hostile to socialism try to turn the development of a given socialist country in the direction of a restoration of the capitalist system, when a threat arises to the cause of socialism in that country – a threat to the security of the socialist commonwealth as a whole – this is no longer merely a problem for that country's people, but a common problem – the concern of all socialist countries.[32]

President Johnson said:

> I understood that there was no time for talking, consulting or delay ... the American nations cannot, should not, and will not permit the establishment of another communist government in the Western hemisphere.[33]

While military conflict became characterised by a superpower confrontation with one of the 'satellite' states, intra-state wars within the sphere of influence tended to diminish,[34] due to the tight control exercised over the region.

Margins of Political Security

Today the use of such terms as the Soviet 'Iron Curtain' or the American 'Backyard' sound anachronistic. They recall the era of international tension, the 'Cold war', an era in which freedom of action by countries within spheres of direct influence was extremely limited. During the initial cold war period, political intolerance was evident within both systems: in the US, McCarthyism; and in the USSR, 'Zhdanovschina'. These phenomena had direct repercussions on the relations between the superpowers and their zones of influence. The Populist ex-President of Guatemala, Juan Jose Arevalo defines the Latin American parallel of McCarthyism as 'antikomunism':

> I write, with a K, this word, to distinguish it from communism, with a C. Communism, with a *C*, is the international current represented by the Communist Party, whose headquarters are in Moscow. Kommunism, with a K, is the political and social democratic current which pretends to defend the interests of the working masses, of the

poor, and of the exploited all over the world; or those who speak about sovereignty and nationalism, or those who dare to censure the United States.'[35]

The Soviet regime found its ideological 'dybuk' in 'revisionism'; Tito and what he represented, was attached on those grounds. Afterwards, during the period of John F. Kennedy and Nikita Krushchev – two leaders classified within their own countries as 'liberals', who followed moderate policies both in the internal and external settings – in apparent contradiction to their outward 'image', their respective governments intervened militarily in Hungary and Cuba.

In analysing the scope and range of the dependency relationship of the nations situated within the spheres of influence of the superpowers, a similar phenomenon becomes observable. One could speak of the existence of a *margin of political security*, which the great powers deem necessary to maintain, restricting the freedom of action of the governments within the adjacent regions. This 'margin' is not systematically expanded or constricted in relation to chronological lines, but it is a function of the changing internal and international situation: the guiding principle is to prevent the East European and Latin American countries escaping, and freeing themselves, from their dependency position.

The 'margin' can be seen as a function of four different factors: (1) the *global situation*, and the level of tensions existing in the relations between the two poles of the blocs, or within the multipolar political relations of the world system; (2) the *superpower internal characteristics*, the political regime at a specific time, the importance and role of the personality of the leaders, the regime's orientation in regard to internal affairs (ranging from conservative to reformist), and the economic and social situation within each country; (3) the *particular characteristics of the subjugated region*, and its possible reinforcement or the weakening of autonomistic drive; (4) on the *national level*, the strength and shape of the political forces supporting change in the relations with the superpower. Obviously, the situation of the Western Hemisphere differs from that of Eastern Europe.

The 'margin of political security' maintained by the USA in Latin America was wide during such periods as the 'big stick' policy of President T. Roosevelt or in the McCarthy period. The inflexibility of those days determined that leaders of moderate parties such as Romulo Betancourt of Democratic Action (AD) in Venezuela, were regarded as being part of a 'communist subversive' plot. The military *coup* executed by Perez Jimenez and his colleagues, ending the Democratic Action's regime in November 1948, received North American support. Ten years later, Perez Jimenez was overthrown, and in the elections of 1959 Romulo Betancourt was re-elected. This time, however, a different president resided in the White House and new political conditions, created by Fidel Castro's success, existed in that part of the world, leading to US support for the new President of Venezuela. During Betancourt's second administration, Democratic Action became a loyal ally to America in its fight against 'communist subversion'.

Similarly the principle of flexibility in the 'margin of political security' is applicable in the case of the Soviet Union. The hostility displayed in Stalin's policy towards Yugoslavia and Tito during the first years of the cold war differs from the position of tolerance and cordiality espoused by Krushchev and Brezhnev towards that same country and its leader. From attacking Yugoslavia as 'non-socialist' and 'revisionist', the Soviet Union came to regard Yugoslavia as a 'non-capitalist' state and even a socialist one.

This resignation over deviant cases risks being interpreted as a sign of tolerance, and therefore it should be noted that a strong reaction of the superpower is often produced when other countries in the sphere of direct influence show signs of *rapprochement* with the undisciplined neighbour. This is illustrated by those governments in Latin America which intended to maintain good relations with Castroist Cuba, such as Ecuador, Brazil and Argentina. The regimes were overthrown, with heavy but discreet assistance from Washington. In the case of Argentina, an invitation to visit Argentina extended by President Frondizi to his revolutionary compatriot Che Guevara, was sufficient notice to his army to prepare for his ouster. Not even the economic concessions granted by the United States could prevent this outcome, and seven months later Frondizi was living in exile on Martin Garcia Island.

Such an attitude was also shown by the Soviet Union, when it severely castigated Czechoslovakia in 1968, already having in the background an undisciplined Romania. Another extreme example is the outbreak of the Hungarian Revolution in October 1956, which was inspired by the independist trend taking place in Poland. The main attention of Moscow was diverted to focus on events in Budapest, thereby displacing attention from Warsaw. Paradoxically, V. Gomulka, the Polish Communist leader, considered as dangerous and unreliable by the USSR until 1956, was permitted to attain power in that same year as a result of the internal situation in Poland. In 1970, in spite of having gradually achieved a high level of control over Poland, the

Soviet Union nevertheless supported his ouster, due to his failure in the economic field and his declining prestige.

The extent of the capability available in limiting the margin of political security to the minimum depends essentially on three basic requirements:

1. The policy or line of action which the rival superpower is under-stood to be willing to follow in the international arena.
2. The existence of, and the dependent government's ability to exploit, the internal contradictions within the bloc, or within the super-power itself, in order to achieve a maximum of liberty without provoking intervention. This line of action has been successfully followed by Romania and Peru; such ability does not necessarily reflect advantageous economic conditions or a favourable military or geo-political situation in relation to other countries within the same sphere of influence. Both the countries that achieved greater room for manoeuvrability took advantage of either the Chinese/Soviet, or the Cuban/United States conflict.
3. Finally, the possiblity exists that the margin may be reduced because of changes in policy by the superpowers or due to a change of international or national priorities.

One can understand, from the Soviet viewpoint, the inherent dangers involved in a 'liberalisation' of the internal system of government of a satellite state, especially if such changes receive popular support; in such a case, both action or inaction on the part of the Kremlin is pregnant in its negative implications.[36] In spite of the theoretical acceptance (which in itself can be questioned) by the USSR of the possibility of 'different' approaches to socialism, the existence of such a model within a satellite country would be interpreted as a tacit accep-tance, by the Soviet Union, as she maintains absolute control over her sphere. The problem of national minorities within the Soviet Union itself could be intensified and aggravated if the USSR in its attitude towards the 'satellites' and the minorities within them, is more tolerant, liberal and willing to accept greater autonomy.

During the Spring of 1968 in Czechoslovakia, the indispensable caution necessary on the part of the Prague government to implement the radical reforms was overwhelmed by popular support and pressures for rapid liberalisation. Czechoslovakia's fate was a warning to the other members of the East European bloc; all the same, it did not hinder Kadar's regime from submitting to the Hungarian Communist Party's

Tenth Congress (November 1970), political and economic reforms,
including the right for more than one candidate to stand for a representative position, the principle of individual responsbility in the management of collective enterprises and the democratisation of the state and
party structures. The caution with which these reforms were proposed,
and the way in which they were initiated, strengthens the possiblity of
success for the Hungerian leadership in a slow but sure progress towards
achieving its policies. This aspect underlines the importance of the
regional situation for the achievement of greater independence by a
country in a sphere of influence. The existence of 'deviationist' states
tends to reduce the possibilities of the establishment of further experi-
ments, so that the point has not yet been reached from which one can
generalise about the cumulative effect of many 'deviationist' states. It is
also interesting that there is a close correlation between increases in, or
lessening of, the margins of political security between the superpowers
in their respective spheres of influence. This emphasises, once more, the
importance of the relations between these powers which is a crucial
factor in influencing the type of relationship between the superpower
and the 'satellite'. This observation will be further developed when
dealing with the options facing the superpowers.

Differences

The degree of dependency and inequality between the 'satellites' on one
hand and the superpowers on the other, varies according to the field
involved. The USSR dominates and enforces its policies basically in the
political field, whether it be internal or foreign affairs, with the
'popular democracies' being strictly controlled by the Kremlin through
the Soviet Embassy, advisers and secret police active in those countries.
In spite of the fact that East European countries are far from being
'equal partners' with Russia in the political sense, in the educational,
cultural, social and economic fields, the differences with the USSR are
minor. In countries such as Czechoslovakia or East Germany, standards
of living are higher than those of the USSR. The inequality between
Latin America and the United States fundamentally expresses itself by
the economic, social and educational differentials. The Gross National
Product, per capita, in the US, is ten times that which exists in Latin
America. (5.073 (USA), to 555 GNP (Latin America) per capita for
1972/3.)[37] Kilowatt production, per capita, per year, for the United
States in 1970 was 6,345, as against 394.4 for Latin America.[38]

   In Latin America, political control by the United States is more
subtly expressed and exercises, with nonconformity permitted, even to

the extent that hostility to 'big brother' in Washington can be openly voiced. With both superpowers, the forms by which control is maintained are linked to the internal political system within those two countries. The internal political structure determines to a great extent the characteristics of the domination over the other countries, with the differences between the oppressing powers being traceable to whether the system is one of 'democratic representation', or 'totalitarian centralism', a state-controlled or free enterprise system, etc.

For the Soviet Union, discipline and docility is the primary requirement from the political leaders of Eastern Europe towards the Kremlin — a country whose internal structure is based on similar principles — rather than concentrating on economic exploitation as a foremost aim.[39] All the same, even at the economic level the USSR enforces its dictates over its satellites through such institutions as COMECON. Here though, the inequality is not so blatant as in the political field. This is illustrated by the following figures: the annual per capita income in the Soviet Union was US $1,200; while in East Germany it is US $1,500; in Czechoslovakia US $1,010; and in Bulgaria US $620.[40] In the Soviet Union there is one private automobile per every 156 inhabitants, in Czechoslovakia one per every 38; in Hungary one per every 88; in Yugoslavia one per every 80; and in Romania one per every 1,288 inhabitants.[41] Comparisons of other socio-economic indexes shows the lack of a drastic difference between the USSR and the East European countries.[42] Even though some of the East European countries started their socialist stage with a more advanced and developed infrastructure than that of the Soviet Union, one could have expected, theoretically, a greater enrichment of the superpower in relation to East Europe during the more than 25 years of domination than that which has resulted.

On the other hand it is an accepted fact that the economic policy of the US in Latin America has produced large profits and earnings for the foreign investors, while the native population failed to receive corresponding benefits.[43] This is illustrated by estimates of the exhaustive exploitation of the natural resources in the region, the preference for short-term investments, the utilisation of cheap hand labour, etc. Even if there are changes now in the rate of industrialisation in Latin America, with a growth in consumer consumption, a wide gap remains between that part of the continent and the United States, with little chance existing for a change in the balance to their favour. Furthermore it has often been asserted that the assets of the US in Latin America are too great to allow them to be jeopardised by a nationalistic regime.[44]

This disparity can be particularised by the large list of minerals extracted in Latin America and consumed or marketed by the US: oil, copper, bauxite, manganese, tungsten, iron, lead, zinc, nickel, tin and nitrates which are considered by Lieuwen as indispensable to the American economy in times of both war and peace.[45] Countries such as Peru, Bolivia, Chile and Venezuela rely heavily on these as their only resources. Other smaller and weaker countries have to rely on an even less vital product, and sometimes a single one, such as cocoa, bananas, sugar, cotton or coffee. The theory of a continuity of exploitation from Spain to the USA (via Great Britain) which has eroded Latin American natural resources has been produced to emphasise that the motives of the United States are not only related to strategic problems but also to the maximisation of marginal profits. It is with such an aim that many Latin American countries are shaken, corrupted or maintained by North American private interests, yet in some of the 'Banana Republics' of Central America, one big company would suffice to run the national affairs for all practical purpose.[46]

In Latin America the restrictions in the ideological and political field are minimal in comparison with the USSR/East European relationship. Political pluralism exists in most countries, and freedom of the press in some; freedom of speech – the overall right to dissent, accepted in the United States – similarly exists in some Latin American countries, in the form of tolerance in their political affairs. Anti-US attitudes ranging from open criticism by the ruling elites to spitting on Vice-President Nixon in a student demonstration are 'respected' as proof of freedom of expression. It is necessary to understand that this phenomenon is part of the superpower ideology which is expressed in the framework of that power's foreign policy. At least from the time of the French Revolution, the 'nation-state', in attempting to increase its influence or establish territorial control over other countries, has not limited itself to purely military conquest, but has also attempted to 'export' its political ideology, in this case pluralistic democracy.

In order to illustrate Latin America's 'freedom of action', frequent references have been made to its acting as an autonomous bloc in the United Nations. Alker and Russet[47] analysed the general characteristics of the political processes within the international organisation. In general terms, as far as is relevant to the problems discussed here, there is a basic division in the UN into two areas: (a) North-South problems (developed countries and developing ones); (b) East-West problems (the Soviet Union and the United States being the polar points). During the

first years of the United Nations' existence, some of the Latin American
countries adopted an anti-Western stance on such questions as 'self-
determination'. However, the presence of newer, more radical, more
powerful (in voting strength) African groupings has pushed most Latin
Americans towards the Old European position which they usually
rejected in 1952 and 1957'.[48] An independent position is usually
adopted by the Latin American delegates at the United Nations, in
opposition to that taken by the United States when problems arise
which divide the Assembly on a North-South line. Under such circumstances, the Latin American majority vote usually resembles the Afro-
Asian one. With the changes that have occurred since the late 1950s,
however, the East-West polarisation has come to dominate the organisation and replace that of the North-South. The Soviet Union has
become the spokesman and supporter of many of the Afro-Asian
demands, which has resulted in the Latin American bloc readjusting its
position and approach in relation to the West. Although not denying
the possible importance of non-economic factors, Richardson in an
exhaustive study clearly shows the inter-relation between the high
dependence of Latin American countries' foreign trade with the USA
and political compliance measured as the agreement to vote along with
the United States at the UN General Assembly (particular on the East-
West issues).[49] At the present time, Cuba, Panama, Peru and Argentina
are exerting their new independent positions *vis-a-vis* the United States.
All the same, quantitatively, such cases can still be considered exceptions to the rule. In spite of this, the trends within the United Nations
should not be taken as an indicator of a change in the relationship
between Latin America and the United States. Most of the problems
affecting Latin American/US relations are discussed within the regional
organisation – the OAS. Latin American support for a resolution con-
demning Portugal for its colonialist policies in Africa lacks the importance for the United States that a similar stand, in opposition to the
US over Cuba, would have.

In spite of an initial policy of reinforcing the agencies of the newly-
organised UN, with its declining influence on that body Washington has
increasingly come to insist that the problems of the Western hemisphere be tackled by the OAS, and not by the UN.[50] Until recently,
within the OAS there have been no important issues on which the US
failed to receive the required majority vote as provided for by the
charter. In the condemnation of communism in Guatemala in 1954, in
the various anti-Cuban resolutions between 1961-2, and in the case of
intervention in the Dominican Republic in 1965, in all of them the US

achieved its desired support.[51] A temporally unfavourable situation —
in 1972-3 — brought the US to a minority position, but a turn to the
right in Latin America has dissipated such fear. It is therefore not
surprising that the present trend is to maintain the discussion in the
OAS or the Warsaw Pact framework. Countries such as Romania
would seek to have the problems raised in other frameworks such as
the European Conference of Security. Panama and Peru have decisively
overlooked this regional tradition and confronted both the UN and the
Neutralistic Conference with their problems, in all cases with favourable results.

This is why as regards jurisdiction over problems occurring in their
spheres of influence, both superpowers adopt a similar approach; they
prefer that the problem be dealt with by the relevant regional organisation rather than by the UN. I.M. Laredo stresses this basic complementary characteristic and emphasises that the regional organisations
' . . . have transformed themselves into instruments with a high degree
of vulnerability to the politics of power and to pressures which operate
without exception within each area'.[52]

In many cases there did not exist unanimous support for the US in
the OAS, but achieving the required two-thirds majority presented no
great problem. This reality can be explained by the basic values of the
North American political system which sees in the existence of an
opposition — not one commanding large support, though — proof of
the democratic functioning of that organisation. It would erode and
undermine the US self-image if on all occasions, within the OAS, she
received unanimous support.[53]

On the political level, the Soviet Union follows a different procedure. The USSR not only permits its 'satellites' to establish diplomatic or other relations with the capitalist countries, but also agrees to
certain 'popular democracies' being the first to make contact with the
'problematic' countries, (i.e. West Germany)[54] or in the cold war
period in which some East European countries, and most notably
Czechoslovakia, could continue to maintain the pre-Second World War
embassies, in countries where Soviet representation was forced to withdraw.[55]

Poland played a central role in proposing solutions to, and bringing
up, problems involved with disarmament, the possibilities of creating a
'nuclear-free' zone in Europe,[56] and the mobilisation of support for the
SALT talks.

In Latin America, many of the regimes were ousted or overthrown
only over the question of establishing diplomatic relations with

Communist Bloc states. The *coup d'etat* against President Frondizi in 1961 and the resignation of Janio Quadros in Brazil, and the subsequent overthrow of President Goulart in 1964, followed because of a refusal to sever diplomatic relations with Cuba. A way in which one could express independence from the US in the Western hemisphere was the establishment of diplomatic relations, or the official recognition of Communist Bloc nations. A recent example was the establishment of diplomatic ties with the Peoples Republic of China by Peru, one of the first Western countries to do so. Undoubtedly, the tighter and more effective political control enjoyed by the USSR in Eastern Europe, in comparison to the more uncertain control exercised by the US in Latin America, provided the Soviet Union with a greater degree of flexibility and range in using its 'satellite' states in the search for achieving international goals.

An inherent structural difference between the superpowers can be found in the degree of central control enjoyed by the Soviet Union in the internal affairs of its East European 'allies'. United States' activities in Latin America, on the other hand, are carried out by numerous government agencies and through more indirect means which further limit the level of control achievable. Firstly, the government agencies involved, in some cases with conflicting interests, range from the Pentagon, Department of State, Treasury, Senate Committees, the White House, etc. Beyond this, there are the intelligence services with their own aims and means, i.e. subversion and espionage — which the CIA has been accused of using, as in Chile in 1970-3 in the overthrow of Allende. In addition, there are private US corporations, with their own economic interests to protect — in many cases they have resorted to the political establishment to protect their private interests and have involved the state in unwanted situations. The means available include economic measures, as with the application of the Hickenloper Amendment (the cessation of aid in retaliation for nationalisation of US enterprises without sufficient compensation), as was threatened in Peru in 1970 after the nationalisation of the IPC oil company. However, these private structures also provide an alternative channel for official government bodies to work through, and thereby avoid official governmental involvements. The ITT corporation, for instance, has been accused of activities aimed at preventing Allende from achieving power in Chile, while at the same time the Pentagon opposed the suspension of military aid to Chile. This presents a picture of either confusion and disorder in the planning and carrying out of policy, or an extremely subtle ploy to cover all possible outcomes. It is only in cases where decisions were

required at the highest levels of government that the policies became
more unanimous and co-ordinated.

For many years there were strong arguments about the existence of
pressure groups in different sectors in the Soviet Union, i.e. economists,
consumers, the military, technocrats, party *apparatchniks,* intellectuals
in dissent, etc. However, there was quite a wide agreement that once
foreign policy has been formulated it takes the form of a unitary
'actor'. Differences are ironed out at the decisional stages, and then the
'line' is carried out by all sectors. When the official position has been
declared, no elements will act against it; this is what permits a greater
centralisation of foreign policy.[57] Another significant difference is the
employment of different means of intervention by the superpowers.
The military way being considered by both as the last resort, the alternatives differ in the two cases. The Soviet Union does not hesitate to
maintain a high level of involvement through a constant clandestine
and military operational presence. The Secret Services' dominance over
the Eastern European authorities is ostensible and in a way, open evidence of surveillance, and involvement serves the purpose of a deterrent against attempts to deviate from the accepted line.

In the case of the United States one could argue that the standard
alternative of forceful compliance is based on the use of political and
economic pressure, leaving the local governments with what appears to
the outsider at least, as a wider room for manoeuvering. It was therefore
a surprise to most sectors of the United States to witness a departure
from this line by the frequent use of the clandestine alternative. What
was regarded as standard Soviet procedure, no matter how much
President Ford called for an acceptance of it as a principle of normal
behaviour of the superpowers[58] met with general criticism. The clear
violation of America's own legal commitments[59] on the one hand, and
the background of trespassing clandestine activities in the United States,
both provoked a considerable reaction. The extent of covert CIA operations in the continent[60] showed that what used to be an *ad hoc* and
restricted activity became common practice, with the advantage of
being less noticeable to local and international public opinion, cheaper
and in most cases successful without disclosure (the possibility of
failure being much smaller). The Congressional investigations can perhaps limit once again this pattern of action which had degenerated to
one similar to that criticised in the rival superpower.

Notes

1. George Liska, *Imperial America: The International Politics of Primacy* (The John Hopkins Press, Baltimore, 1967).

2. John R. Swanson, 'The Superpowers and Multipolarity: from Pax Americana to Pax Sovietica', in *Orbis,* vol. XV, Winter 1972, pp. 1035-63.

3. Albert Wohlstetter, 'Is There a Strategic Arms Race?' in *Foreign Policy,* No. 15 (Summer 1974), pp. 3-20.

4. Henry A. Kissinger, 'The End of Bipolarity', in Kermit Gordon (ed.), *Agenda for the Nation* (The Brookings Institute, Washington, D.C., 1968).

5. Morton A. Kaplan, 'Variants on Six Models of the International System', in James N. Rosenau, (ed.), *International Politics and Foreign Policy* (The Free Press, New York, 1969), pp. 300-301.

6. Ibid. p. 298.

7. *Documents of the 22nd Congress* of the CPSU, 'The Road to Communism', N.S. Krushchev report of the Central Committee of the CPSU (Foreign Languages Publishing House, Moscow, 1961), p. 54.

8. Dean Rusk, 'Why We Treat Different Communist Countries Differently', *Department of State Bulletin,* vol. I, no. 1920 (March 1964), p. 393.

9. *The Times,* London, 7 April 1976.

10. N.S. Krushchev from the speech at the Third Contress of Romanian Workers Party, 21 June 1960, in *On Peaceful Co-existence* (Foreign Language Publishing House, Moscow, 1961), p. 237.

11. 'Prospects for Arms Control in Latin America', *Arms Control Today,* vol. 5, N9 (Washington, September 1975), p. 2.

12. We should also mention that official publications of the Soviet Union have condemned the Monroe Doctrine as a product of 'aggressive capitalism and national militarist bourgeoisie', (See article by B. Dymtryshyn and J.B. Gilmore, 'The Monroe Doctrine: A Soviet View', *Bulletin of the Institute of the Study of the USSR,* vol. XI, no. 5 (May 1964)).

13. *New York Times,* 31 July 1975.

14. The inclusion of these two countries was explained by the White House as '. . . in consideration of the fact that those "Republics" by the numbers of their population, their political significance and the contributions made by them to the common cause of defeating Germany, exceeded in importance some of the States which by common agreement have been placed among the founder Members'. *Keesings Contemporary Archives,* vol. 1943-1946, 7413 A, 7 July 1945.

15. *Keesings Contemporary Archives,* Vol. 1949, 10374. When the same argument was reintroduced in 1956, the United States explained that this 'gentlemen's agreement' was granted only for the first years of the United Nations. (Ibid., vol. 1956, 14667, 20 December 1956.)

16. Jefferson to Monroe: Report to the President of the United States, as an answer to a consultation, 24 October 1823. *Estados Unidos y America Latina,* (documents), Carlos Machado (ed.), (Montevideo: Patria Grande, 1968), p. 15.

17. President Grant's project over Santo Domingo, 31 May 1870, op. cit., p. 38.

18. Marshall R. Singer, *Weak States in a World of Powers,* Free Press, New York, 1972, p. 312.

19. Ibid., p. 57.

20. Paulo Schiling, *El Imperio Rockefeller: America Latina* (Tierra Neuva, Montevideo, 1970).

21. Robert S. Walters, *American and Soviet Aid* (University of Pittsburgh

Press, London 1970), p. 90.

22. See the article by Gabriel Valdes, former Under-secretary of the United Nations Agency for Development in Latin America, in *La Opinion,* 30 December 1972.

23. The flight time of nuclear missiles is still of great importance to the second strike capability.

24. 'Following the United States strategic interest, Latin America is divided in three zones: N-1, the nearest, includes Central America, the Caribbeans, Colombia and Venezuela. Zones II and III the other Pacific and Atlantic South American countries. Zone N-1 constitutes the top security risk and requires a top alarm system. It was necessary to ensure that Cuba will be surrounded by a security belt of eleven anti-communist countries.' see Gabriel Ramirez, *Las Fuerzos Armadas Uruguayas en la Crisis Continental* (Tierra Neuva, Montevideo, 1971).

25. 'The Northern Tier countries which together with the Soviet Union itself formed a quartet sometimes referred to as the first strategic echelon of the Warsaw Pact, were obviously of prime strategic and political importance to Soviet European policy, for not only did their territory lie astride what in war time would be the main axis of a Central European campaign but they were the countries sharing the most immediate geopolitical interests against West Germany.' Thomas W. Wolfe, *Soviet Power and Europe 1945-1970* (The John Hopkins Press, Baltimore), p. 297.

26. It can be argued that there exists a clear difference between a situation where the majority of the citizens of Puerto Rico expressed themselves by ballot in favour of joining the United States and the probable unwillingness of the population in the Baltic states to remain within the USSR framework.

27. R. Nixon, *United States Foreign Policy for the 1970s: A New Strategy for Peace* (Bantam Books, New York, 1970), p. 31.

28. Adam Ulam, 'The Destiny of Eastern Europe', *Problems of Communism,* vol. XXIII, February 1974, p. 3.

29. *Pravda,* Moscow, 25 September 1968. The intervention in one of the member-states of the 'Socialist Community' by a collective force is considered a legitimate self-defence in the case of a member country which is attempting to establish a social-economic doctrine or a policy different from the 'leninist-marxist' principles established by the community and will be considered to be an act of foreign aggression and subversion.

30. The house of Representatives Resolution of 20 September 1965, usually named after its initator, in this case Democratic representative Selden of Alabama − President of the Subcommittee for Inter-American Affairs of the House − includes paragraphs that condemn the direct or indirect intervention of 'international communism' as a policy opposed to the one established by the American Republics. This could bring one or more members, signatories of the Inter-American Treaty of Reciprocal Assistance, to 'exercise the clause of individual or collective self-defense', which could come to the extreme of applying the use of force, ' . . . in order to stop or combat the intervention, domination, control or colonization of any type of subversive forces, components of international communism and its agent in the western hemisphere'.

31. *Time Magazine* , 30 September 1974, reports President Ford reacting to the allegations of US involvement in the overthrow of Allende by stating: ' . . . I am not going to pass judgement on whether it is permitted or authorized under international law. It is a recognized fact that historically as well as presently such actions are taken in the best interest of the

countries involved . . . Our government like other governments does take certain action in the intelligence field to help implement foreign policy and protect national security. I am informed reliably that communist nations spend vastly more money than we do for the same kind of purposes.' (pp. 24-5).

32. Quoted in an article by William Korey, in *Problems of Communism*, May-June, 1969 (US Information Agency, Washington), p. 52, from *Pravda*, 13 November 1968.

33. Johnson's speech on the Dominican intervention, 2 May 1965, in Carlos Machado, op. cit., p. 109.

34. This trend is confirmed by the data on the number of international wars, their duration and number of casualties. David Singer and Melvin Small, *The Wages of War 1865-1965* (J. Wiley & Sons, New York; 1972).

35. Juan Jose Arevalo, *Fabula del Tiburon y las Sardinas, ed.* Palestra (Buenos Aires, 1959), p. 116.

36. Analysing the Soviet invasion in Czechoslovakia, Galia Golan concludes: ' . . . that the Soviet invasion came, not because the Soviets feared the defection of Czechoslovakia from the socialist camp, but because they considered Prague's internal reforms as an unacceptable, dangerous deviation from the Soviet model, a precedent that could well be attractive to reformist elements not only in Eastern Europe, but in the USSR itself.' From a review of G. Golan, 'The Czechoslovak Reform Movement: Communism in Crisis', published by Zvi Y. Gitelman, in *Problems of Communism* (Washington, Sept-Oct. 1972), XXI, p. 94.

37. *The Official Associated Press Almanac,* statistics quoted from data of the Agency for Intern. Development., Newspaper Enterprise Association, Cleveland, 1974, p. 175.

38. Statistics gathered by the New York Times Encyclopaedic Almanac, New York, 1970.

39. Events in Hungary and Poland in 1956 had repercussions on Krushchev's position and nearly brought his overthrow two years later. In Ulam's words, the Soviet Union is ' . . . Today the center of the new empire, though infinitely stronger and more tightly controlled than that of the Romanovs, is still not invulnerable to the echoes of protest and rebellion in its dependencies.' Adam B. Ulam, op. cit., p. 3.

40. An analysis of the given statistics should take into account differences in the real buying power and variations in the availability of goods, both of which are generally to the advantage of the East European countries *vis-à-vis* the USSR.

41. New York Times Encyclopaedic Almanac, op. cit.,

42. Illiteracy in the USSR is approximately 2 per cent, Czechoslovakia 0.5 per cent, Hungary 3 per cent and Bulgaria 10-15 per cent. The Soviet Union has a doctor for every 400 inhabitants, Czechoslovakia 540, Bulgaria 560 and Poland 768. Life expectancy in the Soviet Union is approximately 70 years, in East Germany and Czechoslovakia 71, and Romania and Poland 68.

43. Almost all the politicians and economists in Latin America consider these investments as oppressive, especially where the maximisation of profit has been reached through a situation of extreme exploitation. See, for instance: Guillermo Martorelli, *Las Inversiones Extrajeras en la Argentina,* ed. Galerna (Buenos Aries, 1969), where 50 per cent of the total invest-

ments of American origin have been studied, or the collection of articles published in *Panorama Economico Latino-americano* (Prensa Latina, Habana, 1963), or various statistics of ECLA.

44. '... United States citizens and corporations have invested in the Latin American area nearly $9 billion, also an amount greater than in any other region in the world. So far as the United States government is concerned, the vested interests of its citizens are inseparably intertwined with the security interests of the nation, for the bulk of the investments are in mining and petroleum enterprises, the products of which are indispensable to the American economy in peace and in war.' Edwin Lieuwin, *Arms and Politics in Latin America* (published for the Council on Foreign Relations, by Frederick A. Praeger, Inc., New York, 1960), p. 3.

45. Edwin Lieuwen, *The United States and the Challenge to Security in Latin America,* p. 240.

46. For a description of the relationship between minerals important to the United States and the overthrow of regimes, see Eduardo Galean, *Las Venas Abiertas de America Latina* (Siglo XXI Mexico D.F. 1971) pp. 204-63.

47. Hayward R. Alker Jr. and Bruce M. Russet, *World Politics in the General Assembly* (Yale University Press, New Haven, 1965).

48. H. Alker and B. Russet, ibid., p. 124. This statement is more carefully developed on p. 139.

49. Neil R. Richardson 'Political Compliance and U.S. Trade Dominance', *American Political Science Review,* LXX, 4 December 1976. Among the non-economic factors — not analysed in the study — which may have a positive conditioning effect of compliance, Richardson mentions fear of the military intervention 'propensities' of the United States, and fear of Castro's communist penetration in the region.

50. The United States' preference for the OAS as the unique frame of discussion for the inter-American problems is treated in the essay by Inis L. Claude Jr., 'The OAS, the UN. and the United States', in Joseph S. Nye Jr. (ed.), *International Regionalism* (Little Brown, and Co., Boston, 1968). According to the author, 'Throughout these cases, the Soviet Union appeared in the usual role of champion of the rights and competence of the United Nations, while the United States was cast, in equally significant deviation from normal character, as the prime opponent of a strong and active organization ... The United States did not repudiate the principle of the paramountcy of the United Nations in the international system but it subordinated that principle to the necessity of gaining a free hand for combating communist infilgration in the Western Hemisphere.' ibid., p. 19.

51. 'But the basic reason for U.S. sponsorship and continuing support of the Inter-American system has been to secure hemisphere acceptance of her own national policy of excluding from Latin America extra-continental influence inimical to her own interest. This has been of increased importance since growing commitments in other regions of the world have made it difficult for her to justify the Monroe Doctrine, which in any case has never been popular with her southern neighbours. The existence of the Inter-American system has made it possible for the United States to claim that her own undertakings in other continents give no cause for other powers to interfere in the Western hemisphere.' Gordon Connell Smith, 'The OAS and the Dominican Crisis', in Joseph S. Nye Jr., op. cit., p. 99.

52. Iris Mabel Laredo, *Problematica de la Solucion de Conflictos Intra-*

bloques (Depalma, Buenos Aires, 1970), p. 127.

53. M.R. Singer provides us with a significant example: 'I was once told by a representative of one of the Powers at the United Nations that he wished the delegates of his country's associated states would not always vote with his country on every issue because it exposed those delegates to charges of being "satellites" of the Power and created the impression that the Power was forcing them to vote as they did. He cited a number of instances in which he was approached by the delegates from weaker assocciated states asking him how his country intended to vote on an issue before they would decide how their own delegation would vote.' *op. cit.,* p. 315. These delegates presumably did so because they thought that the Power wanted them to vote the way the Power was going to vote.

54. See the analysis of the foreign policies of the Eastern European countries *vis-à-vis* West Germany in William Clark Potter, *Continuity and Change.*

55. In 1966, taking Bulgaria and Bolivia as two typical cases of dependent countries, we find that the first has 23.4 per cent of its embassies in 'very anti-USA' countries, and 34.6 per cent in 'very anti-USSR' countries, the rest in intermediate countries. Bolivia, however, had 93.3 per cent of its embassies in 'very anti-USSR' countries and none in 'very anti-USA' countries. M.R. Singer, *op. cit.,* pp.198-9.

56. In the UN Debate on Disarmament, (Polish Foreign Minister) M. Rapacki proposed on 3 October 1957 a Central European 'atom-free' zone – if both Germanies agreed to keep nuclear weapons off their territory, Poland and Czechoslovakia would do the same. 5 February 1958 the second Rapacki programme was put forward, more detailed and developed than first proposed, and it seems that at least Poland was serious about it.

57. The impact and progress of interest groups in the foreign policy after Stalin's death has been unmistakeably demonstrated. Brzezinsky refers to some groups with a 'degree of institutional cohesion', such as party *apparat,* consumer goods industries, light industry, military innovators, the conventional army, ministerial bureaucrats, heavy industry managers, economic reformers, secret police and Moscow and Leningrad intellectuals. Sbigniew Brzezinski (ed.), *Dilemmas of Change in Soviet Politics* (Columbia University Press, New York, 1969), pp. 1-34. Farrel and Aspaturian stress the differences from the West to the extent that those forces influence foreign policy making and the lack of 'private' interest involved in the form of pressure groups (see Barry R. Farrell, (ed.), *Approaches to Comparative and International Politics* (Northwestern University Press, Evanston, 1966). R.B. Farrell, 'Foreign Policies of Open and Closed Political Societies', pp. 167-208, and Vernon V. Aspaturian, 'Internal Politics and Foreign Policy in the Soviet System', pp. 212-88.

58. He declared that 'our Government like other governments does take certain action in the Intelligence field to help implement foreign policy and protect National Security', and that in the American cases it still did not reach Russian proportions. *New York Times,* 8 September 1974.

59. This action is believed to contradict the political beliefs of the nation. As Congressmen Robert Drinan expressed it: 'It should also be noted that the CIA has violated basic international law and numerous treaties of which the United States is a signatory' (quoting Article XV of the Organisation of American States rejecting the right of intervention in internal or external affairs of any other state). Letter to the *New York Times,* published 31 July 1975.

60. See revelations disclosed by Victor Marchetti and John D. Marks, *The CIA and the Cult of Intelligence* (Dell Publishing, New York, 1974), and Philip Agee, *Inside the Company – CIA Diary* (Penguin Books, Middlesex, England, 1975).

2 EXTERNAL VARIABLES: POLITICAL MULTIPOLARITY

1 General Features

The present political multipolarity in the international system has allowed the secondary powers freedom of action in penetrating smaller countries, and enabled groups of small states to maintain a relatively independent line. This situation is a result of the balance of terror' existing between the superpowers; the destructive capabilities of nuclear weaponry has led to mutual deterrence and military impotence. Today, France, Great Britain, West Germany, China and Japan all maintain greater independence in foreign policy than in the period immediately following the Second World War, implying a greater freedom of action for these countries from the superpowers.

It is outside the superpowers' spheres of influence where multipolarity is most effectively expressed. The competition or rivalry between the powers for influence and the subsequent benefits accruing from that influence enable the Asian and African countries to minimise their dependency on secondary powers, in contrast to Eastern Europe and Latin America with the superpowers

The influence of secondary powers within the spheres of direct influence is minimal and restricted. In other areas the primacy of the superpowers is determined by the overall extent of their involvement as well as by the considerable effect of the second-rate powers. However, in individual countries of the developing world we can often see one of the secondary powers having a more pronounced penetration than others, including the superpowers (i.e. France in Gabon, South Africa in Rhodesia, China in Cambodia, India in Bangladesh). But these links of dependence are weaker and more limited than those of the countries within the superpowers' orbit. Within the multipolar political system smaller countries, those from the *tiers monde,* enjoy better opportunities for political freedom than those within the sphere of direct influence. Furthermore, with the formation by a considerable number of these countries of the group of 'non-aligned' nations, their ability to play an active international role has been enhanced in relation to the superpowers, the secondary powers and the regional powers. An extreme case is the inverting of relations with the oil-producing countries over the last few years. The heavy dependence of the developed countries on this source of energy — without a viable alternative — and the scarcity of home resources, particularly in the case of the secondary powers, have presented a unique example of the wide margin of action open to the Third World countries. Obviously, this is unlikely to be repeated to the same extent with other less vital goods, but it is still important to stress the independent power of decision that was suddenly found resting in the hands of the oil-producing countries.

With regard to the superpowers' spheres of influence, contacts with other blocs are relatively unimportant — fact that re-emphasises in the case of Latin America that this region is not part of the Third World or 'non-aligned nations'.

This chapter will briefly analyse the role of the three main protagonists: Western Europe, Communist China and the 'non-aligned' or 'neutralist' bloc. These protagonists will be dealt with briefly, emphasising their insignificant role and status in comparison with the superpowers in the spheres of influence.

The growing economic presence of Japan in Latin America, since it does not present a threat to the US dominance in this area shall not be considered among the other intruding subsystems.[1]

One last observation: on certain occasions the superpowers support and foster encroachment of the opposing superpower's sphere of interest by friendly secondary powers, or subsystems. Therefore, one may hear sympathetic support from the USSR for French, Italian or neutralist activity in Latin America;[2] at the same time Washington will encourage Western European countries to develop their relations with the neighbouring Communist Bloc. Still, such efforts do not yet represent a serious threat to the hegemony of superpowers.

2 Western Europe

The interest that has been expressed by Western Europe in both Latin America and Eastern Europe has not entailed a real challenge to the prevailing strength of the superpowers involved. On the contrary, a high level of explicit recognition of superpower political predominance has been shown with the countries of Western Europe restricting their interest mainly to the economic field. Recently, both superpowers have shown interest in increasing economic and financial aid to their subservient regions, especially from the multilateral financial organisations often centred around Western Europe. However, it should be realised that as a collective entity the West European system in principle shares similar goals with those of the regions dominated by the superpowers: the attainment and maintenance of national and regional independence.

However, little has been achieved in practice in helping them to move
in this direction.

In France during the presidency of de Gaulle, the interest shown in
the countries of both spheres was basically for political reasons: in
order to increase national prestige by following policies independent of
the interests and desires of other powers or superpowers. De Gaulle
visited Eastern European countries and supported Romania (a reminder
that in 1918 France was regarded as the protector of many small
nations in that region) he was widely acclaimed in Latin America on a
visit in 1964; French airplanes were sold to Peru and Brazil, and Franco-
phile presidents in the Latin American continent were wooed. All this
indicated that France was not over-impressed by the principle of ex-
clusiveness adopted by the superpowers toward their adjacent regions —
de Gaulle also saw a role for a French presence. This 'irredentist' line
did not noticeably impress any of the superpowers, who in any case
were more concerned with the French stand in the nuclear and conventional armaments race. These French activities have considerably
decreased during the 'apres-Gaullism' and today the individual role
played by France is no different from that of the other European
powers.[3]

The Christian Democratic governments of Italy and Germany supported kindred parties in Latin America, both in organisation and in
the day-to-day running of affairs, and this influence was to a certain
extent well received in North American circles. One of the recent
examples is the dialogue between Latin American governments and
representatives of the EEC (European Economic Community), which
took place at Punto del Este in March 1974, at the initiative of the
'Instituto Italio/Latino Americano' (Christian Democrat influenced),
under the auspices of former Italian Foreign Minister Amitore Fanfani.
Traditional attitudes such as Spain's fostering of 'Hispanism', and of
dictators like Trujillo or Peron, do not worry the United States. The
traditional role of the Vatican as a preserver of the *status quo* permits
to a certain extent the isolation of extremist elements, guerilla members and 'third worldists' by the church in Latin America. The Council
of Europe has recently tried to improve and increase its ties with the
diplomatic representatives of the Latin American countries in the Old
World; such trends do not necessarily damage United States hegemony.
Furthermore, with the oil crisis, most European efforts were concentrated on giving preferential treatment to the Arab oil producing
countries,[4] and the signatories of the Lome agreement.

Economic activity by England or the European Common Market in

Latin America may upset certain economic circles in the United States; however, the absence of political rivalry enables the Old World colonial powers to penetrate this system. Britain's role in Latin America, especially within the southern region, is of specific importance. Following the withdrawal of Spain from the region, Britain stepped in to fill the power vacuum. Her presence was felt most strongly in the economic field up to the Second World War. Argentina in 1938 exported 81 per cent of her industrial production to the UK, and even by 1969 her trade was strongly Europe-orientated — 34 per cent of exports went to the US, 22.3 per cent to Great Britain, 43.7 per cent to Continental Europe.[5] Argentina still buys much of her military hardware from Britain, especially her naval requirements. However, the anonymous character of many of the multinational enterprises makes it difficult to estimate accurately the level of US investments in the region — what is the American share of the European car industries that have established plants in Latin America? Generally it can be stated that the more developed and larger Latin American countries tend to maintain stronger economic relations with Western Europe.

The independence shown by the Western European countries from the United States, can result in tense situations over behaviour within the Latin American subsystem. In 1954 Britain participated in the US-organised boycott against Guatemala and refused to sell that country arms; however, since then changes have occurred, as shown by British continuance of commercial relations with revolutionary Cuba in the face of another US boycott. The extent to which this attitude has gone against official American policy is illustrated by the secret attempts of the CIA to sabotage British trade with the island. In 1973, nevertheless, England was the only country in the Security Council to support Washington, abstaining over the issue of Panama's re-establishing control over the canal.

In issues of great public impact, such as the overthrow of the Allende regime, criticism by Western European leaders (particularly Social Democratic) has also operated against White House policy, but is little different from the stand adopted by many US congressmen, and is perhaps less effective in real terms. European governments can still make an impression about humanitarian concerns (refugees, exiles, etc.), but not much more than this. On the other hand, as shown in Chapter 5 (Sections 3 and 4), the economic activity of individual Western European countries with Eastern Europe is rapidly growing, and is now almost reaching pre-World War II levels. This trend in the economic trade patterns of Europe can be seen in the development of economic relations between Poland and Western European countries.[6]

The role played by Western Europe in this superpower sphere of influence indirectly helps the slow process of economic emancipation by the satellite countries. This process, though, is not accompanied by any revisionist designs with regard to the delimitation of the same region as dependent from the Soviet superpower. Brandt's West Germany was the first to resign itself pragmatically to facing the present reality in the hope of exchanging a recognition of the existing boundaries and *de facto* Soviet presence for vague promises of a long-term reassurance of greater individual freedom in Communist countries. The European Summit meeting in Helsinki legitimised the compromise in a written document. There is still controversy over the comparative gains. One could admit that although the Soviets have more tangible benefits, the change of atmosphere and a lower susceptibility to this superpower might indeed provide an erasing of some of the restrictions in Eastern Europe.

The Vatican has also softened its attitude toward Eastern European regimes, such as Poland, where the Communists granted more power to the Church over the masses in their countries. As in the case of Latin America, no official criticism is expressed from Rome, but from the local clergy who are more politically active.[7]

One can then sum up by saying that Western European presence in Eastern Europe and Latin America was not extensive enough to represent a threat to the superpowers' dominance. To a great extent, some of the Western European actions in both fields merge with the interests of Moscow and Washington. However, no false symmetry should be assumed and the Western European role and influence on her Eastern neighbours is obviously of greater relevance and magnitude than the one played in Latin America. This situation was explicitly admitted by the former Venezuelan President Betancourt when he made clear his disappointment in an interview. 'It seems that Europe is more interested in its former African colonies than in Latin America.'[8]

3 China

In spite of the growing role played by China in the international arena, her effect on the superpowers' spheres of influence is minimal. The policy of revolutionary intransigency followed by Peking and the self-imposed isolation during the cultural revolution were both limiting factors. In 1970 a new policy line began to emerge and China started to 'normalise' its role as a great power, acting according to 'national interests'.

According to Johnson, Chinese political achievements in Latin America, in the period 1959 to 1967, surpassed all expectations.[9] Even though, theoretically, conditions were favourable to China (anti-Yankeeism; preference for violence as a means of achieving political changes; the lack of prestige accorded to the Soviet policy of 'peaceful co-existence', the importance of Marxism amongst the intellectuals; government repression; and poverty and misery among large sectors of the population), an analysis of the situation shows that revolutionary action by, or with the support of, China on the continent of South America was extremely limited if not non-existent. China condemned the regimes of the continent verbally and expressed solidarity with the guerilla movements, but on the material level she did not extend significant aid to the organisations, either in arms or money. Following the Sino-Cuban crisis of 1965, China showed little interest in the guerillas and criticises the 'elitist' attitudes of Regis Debray and Che Guevara. Except for a long period in Colombia, and an abortive attempt in Bolivia, there was no pro-Chinese guerilla group of importance. In Brazil, the MR-8 and other guerilla groups, although showing sympathy towards China, identified themselves with Havana, their centre of revolutionary activity. Halperin says: 'In actual fact, however, Chinese support for the guerillas has so far been largely verbal. The real Chinese effort in Latin America has been directed at a very different and far more modest goal; not against the great imperialist foe, the United States, but against Soviet influence in the area.'[10] The greater part of the Chinese broadcasts to Latin America is devoted to denouncing their 'revisionist' neighbour.

Following the Cultural Revolution and the *rapprochement* with the United States, China has attempted to establish diplomatic relations with the Latin American countries, and to develop the commercial relations which have existed since the 1950s with such countries as Uruguay and Argentina. During the first nine months of 1972 China exported $37 million of goods to Brazil. She established diplomatic relations with Peru, Mexico, Chile, Cuba, Argentina and Venezuela, and it is expected that other countries will soon follow. To gain this recognition China was forced to quieten the vociferous support for the revolutionary cause. As a result China lost much of her popular image and attraction; Maoist groups — never numerous — have been consequently weakened; this is comparable with what happend to the Soviet Union in the Latin American Left following her policy of conciliation with the United States. Paradoxically, it was after President Nixon's visit to Peking that Sino-Cuban relations also improved; in spite of Havana's disillusionment with this act, the Cuban government is now following a more pragmatic policy towards Washington, with the prospect of an eventual establishment of relations. China in her drive to strengthen relations with various Latin American regimes, including Cuba, participated in the July 1970 celebrations of the National Day of the Cuban Revolution — following an absence of five years — by sending a delegation carrying a goodwill message from Chou En-Lai.[11] Closer co-operation between the two countries was instigated by this visit but due to the strong pro-Soviet leaning, Cuba is still politically very distant from Peking. At the same time China — unlike other Communist countries except Romania — did not sever relations with Chile in 1973, following the military *coup*.

In Eastern Europe we also witness a change of policy by the Chinese. With the eruption of the Sino-Soviet conflict, China adopted a protective stance *vis-a-vis* Albania; facilitated Romania's independent diplomatic manoeuvring; and it seems more than likely that it would follow a similar line with any other Soviet satellite showing independent tendencies. The condemnation of the Soviet invasion of Czechoslovakia in 1968 was purely an anti-Soviet demonstration — upholding the principle of non-interference in the internal affairs of another country. Still, what made it more difficult to Dubcek to play the 'Chinese card' were the deep disagreements as to the type of socialist regime he aspired to. This was not the case in Albania or Romania since part of their struggle with Moscow was their determination to remain Stalinist despite Soviet condemnation of this era. With the end of the Cultural Revolution some previous accusations against Tito — considered in the past to be a traitor due to his challenge of Stalinism — were conveniently forgotten, and Peking renewed its relations with Belgrade. She acclaimed the Popular Army of Yugoslavia during its manoeuvres in the Karova zone, stressing 'its glorious tradition in opposing foreign aggressors'.[12]

China's most important involvement in a country within the Soviet orbit is in Romania. According to Romanian sources, Chinese leaders promised to provoke skirmishes on the Russian far-eastern border in the event of eventual Soviet military intervention within Romania.[13]

China's hostility towards the Soviet Union and its successful resistance to any intervention by Moscow in its internal affairs, intensified nationalistic feelings within Eastern Europe to a certain extent; Peking tried to stimulate these feelings, lately irrespective of the type of socialism the various countries support.[14]

By the beginning of the 1970s, in spite of its nuclear achievements,

China still remained, as a power, far inferior to both the United States and the Soviet Union. All the same, the acceptance of the People's Republic of China into the family of nations, and its dynamic *realpolitik* in re-establishing relations with the world, forces one to ask whether, in the not too distant future, the international system will be transformed from a bipolar to a tripolar world. In such a power figuration would the superpowers respect each other's spheres of influence? Shulman foresees that in such a situation a balance of power would exist between the three, creating an equilibrium based on mutual respect for each other's satellite regions.

> The most probable relationships would involve a Chinese hegemonial role within the subsystems of South East Asia, continuing Soviet predominance in Eastern Europe, and American domination of Latin America. So long as the subsystems are dominated by the super-powers, they will probably not be able to affect the power relations or equilibrium among the principal states. However, significant systematic instability would arise in the event that any superpower attempted to exert influence in the subsystems of the other two, generating a possible bipolar coalition against it. This means that one of the fundamental rules for preserving tripolar stability would require each superpower to refrain from intervening in subsystems not recognized as its own.[15]

This drive has been increasingly felt not only with the takeover by Communist regimes in Vietnam, Laos and Cambodia but with the acceptance of Peking's influence in very different regimes, such as Burma or Pakistan.

Returning to the present, and putting aside speculations, we may summarise the situation as one in which Communist China plays a minimal role within the two superpowers' spheres of influence, but with its importance in these regions gradually growing. The Chinese presence which does exist in both zones, though, is basically aimed at undermining the Soviet position and not the American one.

4 The Neutralists

'Neutralist' was a term formulated at Asian Solidarity meetings at the end of the 1940s — a meeting place both of independent countries and of movements fighting for that independence from the colonial powers. The 1955 Bandung Conference of Asian countries extended the scope of the movement, as it included nationalist movements from Africa as as well as established countries such as Egypt, Libya, Sudan, Liberia, Ghana and Ethiopia. It was not until after the Korean War that this forum received superpower support. During his lifetime Stalin was not enthusiastic about them, accusing Asian nationalist leaders of having been 'Quislings' and Fascist collaborators during World War Two. The United States was incapable of understanding how Asian countries, supporting the democratic principles, could fail to join their anti-communist crusade in Korea, and only in 1954-5 did both superpowers change their attitudes. In the search for new allies on other continents, 'The Russian and the Chinese hoped to advance communism by exploiting anti-Western nationalism, while the Americans hoped to exploit fears of communism and of China, and so create new, and if necessary heavily subsidized military groups.'[16]

The overtures made towards the Afro-Asian countries did not have a great impact on the adjacent regions of the superpowers, though in both cases it could be an optimal solution for a switch from a dependency relationship on one superpower, without falling into the orbit of the other. In Eastern Europe, after Bulganin's and Khrushchev's successful visit to Asia, Yugoslavia began to enjoy improved diplomatic ties with the USSR; but at the same time worked towards consolidating the neutralist bloc as a universal group. During Nehru's and Nasser's visit to Tito in 1956, they sealed the friendship that was to become the basis of the future axis of the non-aligned nations. Yugoslavia saw an opportunity for assuming an important international role, and for emphasising its example of an independent socialism. One should also take into account Tito's personality and his similarity in outlook with other Afro-Asian leaders; a correspondingly low standard of living between the regions (especially if compared with other European countries); Yugoslavia's geographical location on the Mediterranean Sea; its proximity to the Afro-Asian bloc on the other side; and, what was more important, the necessity of strengthening its independent position by consolidating a bloc adhering to the same foreign policy. All these factors may have contributed to the development of this phenomenon. As Romania, some years later, searched to play an active role in Europe, Yugoslavia turned to Afro-Asia. In the 1961 Conference of Non-Aligned Nations held in Belgrade, differences appeared for the first time in attitudes towards the role of the bloc — was its outlook to be anti-colonialist and anti-West, or was it to be an instrument for promoting 'peaceful co-existence' and world peace?

The 'internationalisation' of the forum failed to take place. During the short days of the Dubcek regime in Prague, although the official lines of foreign policy remained very much unchanged, and subdued to Soviet orientations, the tone in issues such as the Middle East became different, and the press wrote about the need for the country to achieve a position of neutrality like Belgium.[17] Imre Nagy referred to the Bandung principles during the abortive attempt to install an independent regime in Hungary,[18] and some neutralist argument can be found in Romanian policy, (i.e. elimination of pacts), but Yugoslavia remains the sole Eastern country to be part of the movement, and of the rest of Europe, so far only Cyprus has participated in the conferences.

The impact of neutralism on the Latin American continent can be traced back to the end of the 1950s with the visits of leaders from both regions to each other; Sukarno visited Mexico in 1959 and Janio Quadros, six months before being elected President of Brazil, visited India, Egypt, Yugoslavia and Cuba. It is significant that the origins of neutralism can be traced to Latin America. Latin America supported neutrality from the legal point of view in order to avoid becoming involved in conflicts of other continents. This became a doctrine with the 'Third Position' of Peron, who, almost up to the end of the Second World War, refused to declare war on Germany and maintained a position of 'neutrality'. With the development of the cold war, Peron declared himself opposed to both 'capitalism' and 'communism', but he failed to establish a relationship with the emerging Afro-Asian movement. At the beginning of the 1960s Presidents Quadros and Goulart in Brazil, and Prime Minister Castro in Cuba, added to the local 'neutrality' the interpretation of 'neutralism' of Asia and Africa. Colonialism, and the linked neo-colonialism that followed it, are perceived to be a linked and common phenomenon of all three continents. However, in Brazil and Argentina the presidents did not survive for long and both countries soon returned to the old allegiance with the Western bloc.

Venezuela, because of its oil interest, has maintained close contact since 1959 with the Arab countries, and supported the Afro-Asian conference held in Cairo in 1964. Ex-President Betancourt underlined that the 'main common feature is the fact that our interest coincides with that of the Middle Eastern countries in the common objective of maintaining the price of oil in the international markets at a high price and profitable level for the producers of that raw material'.[19]

Until the middle of the 1960s there was no serious organisational connection between Latin America and the 'neutralist' bloc. It was at the time when the 'neutralists' were undergoing a unity crisis, and disagreements were growing, that Cuba attempted to take over the leadership, by tring to forge a link between the three continents. The differ-

ence was that Cuba attempted to organise the revolutionary elements
into a new 'International' including the subversive and extremist militants to the exclusion of a great number of government representatives
from the region (i.e. among the delegates was M. Ben Barka, main
leader of the opposition to King Hassan of Morocco).

In 1965 in Havana, the Organization of Solidarity of the People of
Asia, Africa and Latin America (OSPAAAL) was created — mainly anti-
imperialist and anti-North American in outlook. This attempt only
intensified existing divisions within Afro-Asia without drawing any new
elements from Latin American regimes into the movement. This continent — with the exception of Cuba — continued to be represented
exclusively by anti-government political forces. The death of Che
Guevara, the collapse of the guerilla movement and the lack of revolutionary 'practice' of most Afro-Asian participants destroyed Castro's
dreams of a combating 'international of oppressed people'. Slowly he
made his way back again to the established Third World framework.

Following a Conference in Belgrade in 1969, a preparation for the
meeting to be held in Lusaka in 1970, the neutralist movement seems
to have returned to its original course. Participants from Latin America
were Cuba, Jamaica, Guayana and Trinidad; while Argentina, Brazil,
Chile, Colombia, Bolivia, Peru and Barbados sent observers. One witnessed at these meetings a certain ambiguity and lack of commitment
towards the Conference's goals from the Latin American contingent.
The Peruvian delegate, Mercado Jarrin, Minister for Foreign
Relations, said:

> I have come here with a desire to inform the conference of the
> common principles of all the Latin American countries concerning
> the right to exploit the sea, the right to explore, preserve and
> utilize national resources of the offshore belt and of the soil, and the
> need for determining the boundaries of sovereignty over the sea in
> agreement with the basic geographical, geological and biological
> characteristics.[20]

As a final word, he added his support for the struggle of people for
liberation from colonial oppression. The Brazilian delegate was even
more lukewarm. He said that, 'with the non-aligned countries we share
the ideals of peace and international security, non-interference in the
internal affairs of other states and non-discrimination'.[21] The participation of right-wing and centrist regimes from Latin America as observers might on the one hand have worried the United States. On the

other hand as they were confident that their control over the countries
of this continent was effective, the problem could be regarded from a
different angle, with the large Latin American participation in this body
looked at as a moderating force of the whole 'neutralist' movement and
thereby in the interest of the United States.

For the first time a 'neutralist' conference was organised to take
place on Latin American soil in Georgetown, Guayana in 1972. In
spite of this, the only new member from the continent to adhere fully
to 'neutralism' was Chile; the only additional guest was the Pro-
Independence Movement of Puerto Rico. Argentina, Barbados, Bolivia,
Brazil, Colombia, Ecuador, Mexico, Peru, Uruguay and Venezuela all
participated only as observers. At this Guayana meeting, political resolutions were adopted concerning Latin America, not only in regard to
independence for Puerto Rico (which had already been adopted at a
previous meeting in Cairo in 1964) but also in relation to independent
Latin American countries:

> The Conference examined the situation in Latin America and
> expressed full support of the Chilean Government of People's Unity
> bent upon consolidating their national independence and building a
> new society; of the nationalist measures taken by the Peruvian
> Government and its efforts to safeguard the nation's sovereignty and
> to promote social progress; and also of the efforts of the people and
> government of Panama to consolidate their territorial integrity.[22]

Another conference which took place on Latin American soil, in Lima,
1975, showed the eagerness of the Afro-Asian organiser to enlarge the
membership with countries from the South American continent. So far,
Panama has officially joined, viewing it as the most appropriate plat-
form from which to see the reclaiming of the Panama Canal applauded
and approved, Argentina has adhered, as a way of mitigating internal
criticism of a move to the right and also loyally following the foreign
policy principles established by General Peron.

Although advances have been made in relations between the neutralists and Latin America, on a more concrete basis this bloc has only
attracted a few countries from the continent. The majority of the
political regimes in Latin America consider themselves of the 'right' or
'centre' and adhere to the basic values of 'Western civilisation' and
'Christendom'; spiritually the ruling elites identify themselves with the
'Old Word' and not with the 'Third World. For them 'neutralism' is
basically an 'anti-colonial' expression with a pro-communist conno-

tation.[23]

At the present time unity between Afro-Asian countries and Latin America seems to be limited to the economic problems shared by both but to different degrees — politically, the countries of the regions have very different outlooks. The UNCTAD Conference in Geneva in 1954 established the bloc of '77', which numerically encompasses the majority of the Latin American nations, whose participation is not only formal, but also active. A more recent unifying factor is Afro-Asia's production of similar raw materials, and together they seek to create a united front in the international market to control production and maintain the world price for the raw materials.[24] A similar reference can be made to the Third Conference of the Right of the Sea that took place in Caracas in 1974, in which all participants of Asia, Africa and Latin America seemed to agree on the extension of the territorial or patrimonial sea, safeguarding and protecting the national resources of the developing countries against the voracity of the more advanced ones.

In short, firmer relationships have been developing between the Afro-Asian and Latin American countries, but mostly on economic or juridical matters, and without showing any particular concern for United States policy. Neutralist appeal in Eastern Europe, no matter how concomitant it might be with some basic aspirations of sovereignty did not go beyond the affiliation of one member only.

Notes

1. For a very interesting and comprehensive article about this question see Yuri Barsukov, 'El Japon en Latinoamerica', published in Russian in *World Economy and International Relations,* no. 7, 1975 and reproduced by Novosti Press Agency's *Panorama Latinoamericano* (in Spanish), no. 212, October 1975. The author elaborates the thesis that greater economic interaction between Japan and Latin American countries helps to reduce the dependence of the Latin American countries from the 'powerful North American neighbour'.
2. 'The fact that the Latin American countries broaden their economic and political relations with the Socialist states and *the capitalist countries rival to the United States* [emphasis added] contributes to weaken the dependence of the Latin American countries with respect to American imperialism.' G. Vishnia, 'The United States and Latin America: Relations in the epoch of Detente', in *World Economy and International Relations* (in Russian) (Moscow, no. 8, 1975), p. 24.
3. 'Unfortunately French aid to Latin America never developed the proportions of an "offensive" and Latin American political leaders have noted on occasions that France provides little material assistance with its gifts of

culture.' Henri Goldheimer, *The Foreign Powers in Latin America* (Princeton University Press, New Jersey, N.J., 1972), p. 182.

4. Latin America receives little beyond tariff preferences granted to all developing countries. Bilateral aid, in small amounts, continues to flow from EEC members (mainly Germany), but most projects at regional group level, having varying Latin American partners (Latin American Free Trade Association, Andean Pact or Central American Common Market) did not go beyond the planning stages. See the *Economist,* 13 September 1975.

5. For a viewpoint that stresses the importance of the European Community upon Latin America, see Jose Luis de Imaz, *Adios a la Teoria de la dependencia,* paper submitted to the 11th Latin American Congress of Sociology, San Jose, Costa Rica, July 1974.

6. 'The Gierek regime has also continued to develop broad contacts with several other West European countries with the dual objective of expanding bilateral relations – especially economic – and paving the way for a conference on European security and co-operation. Poland's relations with France, which had chilled appreciably since President De Gaulle's 1967 visit, have begun to warm, and Gierek has received an invitation to pay an official visit to France in the fall of 1972. In October 1971, Poland signed an agreement with Italy providing for the mass production of small Fiat cars in Poland, and in November a protocol guaranteed long-term Italian credits for the project. In late 1971, a Polish-British venture in the co-production of machine tools was agreed on, and in mid-1972 a contract was negotiated with the British Petroleum Company for the joint construction of an oil refinery at Gdansk. The Swedes, in turn, are to build a luxury hotel in Warsaw.' Adam Bromke, 'A New Political Style – Poland Under Gierek,' *Problems of Communism,* XXI, no. 5 (Sept. – Oct. 1972), p. 16.

7. 'In many ways the most controversial policy of recent years has been the Vaticans attempt to strike bargains with Eastern European countries in the hope that this will ease the plight of Catholics under Communism. Some in the church criticize the policy as fruitless and humiliating.' (*International Herald Tribune,* 13 December 1975)

8. H. Goldheimer, *op. cit.,* p. 183.

9. Cecil Johnson, *Communist China and Latin America 1959-1967* (Columbia University Press, New York and London, 1970), p. 286.

10. E. Halperin 'Peking and the Latin American Communist', *The China Quarterly* vol. 29 (Jan. – March 1967), p. 111.

11. Cecil Johnson 'China's Latin American Policy' in *Problems of Communism* XXI, no. 4 (July – Aug. 1972), p. 56.

12. Stuart S. Smith, 'Russia, China and the Balkans', in *Midstream,* vol. XVII, no. 10 (New York, December 1971), p. 10.

13. Ibid.

14. 'Clearly, the Sino-Soviet dispute, together with the climate of reduced tension in Europe, has intensified nationalistic trends in Eastern Europe, and has encouraged a greater degree of independence in the foreign policies of some East European countries.' Marshall D. Shulman, ' "Europe" versus "Detente"?', *Foreign Affairs,* vol. 45, no. 3 (April 1967), p. 393.

15. Ronald J. Yalem, 'Tripolarity and the International System', *Orbis,* vol. XV (Winter 1972), p. 1055.

16. Peter Calocvoressi, *World Politics since 1945* 2nd ed. (Longman, London, 1971), p. 273.

17. Galia Golan, *Reform Rule in Czechoslovakia* (Cambridge University Press, Cambridge, 1973), pp. 200-17.

18. See Nagy's adherence to the 'Five Basic Principles of International Relations' drafted at the Bandung Conference, stressing the importance of the questions of national independence, sovereignty, territorial inviolability, non-interference in internal affairs. Imre Nagy, *On Communism* (Thames and Hudson, 1957), pp. 20-23.

19. R. Betancourt's speech published in *El Nacional* (Caracas, January 13, 1960), mentioned in Leopoldo Zea, *Latin America and the World* (Univ. of Oklahoma Press, 1969), p. 40.

20. *Review of International Affairs* no. 491 (Belgrade, 20 September 1970), p. 7.

21. Ibid, p. 8.

22. Ibid., vol. 23, no. 538 (Sept. 1972, p. 29). The Cuban hand can be distinguished easily in the formulation of this resolution.

23. See the work by Vladimir Reisky de Dubnic, 'Brazil's New Foreign Policy: From Non-Alignment to Solidarity with the West', in A. Carlos Astiz, (ed.), *Latin American International Politics,* (University of Notre Dame Press, Indiana, 1969), pp. 274-88.

24. This is Viana's principal conclusion when he talks about the reasons for the Brazilian approach to Afro-Asia. Without entering the discussion of political positions, such as that of Brazil's support of Portugal in their question of colonial territories in Africa, the importance of the commercial relations and the opening of markets is pointed out. Mendez Viana, 'The Afro-Asian World: Its Significance for Brazil', in Astiz, ibid., pp. 216-33.

3 REGIONAL VARIABLES: A COMPARISON OF THE SUBSYSTEMS

1 Analytical Framework

In comparing different subsystems an analytical framework is essential, and for this work the approach used by Cantori and Spiegel[1] has been adopted. Their point of departure is to take a region or subordinate system as a basic unit, instead of the individual state or the whole world. Before continuing, it is necessary to summarise their framework, and to adapt it to meet the requirements of this study. As we discussed in the Introduction, subordinate systems or subsystems are generally classified by geographic proximity, but are more accurately defined by the degree of interaction among the component states. Accordingly one could place the countries involved in three major categories: those who belong to the 'core' of the subsystem, maintaining a very high level of interaction among themselves; those who are 'peripheral' in the sense that they are linked with other subsystems by important interactions in different fields, but still maintain a considerable level of contact with their original region; and thirdly, powers whose presence in the particular region is strongly felt and who are considered to be 'intrusive' elements in these subsystems. In most cases, according to Spiegel and Cantori, one could refer to subordinate systems 'intruding' in other subordinate systems, since the superpowers are by definition two bodies of confederate states on the highest level of interaction.

Before comparing Latin America and Eastern Europe with other subsystems, the question must be raised as to whether that system can be called a single unit. As shown by Cantori and Spiegel in Table 1, Latin America[2] is a unified entity, while Africa, Asia and Europe can be divided into two or more subsystems. Although in this particular study, on certain occasions, some Latin American countries are compared to Afro-Asia, and others to Europe, this does not refute the premise that the Latin American continent can be defined as a single entity. The high intensity of interaction between the twenty Latin American countries can be delineated in most socio-economic, political and cultural parameters.

Employing the aforementioned criteria for analysing the frequency of interaction between member countries of a region, Eastern Europe can also be recognised as a distinct subordinate system. Even extending the subsystem to include the Communist Bloc, which is the area in which the majority of transactions between the various countries take place, this proposition is verifiable in all fields: political, economic, cultural, scientific, technological, etc. At the beginning of the cold war, the idea of autonomy in the socialist community was put forward with the aim of placing this subsystem on a self-sufficient basis.

Table 1: Types of Subordinate Systems

	SYSTEMS	CORES
INTEGRATIVE	North America The Soviet Union	West Europe East Asia (Communist China) South Asia (India)
CONSOLIDATIVE	West Europe Southwest Pacific East Europe	Southwest Pacific Southern Africa Latin America East Europe
COHESIVE	Latin America North Africa Southern Africa	Middle East North Africa Maritime Southeast Asia West Africa East Africa Central Africa
COHERENT	Middle East South Asia East Asia West Africa East Africa Southeast Asia Central Africa	Mainland Southeast Asia

Source: Louis J. Cantori and L. Spiegel, *International Politics of Regions,* p. 382.

In order to understand the structure, the level and the distribution of power within this subsystem, it is not enough to state that it is semi-isolated from the rest of the international system; it is necessary to study the internal characteristics in conjunction with the external situation. In regard to the system's relative isolation, this is considered to be the result of the dominance over the countries of the zone by the adjacent superpower, the Soviet Union. However, it is precisely this physical control over countries that has led, for the first time in modern history, to multiple linkages between the countries of Eastern and Central Europe.

A comparison between the different subordinate systems can be made, taking into consideration the structural differences in the type,

level, character and intensity of interactions of the constituent members. There are four pattern variables to be considered, which are of
paramount importance for making a comparative analysis of different
regions, and for drawing the demarcation lines within the regions: (1)
the nature and level of cohesion; (2) the nature of communications; (3)
the level of power; (4) the structure of relations.

The nature and level of cohesion refers to the extent to which the
countries of a subsystem resemble and complement one another, and
to the intensity of their interaction.[3] Of importance is the readiness
with which states are willing to sacrifice national sovereignty in order to
further supranational goals; and in what fields and to what degree co-
operation exists (military, scientific, economic, organisational, etc.).
Furthermore, factors common to several states, both in their formation
and development, are of importance in the field of integration, i.e.
collective defence against external elements during a long historical
process.

The nature of communication can be divided into four aspects:
transportation (road, water, rail and air); personal communication
(mail, telephone and telegraph); mass media (press, radio and television); and exchanges amongst the elite (intra-regional education,
tourism and diplomatic visits within the region). A fifth aspect may be
applicable, that is interaction of the masses (temporary migration between countries for economic reasons, i.e. seasonal work). The greater
the use of the above means, the greater will be the integration in such
fields as economics, social homogeneity, politics, etc.

The level of power of different states is reliant on the combination
of a variety of elements. Hans Morgenthau emphasises: geography,
natural resources (food and raw materials), industrial capacity, military
preparation (technology, leadership. quantity and quality of the armed
forces), population (distribution and trends), national character,
national morale, quality of diplomacy, and the quality of government.[4]
Lerche and Said divide a nation's capabilities into two main aspects: the
tangible elements (geographic position, population and manpower,
resource endowment, industrial and agricultural productive capacity
and military power); and the intangible elements (political, economic
and social structure, educational and technical level, national morale
and international strategic position).[5] Cantori and Spiegel detect seven
types of nation-states, graded according to power and range of
influence: primary, secondary, middle and minor powers, regional
states, microstates and colonies.

What is not clear from this classification is whether a country is placed on a certain level according to its ranking inside the subordinate system or in its position in the world community. The first provides a more accurate estimate but fails to project it without an adequate rescaling for comparison at international level. In our case what counts is the level of power in the subsystem, its type (based on equality or inequality), and its general grade, all of which effect the functioning of the region. In this respect, the existing relations between the countries of the subregions have to be taken into consideration; it is necessary to clarify whether the power of each state can be calculated at the regional level as a cumulative total, or if internal antagonisms neutralise the respective power of the different countries of the region. It is also important to analyse the differences in power capability between the various countries of a subsystem, and to consider whether an equalitarian distribution of power creates greater regional cohesion.

The structure of relations can be characterised according to the relationships between member-states of a subsystem. To do this one needs to determine:

(a) the spectrum of relations, which varies from: bloc relations to alliance, limited co-operation, equilibrium, stalemate, limited crisis to direct military conflict.
(b) the causes of relations — it is important to evaluate the significance of major issues, which may be the cause of either conflict or co-operation between various states in a subsystem (e.g. border disputes, competition over the same primary product, ideological affinity/ antagonism, linguistic relations, etc.).
(c) the means of relations — whether pacific or military means are used, or economic, organisational, political, cultural or subversive means.

Finally, the authors suggest four types of subsystems, in respect of the four pattern variables, ranging from : integrative systems, coherent systems, consolidative systems, to cohesive systems. The integrative systems have relatively high degrees of cohesion, communication, power and co-operation, with each of the other types of systems representing a lower level of rank according to the four pattern variables.

To the right of the column dealing with the subordinate systems we find a second one defining four levels of relationship, but this time taking into account only those states that belong to the 'core' of the subordinate system, excluding the 'peripheral' ones which, because of their links with other subsystems, blur the issue.

While Spiegel and Cantori's framework is useful for assessing the structural differences and similitudes among subsystems it does not provide all the elements required for an analysis of the role they play in the international system. The four criteria for comparison (pattern independent variables) are all related to the internal setting of the subsystem (level of cohesion, level of power, level of communications and structure of relations among the countries inside the subsystem). Without the inclusion of the variables of the international system — as in Chapter 1 — it becomes difficult to present a relevant ranking of subsystems. In Spiegel and Cantori's table, following the four mentioned criteria, integrative subsystems rank higher than consolidative, cohesive and coherent ones. They explain : 'The generally low level of power in the cohesive and coherent regions contributed to the ease with which external powers intrude. Yet, local competition and lack of regional cohesion — if not consolidation — facilitates intrusion, as the examples of the more powerful East and South Asian regions suggest.[6] The inference then of this table is that subsystems of the lower rank are more subdued by foreign powers, and therefore more dependent. In other words, they seem to present a linear process in which ' . . . we find that as we move from integrative to coherent regions, the conflict among intrusive powers becomes greater. Thus, integrative regions are distinctive for the near absence of competition among external nations.'[7]

This assumption is distorted by the fact that only internal determinants are taken into consideration and major intervening variables — the international system and the superpowers — are omitted. These variables have, in fact, the power to make the supposed linear process into a curvilinear one, in which at the lower point of relative independence in the international system we find subsystems that have been penetrated exclusively by a single superpower (the cores which are considered by Cantori and Spiegel as 'consolidative'). These are the cases of the two spheres of direct influence of the superpowers, characterised by the absence of the rival power and the low interaction with other secondary powers. The graphical representation of the amended proposition as shown on p. 67.

In more concrete terms, it means that a hypothetical country in a sphere of direct influence, ranking on a level with one in another subsystem, measured by internal elements of power, will most probably rank *lower* in the international system, by the mere fact of belonging to an area with limited superpower competition.

When comparing Latin America with Asia and Africa, although in general terms we shall demonstrate that the first represents a much

Relative Independence HIGH
in International   USA
Systems   USSR

                                      WESTERN EUROPE

                                                        ASIA
                                                        AFRICA

                              LATIN AMERICA
                              EASTERN EUROPE

                LOW   Number of Intrusive
                                          Powers

                     No intrusive   One intrusive Competing
                       Powers   Power   Intrusive
                                                   Powers

higher rate in the four pattern variables — a fact that is admitted in
Spiegel and Cantori's table — it nevertheless plays a lesser role in the
international system. On the other hand, while a comparison between
Eastern and Western Europe generally presents slightly lower rates of
the four variables in the first subsystem, its real level of 'power' in the
international system will tend to be drastically low.

Nevertheless, as the present chapter attempts to show, the comparison of subsystems based on structural internal differences can be
useful to demonstrate how these elements can influence different
degrees of resistance to the intrusive powers. Some of the differences
of those elements can elucidate the importance of the four pattern
variables in Eastern European and Latin American nations when facing
their paramounts. Furthermore, as shown by Spiegel and Cantori, since
both carry a similar weight in the suggested ranking of subsystems,
these tests might single out the common and distinctive elements.

The comparison between Latin America and the more currently
related subsystems of Asia and Africa will enable us to appraise some

of the 'developmental' comparative studies in which the three continents are presented in one category. Differences are great and
although it might be legitimate to take them as a whole in terms of
patterns of development, when focusing on the role those countries
play in the international system, it might prove better to exclude Latin
America from a unitary framework. The comparison between Eastern
and Western Europe is made to show the growing differences between
areas that were in the past, to a great extent, on approximate levels. By
way of both direct and indirect comparison, the similarities and differences between the two spheres of direct influence can be best
identified.

2 Latin America and Eastern Europe

While in the last section the emphasis was placed on analysing the
influence of external variables on the behaviour of countries in the
sphere of direct influence, by comparing the regional characteristics of
Eastern Europe and Latin America we might understand how structural
components can enable such subsystems to face superpower domination with a greater or lesser measure of success.

The level of cohesion in both subsystems is high in many respects.
Latin American countries are geographically contiguous and the majority of their economies are monoproductive and based on similar
single crops or natural resources. They tend to interact extensively in
attempts to co-ordinate exporting strategies towards countries outside
the subsystem and geo-political demands such as the claim for sovereignty over the patrimonial sea.

The cohesiveness of the Latin American region can be traced back
to common historical links, religion, race and culture, not only inside
the component states but crosscutting them.[8] The continent has also
experienced common political processes. It can be argued that any
event in any place in the world has an impact on every other part; however, if the intensity of the actual influence could be verified, it might
be said in our case that events which occur on one continent tend to
have an increased effect on the other countries within that continent.
The triumph of the Cuban revolution caused the United States to
follow a new economic policy on the continent, the Alliance for Progress which aimed at preventing the spread of communism to other
regimes. The anti-Cuban attitude of the inter-American organisation
was justified by opposing all totalitarian governments, using as scape-
goats the extreme dictatorships of the Dominican Republic and Haiti.
Another interesting example was the invasion of Guatemala in 1954 to

depose the leftist regime; as a consequence there was greater repression of communist elements in other Latin American countries. Martin Needler has demonstrated that certain political phenomena, such as changes from military dictatorial governments to civil-democratic ones, have a cyclical character in Latin America.[9] Lately, phenomena such as guerilla warfare, the radicalisation of the clergy and an increase in military intervention in politics have affected most Latin American countries.

However, heterogeneity is also found in Latin America. Different types of government exist on the continent, but there is no regional connection between their locations. The military Central American dictatorships resemble the regimes of Paraguay and Bolivia; Costa Rica's civilian system, until a few years ago, took after the former Uruguayan and Chilean democracy rather than any other country of the continent; and Cuba's socialist regime found its closest ally in Chile, the most distant country geographically. In the same way the problems of population distribution, based on ethnic composition, do not correspond to the location of these geographical units. Countries with a high Indian co-efficient are Guatemala, Bolivia and Ecuador; countries with an almost totally European population are Costa Rica, Uruguay and Argentina; Mexico, Colombia and Venezuela have a high percentage of *mestizos,* and Brazil follows Haiti in black population percentage. Neither can Latin America be divided economically into subregions. In spite of the fact that the countries with the highest gross national product per capita are concentrated in the southern area, Mexico and Costa Rica are not far behind, and Venezuela has the highest GNP on the continent. Therefore, the factors differentiating the various countries do not correspond to geographical proximity, making it impossible to divide the subsystem into smaller regions.[10]

In Eastern Europe physical affinity is manifested, from a geographical point of view, by an area of territorial continuity delimited by powers or alliances that occupy, or hold ambitions to occupy, this region: Russia in the East, the Central Powers in the West, and Turkey in the South. However, by observing the internal geo-political structure, three distinct regions become discernible: the Balkans, Central Europe and the Baltic countries. In all three cases there is a continuity with the past. The Baltic countries were annexed by the Soviet Union; Central Europe is now changed, with Germany divided and Austria associated with the subsystem of Western Europe; in the Balkans, Greece sits outside the subsystem, and Yugoslavia, Romania and Albania show only varying degrees of participation. If one compares the last two zones

from the economic, cultural and technological point of view, regional
differences are discernible. The Balkan countries are less industrialised,
have a lower GNP and a lower socio-cultural level. Before the Second
World War, Germany and Czechoslovakia were among the major impor-
ters of agricultural produce, and exporters of manufactured goods to
the Balkans.[11] The fact that changes in the physical organisational
unity of a region have occured does not necessarily imply the disappearance of established differences between the various subregions of a subsystem.

Countries which escape partially or totally from the severe control
of the superpower have adopted different allegiances: Albania to China,
Yugoslavia to the neutralists and Romania partially to the West.
Furthermore the historical and political internal problems of these
neighbouring countries are not a positive incentive for co-operation
among the three. In Latin America it seems that escape from superpower domination is in one direction only: although with different
shades and degrees of intensity, Peru, Chile and Cuba have been the
core of neutralism in the continent, with Cuba grossly bypassing them
by allying with the Soviet Union and Peru remaining at the other end
of the spectrum retaining closer links with the Third World. But all
three deviant cases maintained close ties of co-operation and understood that such a common front could strengthen them in their conflict with the United States.

The heterogenic languages, religion, ethnic and cultural characteristics of Eastern European countries not only separate the countries,
but also weaken the domestic structure of most of them. Indeed, the
unifying factors of all four elements can also be found in the Soviet
Union. The main spoken language is Russian, the orthodox religion
is represented in different proportions in most East European states,
and the USSR also includes religions shared by many other groups
in Eastern Europe. The Slavic element is in the majority over any other
ethnic group in the area; the seven large Eastern European groups are
Slavs (Poles, Slovaks, Slovenes, Croats, Serbs, Bulgarians), while
others (Romanians, Germans, Macedonians, Albanians) have an insufficient common bond of race and tradition. Many of these disinte-
grative elements can be traced far back into the past. Among the
countries of Eastern Europe there have been republics and monarchies,
collaborators and opponents of Fascism, regional rivalry, minorities
who do not conform with the immediately dominating ethnic groups;
a history of opposites and discord involving the nationalist populations
of the Baltic countries, and Ukranians, Tartars and other groups within

the Soviet Union.

Common political processes are phenomena that affect zonal relations, as can be seen in the inter-relationship between, for instance,
the *rapprochement* of Yugoslavia and the USSR in 1955 and the Hungarian invasion of 1956, or the independent position taken by Romania
and the invasion of Czechoslovakia in 1968. In all cases, the common
denominator is the level of the relations with the Soviet Union. It is
interesting to point out that in spite of a strong and oppressive superpower common to all the countries in the zone, nearly all of them have
witnessed attempts to gain increasing independence at one time or
another, but their efforts have been separate and unco-ordinated, with
mutual help never exceeding limited vocal support. The rigorous control of the USSR does not facilitate such action, and the background of
these countries does not stimulate close co-operation.

Almost all of the Latin American peoples have a similar Indo-Iberic
background, which throughout the years has provided a common factor
unifying the populations. The similar historical experience of emancipation from the yoke of the Spanish Empire produces an added feeling
of common identification. Generals such as Jose de San Martin or
Simon Bolivar are not considered the liberators of one country zone,
but as regional heroes who participated in the general movement of
independence from Spain. They are therefore considered the saviours
of all the countries of the continent, and represent the ideal of continental unity. Even in the twentieth century, popular leaders such as the
Nicaraguan Julio Cesar Sandino, the Mexican Lazaro Cardenas, or Fidel
Castro, have been considered as personalities on a regional scale.

In Eastern Europe from the point of view of cultural heritage, many
countries have had a different historical-cultural experience. In the
struggle for national liberation, there was no common foreign exploiter,
and the struggle occurred at different times. Also, a fragmented nationalism resulted from most of these countries gaining independence
relatively late (Romania in 1866, Bulgaria in 1876), and only then
achieving national unity. With the end of the First World War, Czechoslovakia, Poland, Estonia, Latvia, Lithuania and Yugoslavia gained independence. The Austro-Hungarian Empire was split up, Hungary being
reduced in size and established as an independent unit; Rumania
receiving new territories and Bulgaria losing some. The problem of
national unity for these new states was made more acute as a result of
the foreign domination that had preceded independence. Until recently,
the Soviet Union attempted to divert the potential nationalist attraction of the Eastern European countries towards Western Germany by

recalling memories of Nazi occupation; this policy was undermined by Bonn's *Ostpolitik,* and by now there are very few countries who do not see emancipation from the Soviet Union as the main direction for their nationalistic forces.

At the organisational level Latin America is less united than Eastern Europe, but its major difference is that it has a series of regional institutions from which the dominating superpower is absent. In Eastern Europe the formal structures are linked by a series of multilateral organisations, covering practically all possible fields of intercourse. However, it is noticeable that in all of them the Soviet Union fulfils a dominant, central and monopolising role. Because of this, Moscow has opposed all regional projects within Eastern Europe, e.g. Tito's proposals for a Balkan Federation between 1945 and 1948, and the Danube Federation, proposed by Hungary in 1965. In order to understand the separationist tendencies and subregional alliances disrupting subgroups or neighbouring powers, it is necessary to understand the pre-Communist situation of the region. In 1912-13 the Balkan Alliance against Turkey was formed between Bulgaria, Greece and Montenegro; however, in 1913 Romania and Serbia united in a war against Bulgaria. Czechoslovakia, Romania and Yugoslavia formed the Little Entente as a counterbalance to the revisionist countries of the region at the end of the First World War; yet, Czechoslovakia was handed to Germany in 1938 without any move from her allies. In 1921 Hungary signed an agreement orientated against the Soviet Union, but ten years later Poland signed a non-aggression pact with the USSR, and soon after that with Germany. The instability of the alliances and the fact that they did not geographically cover all the countries of the subsystem weakened regional and internal cohesion. On the other hand, the rapidity of the changes of political regime in all those countries only interfered with the process and its continuity, which in itself was not lasting. Furthermore the external problems of these countries were accentuated by the lack of internal legitimisation of their established regimes at the end of Second World War.

Even if we accept that the Communist ideology, which is shared by the ruling elites of all East European countries, should be a unifying factor, its existence in the Soviet Union undermines its potential as a homogenising force among the satellite states. The term 'Balkanisation', originating in the area is perhaps appropriate to describe the type of relationship existing between the countries of the region, which was weakened by lack of cohesion and the threat of strong external domination.

Latin American organisational unity is not a new phenomenon; the inter-American organisation is the only regional body among the twenty-three presently existing that precedes the Second World War. In spite of the fact that many of these organisations, such as the Organisation of American States, include its northern neighbour, there is a clear polarisation between the Latin American countries on the one hand, and the United States on the other. J.J. Arevalo, a former Guatemalan President, referred to this relationship as 'the shark and the 20 sardines'. All the same, the Latin American group is strengthened by the existence of a wide variety of regional organisations: there are governmental economic associations, i.e. the Latin American Area for Free Trade (ALALC); non-governmental, cultural or political associations, such as the Latin American Organisation for Solidarity (OLAS), which is pro-Cuban, the Latin American Center for Democratic Studies (CEDAL), which is pro-populist, the Latin American Sociologist Association (ALAS), etc. It is also important to point out that Latin America is recognised by the international community as a bloc, represented both through regional bodies, such as the Economic Commission for Latin America (CEPAL), and as a caucus in international representative meetings, such as at the United Nations agencies.

Regional self-determination reflects the desire of the people of the area — the political elite as well as the people — and is seen in the determination to establish a supranational framework, to emphasise the separateness and autonomy of Latin America. Many consider Latin America to be nothing more than a 'broken country' of 'dismembered people, by lack of communication and feudalism since a century ago'.[12] Politically, such expressions as Haya de la Torre's 'Indo-America', Hispanic, Ibero or Latin America, represent an ideal accepted by the forces of both the right and the left. The expressions 'Latin American nationalism' or 'Latin American internationalism', commonly used by both politicians and statesmen of the continent, emphasise the importance of Latin American unity, and the high cohesion in the international system. This is a phenomenon called by Herrera, 'regional nationalism', 'Pan-nationalism', or 'continental nationalism'.[13]

Finally, it is difficult to ascertain the 'true' feeling toward regional self-determination in Eastern Europe, as all sources which could be used to measure public opinion are unavailable. It is understood that large sectors of the population of the countries of Eastern Europe are dissatisfied, both at being classified as a subsystem, and at the consequences of their physical proximity to the Soviet Union; apparently they would prefer alternative structures, either on a more localised regional basis with their immediate geographical neighbours, or as part of a 'United Europe' that would include the West European states as well.

Eastern Europe can be described as a subsystem, the functional element in this situation being the penetration of the region by a foreign power, or as Cantori puts it, 'an intrusive subsystem'. He considers that ' . . . indeed, were it not for Soviet willingness to use force (including the nominal participation of its East European allies) in the form of the Czechoslovak occupation of August 1968 to maintain political cohesion, this region would be on the verge of developing into two competing *ententes* (Yugoslavia, Romania and Czechoslovakia vs. the more orthodox communist states)'.[14]

The level of communications, transportation, and personal communications is higher and more developed in Eastern Europe. However, as a result of linguistic similarities and the free and in most cases unrestricted use of the mass media at the regional level, Latin America is more advanced than Eastern Europe in these fields, thereby balancing out the difference. Illiteracy rates are higher in most Latin American countries restricting the possible use of written communication. However in the most developed countries of the continent (Chile, Argentina, Uruguay and Venezuela), higher education rates are not different from Eastern European ones, and this in turn produces comparable levels of newspaper circulation (see Table 2).

When analysing the *level of power* in absolute terms, the total population of Latin America — double that of Eastern Europe — is found to be larger than that of the United States, while the Soviet Union outstrips the number of inhabitants of the adjacent subsystem. Surely, one has to qualify any numeric conclusion about the real level of positive manpower, when skill and education convert large figures into an advantage. From this point of view, the abysmal differences between the two Americas make any possible inference about a major Eastern European weakness unfounded. Eastern European countries rank higher than Latin American, if all states in this continent are considered; however, when drawing parallels with the seven most developed countries of Latin America (Argentina, Brazil, Chile, Costa Rica, Mexico, Uruguay and Venezuela), socio-economic indicators tend to show similar rates for both areas. The fact that these seven represent in the main 75 per cent of the continent makes this comparison interesting; besides, it will be useful in banishing the effect of any distorted stereotypes about the general Latin American level of development. Much of Latin America is closer in these indicators to some of the poor European countries, especially to their so-called 'mother countries', Spain and Portugal. It is in the analysis of many of the tangible components of power that Table 2 should be incorporated. (Communist countries also include Mongolia).

This data do not help to explain, though, the socio-economic differences between Eastern Europe and Latin America. In the latter subsystem there is a greater and more varied polarisation of social groups, with less mobility between them. Eastern Europe, as far as distribution of wealth, land ownership and relative educational opportunities and economic means are concerned, presents a much more egalitarian society. Because the data are presented in national averages, they prevent us from appreciating existing differences inside the countries of the two subsystems, resulting from disproportionate distribution rates.All the same, it is still beneficial to analyse the enclosed indexes, as it provides an indication of the development levels reached.

In general terms we could consider that the percentage of urban population in the seven Latin American countries mentioned is higher (above 50 per cent), than in the whole of Eastern Europe (with the exception of East Germany, below 50 per cent). Furthermore, Latin Americans enjoy greater benefits from some consumer-orientated technological products. The United States, in her efforts to increase domestic markets, has facilitated the introduction of mass consumption items. The 'passenger cars per inhabitant' category in the mentioned table provides a sharp example of this.

Obviously, differences arise as a consequence of the disparate political systems and of the extent to which there is a monopolistic rule. Many Latin American regimes restrict human rights in proportions that do not differ greatly from the standards of Eastern Europe, although they are prevailingly less totalitarian. Still, many of the governments rule more or less in accordance with the principles of pluralistic democracy, representation through free elections is granted, and pressure and interest groups play an open and major role in the process of political and economic decision-making. In these cases, and in others ruled by charismatic personalist leaders, the degree of legitimation is far higher than in most of the non-deviant cases of Eastern Europe.

An important element of political power is the extent to which the population is homogenic in ethnic, religious and linguistic terms. The scene in our two subsystems is utterly different. Nearly all Eastern European countries present an heterogenous population from the religious point of view, as shown in Table 3.

Table 2: Comparative Figures of 7 Latin American Countries with Eastern European States

Country	Passenger Cars per inhabitant	Population Urban %	Rural %	Telephone x 100 inhab.	p/Capita income $ US	Higher Education x 100	Newspaper Circulation x 100	Life expec. years	Illiteracy %	Hospital bed per inhabitant	Physician per inhabitant
Albania	1 × 2300	35	65	0.31	$300	0.7	45	65-67	*	210	1300
Argentina	1 × 22	70	30	6.66	709	1.19	300	65	8.5	156	711
Brazil	1 × 51	53	47	1.6	215	0.19	33	56	39	275	2370
Bulgaria	1 × 857	48	52	4.5	620	1.0	172	70	10-15	158	560
Chile	1 × 145	70	30	2.5	510	0.4	118	59	12	233	2100
Costa Rica	1 × 63	34	65	1.69	426	0.4	77	63	16	243	2000
Czechoslovakia	1 × 38	48	52	11.71	1010	1.02	280	71	0-5	128	540
East Germany	1 × 92	70	30	10.42	1500	0.66	475	71	0-1	80	750
Hungary	1 × 88	40	60	6.2	800	0.5	178	70	3	129	509
Mexico	1 × 60	51	49	2.25	527	0.32	83	58-64	30-35	500	1810
Mongolia	*	25	75	1.0	390	0.75	103	64	25	117	800
Poland	1 × 118	50	50	2.5	730	0.80	167	68	5	168	786
Romania	1 × 1288	39	61	1.6	650	0.68	110	68	11	130	682
Uruguay	1 × 24	82	18	7	622	0.94	310	65-70	8	256	850
Venezuela	1 × 25	67	33	3.2	850	0.5	70	65-70	34	189	3520
Yugoslavia	1 × 80	41	59	2.2	510	0.95	90	65	20	227	1336

Source: Data compiled from *The New York Times Encyclopedic Almanac 1970,* section on individual 'World Nations'.

* Figures not available

Table 3: Main Religions in Eastern Europe

	Poland	Romania	Czecho-slovakia	Hungary	Yugo-slavia	Bulgaria
Catholics	90%	6%	73%	64%	37%	
Greek Orthodox		70%			49%	86%
Protestants			26%	8%		
Moslems					11%	13%

Source: Yigael Gluckstein, *Stalin's Satellites in Europe* (The Beacon Press, Boston, 1952), p. 211. Other minor religious groups are not represented in the table (Greek Catholic, Orthodox, Jews and Protestants in Poland; Greek, Orthodox, Jewish, old Catholic, Konfessionslos and Czechoslovak Church groups in Czechoslovakia, etc.).

Furthermore, the existence of numerous national minorities increases fractionalism and weakens internal cohesion in the subsystem, with the exception of East Germany: Magyars, Albanians, Slovenes, Slovaks, Croats, Serbs, Jews, Gypsies, Germans, Turks and Tartans, Armenians, Greeks and Bosnians remain attached to their own ethnicity. Seton-Watson[15] refers to three types of minorities: (a) national minorities in border regions, like the Germans in Bohemia, Albanians in Yugoslavia or Magyars in Romania; (b) minorities separated by a great distance from their own country, like the Greeks in Yugoslavia or Germans in Poland; (c) inhabitants of regions with exceedingly mixed populations; i.e. Banat, Transylvania or Macedonia.

The existence of ethnic groups who dominate in one country but live as a minority in another, has resulted in serious problems in the bilateral relations between those countries. 'A series of migrations, conquests and reconquests have caused an intermixture of national-alities in certain areas, which cannot be straightened out by any "ethnic frontier." '[16] The religious composition of Latin American countries is homogeneously catholic, the race differences have been gradually obscured by transitional types of mixed blood, and indigenous linguistic groups have tended to become integrated in the Spanish speaking majority.

The fourth pattern variable relates to the type of relations among the members of the subsystem. Again, the 'block' network in Eastern Europe is closely interwoven with the paramount superpower's, while the less strong 'alliance' type of relation in Latin America is in many cases free from superpower participation.

In comparing the characteristics of the subsystem relations, there seems to be a relative lack of conflict between the system countries in both cases. In each zone it is basically the superpowers' intrusion which prevents conflict situations arising between member-states; and where tension does exist, it is usually between the superpower and the 'satellite state'. In both subsystems there are still latent frontier problems, although in the case of Latin America they are generally not the result of demography, but simply of historical claims.

While most objective comparisons of internal conditions emphasise significant differences between the two subsystems, there is nevertheless a striking similarity of attributes resulting from the type of relationship between superpower and dependent state. It is characterised by economic stagnation, the maintenance of unpopular political regimes, and by the foreign policies of the countries subjugated to the interests of the superpower. This aspect cannot be analysed solely by the use of statistical data, but can be better understood by defining the images perceived by the elite sectors in the local countries, those which determine decisions and policies.

Even if we assume that a certain percentage of the population of East European countries 'collaborate', and are favourably inclined toward the USSR, and that in most of Latin America we find a pro-American elite, in most cases it is a totalitarian authority that maintains such an allegiance. It is also evident to any observer that a large number of the citizens of both 'empires' have strong feelings of resentment and antagonism toward their respective 'metropolis'. 'Anti-Yankeeism' in Latin America is such a widespread phenomenon that the majority of the candidates in democratic elections, even when belonging to the centre or conservative parties, feel obliged to use anti-imperialist terminology and to exploit anti-American feelings. This feeling in Latin America is easy to corroborate, as an enormous number of declarations and speeches can be shown expressing this sentiment. The existing restrictions in Eastern Europe control such open expression which often appears more subtly in theatre plays, like the Polish *Dziady* and other literary forms. Examples of this are the Czech exile Goldstucker, a writer who sees an analogy between East European-Soviet relations and Orwell's *Animal Farm;* and Pelikan, past director of Czechoslovakian television and former party leader, who released a publication criticising Soviet domination.[17] Perhaps it is Radio Tirana who openly expressed this feeling most accurately:

Following the socialist imperialist policy, the Kremlin (leaders) will use the new agreement to secure . . . and to consolidate its sphere of influence, especially in Eastern Europe, by increasing its control over an enslavement of these countries.[18]

There have been numerous expressions of 'Anti-Yankeeism' in Latin America, from Simon Bolivar[19] until today. Even in the eyes of certain politicians in the United States, this reaction is understandable. David Bronheim, one of the officials who worked for the implementation of the 'Alliance for Progress', relates:

> When I was in the government, I used to watch our Foreign Service officers trying to explain to serious Mexican officials the dangers of the Communist threat. The Mexicans were polite, and you could see them trying to work out how they could possibly make us believe they were worried about the Russians. Yet it is not the Russians who bother them. We have at various times invaded Haiti, Nicaragua, the Dominican Republic and Cuba. We provoked the secession of Panama, and we have arranged for armed invasions of Guatemala, and recently, Cuba. Our troops sit astride the Panama Canal. This is something that, as I say, we the United States, do not keep before us. Latin Americans do. Their memories of these things are much better than ours, and those memories do shape their view of us.[20]

Senator William Fulbright said:

> And in recent years some of the Eastern European governments have demonstrated that despite the communist ideology which they share with the Soviet Union, they still wish to free themselves as much as they can and as much as they dare from the overbearing power of Russia. It is natural and inevitable that Latin American countries should have the same feelings towards the United States.[21]

Latin Americans are not generally aware of the restrictions imposed on Eastern European citizens and vice versa. An outstanding exception, a Venezuelan ex-minister, commented: 'We are, in relation to the USA, in the same position of confrontation as Czechoslovakia *vis-à-vis* the USSR.'[22]

From the other end, strong evidence of similar feelings can be found in an open letter signed by 30 former Czechoslovak political prisoners, gaoled in the aftermath of the Soviet invasion of 1968. Reacting to a press statement issued by the Society of Czechoslovak Lawyers against the military Junta in Chile on 14 June 1974, the letter goes:

... All progressive people in the world should do everything in
their power to provide Chilean revolutionaries and democrats with
full material and moral aid in their just struggle for a democractic
society and socialism. If we are rather late in expressing our views it
is because many of us have had no opportunity until now. We
hereby proclaim our wholehearted solidarity with the progressive
forces in Chile and unequivocally condemn the brutality of the
fascist junta.

We claim the right to express our solidarity because we are linked
with progressive Chileans by common ideals and aims and in many
cases by a common fate. But we emphatically deny you, gentlemen
of the Society of Czechoslovak Lawyers, the right to express
support.

We do not know of a single case in which you have defended
human rights or civil liberties or have insisted that the norms of
legality be observed in your own country — Czechoslovakia ... [23]

It is not surprising, therefore, that in general, in Latin America the
Soviet Union is idealised by large political segments, while in Eastern
Europe the US is looked upon as representative of freedom and demo-
cracy.

When comparing the economic growth rate of these countries with
other regions, one finds a picture of economic stagnation. In Eastern
Europe, countries such as Czechoslovakia were, before the Second
World War, among the ten most highly industrialised countries in the
world. Likewise, Argentina in 1930 ranked ninth in the world in
foreign trade, and tenth in total industrial trade; furthermore, in the
years 1939-45, Argentina was nearly equal to Canada in per capita income, while today Canada's income is three times that of Argentina.[24]
In 1918, Argentina was seventh in the world according to per capita
income, and in 1944 was eighth in relation to gold reserves.[25] A similar
comparison could be drawn between Czechoslovakia and Austria before
and after the Second World War. Latin America is now falling behind
European development levels, and slowly approaching the Afro-Asian
level. Table 4 emphasises this position.

This stagnation is attributed to the exploitive policy followed by the
superpowers, who benefited from the economic vulnerability of the
countries in the zones under their influence.[26] At the same time that
they are economically exploiting their own sphere of influence, the
superpowers expend their economic resources in the form of foreign
aid to other world zones, as a result of the rivalry to gain influence; and

in the case of the USSR, Eastern Europe is also compelled to extend such aid. This stagnation has led to demoralisation, resulting from the realisation of the negative developmental trend: it usually results in inefficient public services, failure to maintain public property or replace worn-out equipment, and in corruption becoming the most effective (and accepted) method of gaining what is required from officialdom.

Table 4: Gross National Product per capita of some developed countries and Latin America, 1956 and 1967

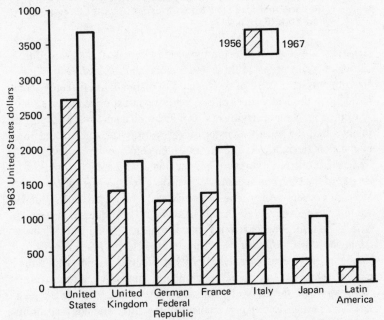

Source: Banco Interamericano de Desarrollo, Division de Desarrollo Económico y Social, Sección de Estadistica, *Tendencias del Desarrollo Económico de America Latina, 1950-1968* (Washington, D.C., July 1969). Table taken from Helio Jaguaribe, 'Dependencia y Autonomiá en América Latina' in Jaguaribe, Ferrer, Wionezek and Dos Santos, *La Dependencia Politica-Economica de America Latina* (Siglo XXI, Mexico) 1969, p. 8.

There has been a decline, in absolute terms, in the GNP of Latin America:

Table 5: Stagnation in Latin America

Period	Gross National Product absolute annual growth rate %	GNP annual growth per capita %
1950-55	5.1	2.2
1955-60	4.7	1.7
1960-65	4.5	1.5
1965-66	3.0	0

Source: CEPAL, Estudio economico de America Latina 1963 (E/CN12/696) and 1966 (E/CN12/1967). These statistics are taken from Frederico G. Gil, *Latin America-United States Relations* (Harcourt Brace Jovanovich, New York 1971), p. 247.

Generally, superpower intervention in the internal affairs of satellite countries is concerned with the undermining and replacement of governments, as a result of their failure to maintain a satisfactory commitment to the basic values of either a Communist or capitalist society. The consequence of carrying out its policies through loyal and 'puppet' rulers is that the superpowers reject and remove nationalistic and popular leaders from power. The Soviet Union achieves this policy of leadership control through internal manipulation of the Communist Parties of East European countries, who as a general rule follow Moscow's orders closely. The United States' methods in Latin America are more varied and subtle, usually involving the support of several elites. The traditional elite was formed from the 'sacred trilogy': the landowners or *Latifundist;* the army and the clergy. Recently the character of the established oligarchy has changed, particularly in the more developed countries of the continent. The fragmentation within the Church and the army hierarchies, especially in the last decade, is a sign of the radicalisation of a segment of the elite, which is a result of confrontation in the political process within their societies. In some, this change has been so radical that segments have come to join extreme anti-US forces, such as the guerilla movements in Brazil or Guatemala. On the other hand, interest groups inside the United States have also extended their support and protection to industrialists and submissive labour leaders. This policy is the result of diversification of participants in the formation of foreign policy in the US with regard to Latin America: the State Department, the Secretary of the Treasury, economic circles, the Pentagon, the CIA, the White House, the universities, exile groups, etc. Juan Bosch, the ousted ex-President of the Dominican Republic, considers that in Latin America the Pentagon acts as an independent factor, cultivating loyalty among the local military elites, in competition with their own national governments.[27]

The renouncing of their own interests by national governments in favour of those of the dominating superpower in the sphere of foreign policy is visible in the automatic adherence of the 'popular democracies' to the Soviet position in any international forum,[28] and on any issue. In Latin America, in matters considered to be of paramount importance to US foreign policy, Washington could formerly mobilise the automatic support of the majority of the countries. Fulbright summarises this situation in Latin America where in his opinion the dominant force is

> the aspiration of increasing numbers of people to personal and national dignity. In the minds of the rising generation there are two principal threats to that aspiration: reaction at home and domination from abroad . . . the United States has allowed itself to become associated with both.[29]

In brief, the differences inherent in the structural characteristics of the two subsystems are great, but an overall weighing of the four pattern variables results in a similar ranking of them as subsystems with a consolidating core. The internal cohesion of Latin America seems firmer as does its adherence to regional organisations separate from the superpower. However, when we measure the tangible elements that determine the level of power of the component states, Eastern Europe stands higher in most socio-economic indicators, although perhaps not as much as could be expected by some preconceived views about Latin American development. Communication levels show more prominent interaction in Eastern Europe and, finally, intra-regional conflicts have been drastically reduced due to the presence of the superpowers, although disintegrating elements in Eastern Europe remain far more latent than in Latin America.

Some of the domestic weaknesses in the countries in the sphere of direct influence of the superpowers are related to the processes of modernisation in both areas. Although this is usually accepted in the Latin American case, it is significant to quote Seton-Watson explaining the instability in Eastern Europe after the decline of the old empires as 'the distortion of economic, cultural and political forums arising from the impact of the West on the East, the conflict between the sixteenth and twentieth centuries which exist side by side in Eastern Europe'.[30]

Finally, the dominance of the superpowers created the feeling among great sectors of the populations in both spheres of direct influence that their particular misfortune could be attributed mainly — or exclusively — to the exploitative type of relationship. Some perceptions on both sides seem to be very acute: economic stagnation, the maintenance of unpopular non-representative political regimes with subjugated foreign policies, caused by unilateral foreign intervention. But perhaps this could be better corroborated by pointing out that those countries which became the deviationist exceptions — Yugoslavia, Cuba, Peru, Romania or Albania — have had more rapid economic development than before emancipation, the regimes tend to receive more popular support than the neighbouring ones and achieve a more independent position of the international system. It is to the characteristics of these exceptional cases that Section 3 is devoted.

3 Latin America and Afro-Asia

In political circles it is common to treat the Third World as an integral unit, a term encompassing three continents — Africa, Asia and Latin America — and many social science scholars who are searching for theories to apply to the developing countries accept this assertion in the formulation of their works.[31] One of the experts, James Coleman, recognises that in many cases such a generalisation limits the typology of each of these two areas.[32]

Certain leftist groups classify the three continents as being of the same status in their fight against 'imperialism',[33] however Soviet representatives[34] and Regis Debray[35] all reject the theory that Latin America and Afro-Asia share equal attributes.

Many of the points differentiating Afro-Asia from Latin America are formulated in articles by John D. Martz and Edward Williams[36] Because of the controversial character of such a comparison it might be worthwhile to examine it in depth. In this work we shall attempt to show systematically the differences between the two areas Latin America vis-à-vis Afro-Asia, in almost all fields. Still, in spite of the more advanced stage of development of Latin America, the awareness of a common lot with Afro-Asia is steadily evolving. Of the 20 countries of the continent, we could say that seven countries — with a combined total of 185 million people, more than three quarters of the continent — are more suitably classified at the same level as such countries as those of Eastern Europe, Portugal, Greece or Spain.[37] The others have similar characteristics to those of Afro-Asia in the economic, cultural and social fields, although in certain cases at a higher level. The coefficients shown in the following table should then be understood as representing the *average* picture of Asian and African countries, drawing parallels with the *less* developed and *smallest* sector of Latin American society.[38]

The level of cohesion. The Latin American subsystem is a more cohesive and homogeneous unit than that of Afro-Asia. This fact is exemplified by Spiegel and Cantori, who take Latin America as a single subsystem, while Africa is divided into five, and Asia into four such systems. This cohesion is based on the unifying nature of the structure in Latin America, for which there are a variety of reasons. Historically, the independence movement and the process of national unification in Latin America started more than 150 years ago, and was completed by the end of the nineteenth century, the exception being Panama, which seceded in 1904 from Colombia. Many of these countries achieved their present position of statehood even before some of the European countries, e.g. Italy, modern Poland and others in Eastern Europe, countries considered today to have stable structures. The African and Asian continents, on the contrary, consist in most cases of countries which have only recently gained their independence, and still face problems over internal cohesion and national unity.

As regards geographical borders, recognised and accepted in most Latin American cases, Afro-Asia is still suffering from conflicts resulting from borders arbitrarily drawn by the colonial powers, which do not generally follow geographic or ethnic criteria. Border conflicts exist between Ethiopia and Somalia, and Kashmir is at issue between India and Pakistan. Clashes resulting from the desire of ethnic groups for self-determination were seen in the bitter fighting in Biafra, in the search for autonomy by the Kurds in Iraq or the black Catholics in Sudan. Wars of secession also rage among the new states, as in the recent Indo-Pakistan war, which gave birth to Bangladesh. These internal disputes weaken the attempt to build up nationalism, and therefore limit the government's ability to renounce sovereign rights in order to strengthen supranational regional organisations. Since the creation of all the new independent states in Afro-Asia, only Tanzania (Tanganyika and Zanzibar) has managed to create a single unit from what was formerly two separate units. Generally the trend was in the opposite direction: India split into two on gaining independence, Singapore left the Malaysian federation, the Mali federation broke up into Mali and Senegal.[39]

In Latin America, the fact that nearly all the movements for national independence had the same colonial enemy to overthrow (Spain) was a unifying factor, and this was a common nineteenth-century experience. In Africa and Asia, the new nationalism, or nationalistic movements, were against various colonial powers : France, Britain, Holland, Spain, Portugal, Belgium and formerly Germany and Italy. This fact de-

Table 6: Comparative Figures of Remaining Latin American Countries with Average African and Asian States

Country	Passenger Cars per inhabitant	Population Urban %	Rural %	Telephone x 100 inhabitant	Per capita income $ US	Higher Education x 100	Newspaper Circulation x 1000	Life expectancy years	Illiteracy %
Bolivia	1 x 700	34	66	0.62	$121	0.232	30	51	65	4,000
Cameroon	1 x 268	15	85	0.09	104	0.04	0.3	43	80-90	28,600
Colombia	1 x 182	53	47	2.00	280	0.2	56	55	37	2,400
Cuba	1 x 50	60	40	2.92	330	0.4	88	*	22.8	1,180
Dahomey	1 x 385	16	84	0.18	75	0.04	0.9	37	90-95	20,400
Domin. Rep.	1 x 134	70	30	0.87	266	0.5	27	50	36	1,680
Ecuador	1 x 341	35	65	0.89	190	0.24	47	53	31	3,473
Egypt	1 x 310	38	62	1.07	160	0.7	2	51-54	70	2,368
El Salvador	1 x 110	39	62	1.18	284	*	47	57-61	52	4,430
Guatemala	1 x 140	34	66	0.7	308	0.15	31	50-60	62	3,690
Haiti	1 x 915	12	88	0.09	80	0.03	2.2	40	90	14,000
Honduras	1 x 200	26	74	0.41	227	0.2	19	46	55	5,400
Indonesia	1 x 712	9.4	90.6	0.15	100	0.25	15	44	55-60	34,920
Nepal	*	12	88	0.04	66	0.05	3	25-40	88	72,000
Nicaragua	1 x 126	41	59	0.7	350	0.2	49	54	50	2,560
Nigeria	1 x 968	19	81	0.12	63	0.16	7	40-50	80-88	32,800
Panama	1 x 41	42	58	4.28	568	0.42	81	59	22	1,990
Paraguay	1 x 198	40	60	0.62	200	0.17	*	55	25	1,850
Peru	1 x 59	48	52	1.1	325	0.50	47	55	32	1,960
Phillippines	1 x 200	80	20	0.55	160	0.13	27	50-60	40-50	1,330
Somalia	1 x 509	89	11	0.17	50	0.24	*	*	95	31,900

Source: The data were compiled by the author from the *New York Times ENCYCLOPEDIC ALMANAC 1970*, Section on individual 'World Nations'.

*Figures not available

emphasises the common struggle aspect, with each new nation experiencing a different road to independence — the road being very much dependent on the colonial regime. Furthermore, the formation of new elites has not crystallised, and has led to a discontinuity and lack of of stability — not of the personal type as represented by the head of government, but within the competing elites, retarding the development of more stable relationships with the countries of the zone.

Similarly, the very fact of having recently achieved liberation has left a legacy of fundamental barriers: idiosyncratic differences, different cultural traditions and a variety of languages. The problem existed even in cases like those of Togo and Cameroon, where three different colonial powers ruled. Latin America differs not only in a historical-cultural perspective, as the modern economic development problems it faces are different; its efforts to achieve political and economic emancipation are mainly related to the creation of new links with one power, the United States. Afro-Asian states, on the other hand, are still trying to achieve full emancipation from the previous colonial powers; they now face the problem of neo-colonialism, as well as fending off penetration, economic and political, by the new superpowers.

Latin America's homogeneity in various fields favours unity in action, as well as a stable structure. The population is 90 per cent Catholic, proportionately distributed in the same ratio in all areas of the continent (there are more than 200 million Roman Catholics, the greatest concentration in any one area of the world). Asia and Africa are riven by different religions and sects, which divide state from state, as well as countries internally. In many cases these are minorities, whose religious centres, from both a population and a spiritual point of view, are located outside their own subregion. The same is applicable to cultural and linguistic homogeneity. Although there is a heterogeneous ethnic population in Latin America, the existence of mixed types such as the *mestizo* and the *mulato* modifies the racial differences by acting as an equaliser over the generations. In Asia and Africa, racial composition in the regions is basically homogeneous; however, strongly-felt identification with sects and tribes acts as a divisive element, an element which is stronger than the potential racial homogeneity. In the case of countries with a multiracial composition, the existing tensions are generally increased.

As a result of these circumstances, Latin America shows greater institutional cohesion, manifested in the existence of permanent, regional and *ad hoc* organisations. However, the greater institutional activity in the area is basically of an inter-American character: the

Organisation of American States includes the intrusive subsystem, the United States. This implication is stressed by Nye

> It is interesting to contrast the record of the OAS with that of the Organization of African Unity (OAU) in peacekeeping. In several cases, particularly in Central America, the OAS has been successful — a major reason for this success however has been the dominant role and leadership of the U.S. within the organization.[40]

Although this definition of the relationship may be accurate when applied to conflicts between Latin American countries, in cases of confrontation between those countries and the dominant superpower, the situation is different.

Latin American regionalism is also reinforced by the existence of institutions such as the Economic Commission for Latin America (ECLA), established by the United Nations, ' . . . an organization in which the United States has usually been a minor dissenting participant, [it] has been enhanced by the fact that the OAS is widely viewed as a United States dominated institution.'[41] When comparing the ECLA with the Economic Commissions of the United Nations for Asia and the Far East, and for Africa (ECAFE and ECA, respectively), Gregg considers that ECLA has been more successful in the integration process.[42] Also in the economic field, ALALC (Latin American Free Trade Area), and the MCCA (Central American Common Market), have made greater progress than similar movements to create markets and free trade areas in Afro-Asia. In the Afro-Asian continents as a result of traditional colonial relationships, the various supranational organisations, whether based on geographic, religious or economic criteria, were unable to agree due to conflicting loyalties to various organisations incompatible with one another, thereby harming the internal cohesion of the subsystem countries as in the case of linguistic or ideologic based groups.[43] An interesting example was the situation of having both South African and Black African countries as members of the British Commonwealth, and the friction that arose over the issue of the expulsion of the Praetoria regime.

In Latin America, regional organisations are orientated towards a Latin American or inter-American goal, a complementary and not contradictory target. Even subregional organisations, based on a specific geographical unit, such as the Andean group (Venezuela, Colombia, Peru, Ecuador, Chile, Bolivia), or the smaller Central American Republics, do not seriously oppose or put pressure on overall regional inte-

gration (like the Benelux countries in the Western European subsystem). In Africa and Asia, on the other hand, regional groups have
had a negative effect on the continental organisation.[44] However, the
relative insecurity of the foreign politics of individual countries — a
consequence of the internal infrastructure detailed above — results in
many of the countries identifying with collective political goals in the
international arena. Such aims do not necessarily manifest themselves
within the framework of the regional or continental subsystem; they
may involve a supracontinental structural-neutralism, being generally
represented within, and by, the Conferences of Non-Aligned Nations.
Finally, greater awareness of the need for unity exists amongst the population of Latin America, and this is a contributing factor to the cohesion of that subsystem.

The *level of communication* is conditional upon an adequate infra-
structure. The lack of a common language, and illiteracy, are great obstacles to regional intercommunication. In Latin America the Spanish
language is a unifying link for eighteen of the countries, while Portuguese and French (the language of the remaining two) have not con-
constituted an insurmountable barrier to mutual understanding. The
linguistic factor hinders communication in Afro-Asia, even to the
extent of resulting in internal wars by linguistic minorities, e.g. the
Kurds of Iraq. One of the most outstanding exceptions where language
has served as a unifying factor is the Arab League, representing all
Arab-speaking countries. The differences in the educational level can be
seen in the table on p. 90.

This table enables us to appreciate clearly the differences between
Latin America and Afro-Asia. While 50 per cent of the countries to the
south of the United States have less than 30 per cent illiteracy, in Africa
77 per cent of the countries have more than 70 per cent illiteracy, while
in Asia the rate is 50 per cent. It is also relevant to analyse the rates of
high school and university education, as it has a bearing on communication between elites. Out of the 28 Latin American countries, in 15
more than 1 per cent of the total adult population are university students; of the 44 African countries, in only 4 countries 20 graduates
number more than 1 per cent; and from the 25 Asian countries, only
ten had a higher percentage than 1 per cent of university students.[45]

In Latin America the transportation system is relatively well
developed, especially in major urban areas and in the coastal regions. A
pan-American road network has almost been completed, unifying the
countries of the continent from north to south. Sea transportation
amongst the ports of South America is also important, in addition to

Table 7: Distribution of Countries According to Educational Status
Around 1960

Range	Developing countries				Rest of world
	Total	Western hemisphere*	Africa	Asia	
Number of countries in which the proportion of literates was (percentage of population 15 years of age and over)					
Under 10	16	—	14	2	—
10-29	30	1	22	7	—
30-49	16	5	7	4	1
50-69	11	7	1	3	2
70-89	18	9	—	9	7
90 and over	3	3	—	—	9
Total	94	25	44	25	19
Number of countries in which the proportion without formal education was (percentage of population 25 years of age and over)					
Under 10	1	1	—	—	12
10-29	4	3	—	1	4
30-49	5	3	—	2	3
50-69	12	7	1	4	4
70-89	20	10	6	4	2
90 and over	14	1	7	6	—
Total	56	25	14	17	25
Number of countries in which the proportion whose formal education extended beyond the primary level was (percentage of population 25 years of age and over)					
Under 5	36	14	12	10	1
5- 9	10	7	—	3	7
10-19	8	4	1	3	12
20-29	1	—	—	1	4
30 and over	—	—	—	—	3
Total	55	25	13	17	27

Source: Figures selected from *Yearbook of National Accounts Statistics 1969,*
vol. II, 1 (UN Dept. of Economic and Social Affairs, Statistical Office,
New York), p. 61.

*Includes all countries south of the United States. The additional five of the
twenty so analysed in our Latin American subsystem are not believed to alter the
general picture.

the Panama Canal, which provides an inter-ocean maritime route. All the same, transportation problems still exist in South America, especially between the coastal regions of the different countries and the interior of the mountainous and jungle regions (in the case of Brazil and Peru). Aviation is an important aspect, with an efficient airline service daily linking the capitals and main cities of Latin America.

Overland transportation creates tremendous difficulties in Afro-Asia due to natural obstacles not yet overcome, and the lack of highway routes. Even air transportation is severely limited in the region; this is highlighted by the poor air service existing at present between Western and Eastern Africa.

Mass communication is related to the publication of journals or books which have a market beyond their national frontiers. Mexico, Uruguay and Argentina are known as great editorial centres for books distributed over the whole continent; newspapers such as *La Prensa* and *La Opinion* of Argentina, *Marcha* of Uruguay, and *Excelsior* of Mexico are read by the elites of other Latin American countries. Radio broadcasting is not an important means of communication with the outside world; it only becomes signficant when, because of censorship in a dictaroal regime, certain sectors of the population start to rely on foreign stations. The Mexican and Argentinian motion picture industry supplies the majority of Spanish-speaking countries with their films. Newspapers in Argentina are read by 300 of every 1,000 inhabitants, in Uruguay 310, Panama 81; Colombia 56 and Guatemala 31. Mass media communication in Afro-Asia is more restricted, both in relation to inter-regional contacts and also within the countries themselves. The newspaper circulation for the Cameroons does not even reach 0.3 per 1,000, Egypt 2, Nigeria 7, Indonesia 15 and the Philippines 27 per 1,000 inhabitants.

In other mass media channels the difference between the three continents continues to be marked by a higher level of development in Latin America. The data on the next page shows the number of countries above the median in radio and television receivers.

Data about individual countries varies between 1959 to 1966. It should be stressed that some of the African and Asian countries heading the 'above median' category are rather small states (Hongkong, Singapore, Kuwait and South Yemen), while in the case of Latin America, many of the leading countries (Argentina, Chile, Mexico, Venezuela) also represent a large percentage of the continent's population. The disproportion shown in the statistics for TV receivers should be mentioned. Many Asian and African countries and a few Latin American ones which most probably belong to the 'below median' category do not provide figures.

Table 8: Radio and Television Receivers in Latin American, African
       and Asian countries

		Latin America	Asia	Africa
radio receivers (median : 100 per 1,000 inhabitants)	above median	13	8	3
	below median	9	16	38
TV receivers (median : 13 per 1,000 inhabitants)	above median	10	5	2
	below median	9	15	24

Source: Data compiled by Charles Lewis Taylor and Michael C. Hudson, *World
       Handbook of Political and Social Indicators* (Yale University Press, New
       Haven, 1972), pp. 242-7.

In regard to indirect personal communication, the comparison between
the subsystems in the number of telephones once again illustrates the
gap between them. Uruguay has 7 telephones per 100 inhabitants;
Mexico, 2.25; El Salvador, 1.18; and Paraguay, 0.62. On the other
hand, Dahomey has 0.18 per 100; Indonesia, 0.15; Egypt, 1.07; the
Philippines, 0.55.[46] Furthermore, the use of the postal services is institutionalised to a greater degree in Latin America, while Africa and Asia
are handicapped by linguistic differences and a high illiteracy rate.

Inter-American tourism by the elites of the various countries of Latin
America is an accepted practice, which has resulted in the development
of resort cities: Punta del Este in Uruguay; Viña del Mar in Chile; Rio
de Janeiro in Brazil; Acapulco in Mexico; these are just the main centres
of attraction on the continent. In Africa and Asia, instead of an inter-
change of elites between countries on a tourist basis, the centre of
attraction is usually the metropolis of the ex-colonial power.

On the political level, exchanges of official visits is an accepted practice in Latin America, not only restricted to the upper political elite; it
is a form of intercourse used by representatives of official bodies,
public organisations, parliamentary groups, etc. In Africa and Asia,
exchanges are almost totally limited to visits by the high-ranking political elite (Presidents, Kings, Prmiers, Ministers, etc.) to their opposite
numbers. In Latin America, in order to facilitate inter-regional travel,
most of the countries have abolished visa requirements for nationals of
the region.

The phenomenon exists in Latin America of the temporary migration
of workers from the underdeveloped countries to those with a higher

degree of economic development.[47] Thousands of Paráguayans work in
Argentina, and hundreds of Argentinian professional work in Sao Paulo
and other propsperous centres in Brazil. In Africa, with the exception
of the Southern subsystem, the urban centres have not yet reached a
sufficient degree of industrialisation to act as a migration centre for
more than a small part of the rural population of that country; migra-
ting workers, both skilled professionals and labourers, are more likely
to be attracted to the urban centres of the ex-colonial power.

When comparing the *level of power* in Latin America and Afro-Asia,
it is important to stress the differences in the power and its stages of
development, but not in terms of rivalry and military strength. For the
majority of the countries in those subsystems, cumulative military
power alone does not constitute a major goal.[48]

In the field of economic capacity, what is important is not the comparison of natural resources, but the exploitation of them, and the level
of industrialisation and productivity.[49] Table 9 enables us to understand the individual economic level and the total power of the regions.

Table 9: Estimate of the Total Gross National Product, and Per Capita
         Income (US dollars) 1968

	1958	1963	1965
Africa [a]	30,400	42,000	48,400
[b]	110	140	150
North America [a]	488,854	639,839	744,494
[b]	2,546	3,071	3,476
Latin America [a]	56,100	78,000	93,700
[b]	290	350	390
Asia [a]	101,000	161,200	197,700
[b]	120	160	190
Asia (Without Japan) [a]	69,000	93,300	109,400
[b]	90	110	120

Source: Yearbook of National Accounts Statistics, op. cit., pp. 15-18.
[a] Gross National Product in the National market (millions of dollars)
[b] Gross National Product per capita (US dollars)

One important indication of the level of development and industrialisation is the production and degree of electrification. Latin America, as
a whole, produces 394.4 kilowatt hours per person per year, the Middle
East 169, Africa 75.4 and Asia 63.6.[50] Labour statistics for Latin
American countries indicate an average of 13 per cent of the work-force

located in industry, while Africa and Asia show only 9 per cent.[51]

Table 10 provides an indication of the levels of private consumption. Though not necessarily positive proof of affluence, it still closely correlates with the level of development. Latin American countries (Western Hemisphere) present in all quartiles a level two or three times higher. Figures representing the average annual rate of increase show Latin America leading in all but the lower quartile, where Asia is progressing faster.

At the other extreme, data compiled about the 32 states which come into the category of the 'poorest nations of the world' where there is a danger of hunger leading to massive numbers of deaths, include four in the Western Hemisphere (Haiti, Guyana, El Salvador and Honduras), eight Asian countries (Bangladesh, South Yemen, India, Cambodia, Laos, Pakistan/Sri Lanka and Yemen) and twenty African countries (Central African Republic, Chad, Dahomey, Ethiopia, Ghana, Guinea, Ivory Coast, Kenya, Lesotho, Madagascar, Mali, Mauritania, Niger, Senegal, Sierra Leone, Somalia, Sudan, Cameroon, Tanzania and Upper Volta).[52] Excluding most Arab countries, the list includes vast African and Asian regions, while in Latin America it covers approximately 3 per cent of the total population of the subcontinent.

In the political process in Latin America, the participation of the masses is at a higher level than in almost all of the Afro-Asian countries. It should be understood, though, that this involvement is not always in support of the system; in many cases it reflects a strong and articulated opposition. In the electoral campaign in Argentina, three months before the elections in March 1973, 40 political parties were listed and four party fronts (the first with 5 parties, the second with 3, the third with 29 provincial parties and 1 national, and the fourth with 10 provincial parties).[53] This might be an extreme case, but it underlines the fact that in Latin America, with few exceptions, the multiparty system is an accepted and established fact. Latin America is similar to many Latin European countries in its wide range of political pluralism. On the other hand, most African and Asian countries not only lack a multiparty system, but legitimate a single party regime as an effective way of accelerating the development process, and as an additional instrument in the integration and identification of the people with the ruling power. In Africa in many cases even the 'one party' system is no more than rule by a small 'oligarchical' group or clique, who have adopted the trappings of a party. These so-called 'parties' scarcely resemble the European meaning of the word; the necessary preconditions for a party system do not exist, as a result of a lower development level.[54] In

Table 10: Private Consumption in Developing Countries, 1960-1968

Item and region	Average (dollars)	Distribution					
		First quartile		Median		Third quartile	
		Dollars	Population in countries below this level (millions)	Dollars	Population in countries between the first and third quartiles (millions)	Dollars	Population in countries above this level (millions)
Per capita level of private consumption 1967							
Developing countries	131	85	853	143	599	252	204
Western hemisphere[a]	315	205	32	282	170	436	46
Africa[b]	93	60	139	90	139	143	30
Asia[c]	97	87	676	139	278	200	47
	Average (percentage)	Percentage		Percentage		Percentage	
Average annual rate of increase							
Developing countries	4.3	2.7	211	4.2	1,023	5.4	308
Western hemisphere[a]	5.0	3.9	32	5.0	135	5.5	81
Africa[b]	2.3	2.2	147	3.1	124	4.6	37
Asia[c]	4.3	3.0	55	4.3	865	6.6	67

Source: Yearbook of National Accounts Statistics, p. 32
[a]Twenty-six countries
[b]Forty-four countries
[c]Twenty-six countries

Latin America, even in the case of dictatorial regimes, the importance of democratic-representative institutions, or at least the principle that they represent, is so ingrained amongst the population that Stroessner in Paraguay and Somoza in Nicaragua maintained a form of parliamentary institution, which included nominal opposition parties. Where the constitution denies the right of re-election to presidents, dictators in that position will in many cases resort to a multitude of tricks in order to circumvent the constitution but remain 'within the confines of the law'.

European political ideologies have a well-established tradition in Latin America. In 1833, Esteban Echeverria wrote the 'Socialist Dogma' in Argentina which followed the utopian thinkers; in the process of independence, the influence of the French Revolution and the American War of Independence was great, especially on the *criollos*. Many of the Latin American political parties based their names and programmes on European parties, e.g. the liberals, the conservatives, radicals, Christian democrats, socialists and communists. In Africa and Asia the process was different, with the political elite and organisation being drawn from the native element which violently opposed the domination of European powers. As a result, in most cases the political structure is of a local character, with European distinctions absent, and with it the following of an independent integrative process. Furthermore, the transfer of the European multiparty system to Latin America also brought political problems similar to those experienced in some of the European countries, e.g. France which faced the problem of the separation of Church and State. In France it was the Radical party that raised the anti-clerical banner, which also happened in Argentina and Chile at the beginning of this century.

Williams presents a comparative table, indicating the differences in political systems between Latin America and Afro-Asia (Table 11).

As regards social stratification, we find in Latin America numerous pressure groups which resemble the Western countries, in their organisation differentiated by economic, professional, religious, cultural or political affinities.

Trade unions in countries like Cuba, Argentina, or Chile have been important factors in political change. On the continent as a whole the trade union movement, in the furtherance of its aims, adopted similar methods to Europe, i.e. use of any known type of strike.[55] The student body in Latin America is also an important factor in the process of social and political change; they have been known to use a variety of means, ranging from participation in the university government to guerilla warfare. There is also almost no known political ideology which did not find followers amongst the students of the continent — Trotskyism, Castroism, Maoism, pro-Soviet Communism, anarchism, populism, 'Third-Worldism', etc. This further illustrates the continent's ideological pluralism, this time in the fragmentation of the left, which is no less drastic than in the European countries. In the majority of Afro-Asian countries, similar pressure groups are not so vociferous or acceptable; where they do exist, they usually reflect personal linguistic or ethnic loyalties. In Africa and Asia the variety of pressure groups is more limited; and if one can say that the existence and activity of more articulate groups is a sign of higher development, the lack of such groups in Afro-Asia conforms with the general picture.

Table 11: Political Party Systems: Latin America vs. Afro-Asia

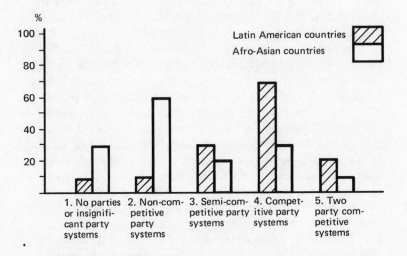

Source: Fred R. von der Mahden, *Politics of the Developing Nations* (Englewood Cliffs, New Jersey, Prentice-Hall Inc., 1964), pp. 54-63.

In a certain number of Latin American countries there exists a middle class which is relatively well-developed. According to Johnson, the middle sectors make up 35 per cent of Argentina's population, 30 per cent in Chile and Uruguay and 15 per cent in Brazil and Mexico.[56] Another source reports that the mean size of the middle class in comparative terms was in 1970, 71 for Latin America, 62 for the Middle East and North Africa, 51 for Asia and 37 for Tropical Africa.[57] This fact presents a stratification pyramid more 'normal' than that of Afro-Asia, in which mobility in Latin America is higher in absolute terms.[58]

Of importance in Latin America are the demographic changes that have taken place in the last few years, transforming the Latin American population from a rural to a more urban society. In 1970 there were in Latin America (population 240 million), 24 cities with more than half a million inhabitants, while in the US (200 million) there were only 21 such cities. Sao Paulo in Brazil had a population of 8 million; it doubled in size in less than a decade. This sign of modernisation, if such it can be called, brought with it the problem of urbanisation; an ex-rural population, improverished and surviving in the 'misery belts' surrounding the major cities,[59] became a sub-proletarian 'urban poor', racked by social problems. In Africa the situation is completely different; there are very few cities exceeding half a million inhabitants. In all of Black Africa (37 countries), no city exists with a population greater than 1 million, and there are only four cities exceeding half a million; in 11 countries there are no towns even reaching 100,000 inhabitants.[60] In Asia the cities are generally over-populated, but this is a result of the population density of that continent; all the same, the rural population is still higher than the urban one. In the field of public health there are also great differences. In Latin America, 90 per cent of the countries have a doctor for at least every 5,000 inhabitants; in Africa, this is the case in only 12 per cent of the countries, and in Asia 15 per cent.[61]

A further element of power is related to the quality of diplomacy. In this case, Afro-Asia's greater success in making these regions more independent factors in international politics cannot be attributed to a more skilled and professional diplomatic body — in both regions diplomats are not usually chosen in many states on the grounds of merit or aptitude, and a body of specialised personnel does not usually exist. What considerably limits independent action by the Latin Americans is not the difference in the quality of diplomacy, but the objective conditions of the world system.

Finally, a comparison of military power between the different regions should not be oriented to calculating what the result of a possible rivalry between these two entities would be, but to see how the military powers of the countries of Afro-Asia and Latin America strengthen their policy potentials vis-à-vis the superpowers. In almost all cases, even in a purely defensive situation, few of these countries could forestall superpower action militarily. It is also necessary to analyse the extent to which military power is a divisive factor between countries of the various subsystems. In Latin America, as a result of the wars of the

nineteenth century, and such conflicts as those between Bolivia and
Paraguay, and between Ecuador, Peru and Colombia in the twentieth
century, there now exists 'a tacit acceptance of a balance of military
power, particularly among the South American countries'.[62] However,
in Afro-Asia there is no such institutionalisation of the balance of military power; tension does exist between neighbouring countries, and in
many of the poorer ones it is only the economic limitations that prevent such tension from degenerating into military conflict. The disruptive role of military power in developing countries, as far as regional
matters are concerned, is minor, as long as international goals do not
include territorial expansion, and there is relatively little danger of invasion. This is the case in the majority of Latin American countries,
where the military is basically an active power factor only in the internal structure, i.e. on the political level, in the anti-subversive
struggle against guerillas, or in pressurising the extra-continental common enemy, the Soviet Union. This is a contributing factor to greater
regional cohesion.

The *type of relation* existing at the inter-regional level in Latin
America is, on average, one of limited co-operation, reaching the level
of alliances in certain fields or specific cases, or the formalisation of
neutral relations. A stalemate relationship between the countries at the
centre of the subsystem seldom occurs, nor does the outbreak of
limited crises. During the present century, besides the Salvador-
Honduras 'football war', the War of Chaco between Paraguay and
Bolivia, and the Leticia border dispute between Peru and Colombia,
there have not been any serious prolonged confrontations. Conflicts in
Asia, Africa, and the Middle East seem to have broken out with greater
frequency than in Europe and the Americas in every decade of the
twentieth century, with the exception of 1908-17, when Europe surpassed all.[63]

The few cases of conflict that arose in Latin America were basically
frontier disputes, but frontiers that have been in existence for over a
century. Most of the conflicts are not based on latent emotions, but on
principles deriving from historical claims. However, these opposing
claims do not generally result in negative relations between neighbouring countries. This can be seen in the cases of Chile and Argentina,
and Peru and Ecuador, whose territorial claims have not harmed their
relations with each other.[64] Sometimes the disputes were intensified as
a result of internal problems in the countries involved, as in the case of
the Chile-Bolivia, Chile-Argentina, Argentina-Uruguay and Salvador-
Honduras conflicts.

Another cause of antagonistic relations, is a country becoming isolated, or attached, for ideological-political reasons. This was the case in Guatemala in 1954, which was the target of hostility from Honduras and Nicaragua. Revolutionary Cuba also endured attack by exiles operating from Central American countries during the stages leading up to the invasion in 1961, which later resulted in the rupturing of ties and an economic boycott. However, it should be pointed out that in these cases the initiative came from the United States, who used other Latin American countries as an indirect instrument for the attainment of her own aims. Argentina and Brazil, two countries with aspirations to subregional supremacy, restricted their competition to a level that avoided outbreaks of crises in the twentieth century; they managed to maintain relations of limited co-operation, and when the opportunity presented itself, also showed a united stand against the United States' hegemony in the region. Until a few years ago, the similar level of power in the two countries neutralised the possibility of a polarisation of the countries in the zone.

Afro-Asian relations show a greater tendency to conflict situations than Latin American. Within the core of the subsystems, we have a polarisation of countries between the radical and the pro-Western regimes. In West Africa, for example, Mali and Guinea are on one side and the Ivory Coast on the other. Open conflict on a relatively large scale, for nationalistic or ethnic reasons, has broken out in both the Middle East and Southern Asia. In many cases these crises continued at varying levels for an extended period of time, due to the failure of the withdrawing colonial power to define frontiers adequately. This was the basis of the dispute between Malaysia and the Philippines, and later Indonesia. As the last vestiges of the Portuguese and Spanish empires fall, Mauritania, Morocco and Algeria dispute the Spanish Sahara, Zaire presents claims in Angola and Indonesia in Timor, while inside those former colonies, civil war is already preceding independence.

The basis of Latin American inter-regional relations is the multi-dimensional development of the infra-structure of the continent, in contrast to Afro-Asia. This is a result of having a longer time period to create a substructure of a community of aims, both on a political level (independence *vis-à-vis* the USA), as well as common needs on a sub-regional technological level (development of postal communication, transportation, similar economic aspects, etc.).

As regards policy implementation, in order to achieve aims in Latin America generally, there has been a decreasing use of violence and a greater appeal to international law and organisations. Dowty and

Kochan report for 1945-65 a general consensus (Denton, Huntington, Kende, Ward, Wood, Wright), about a decline in conventional inter-state wars fought in Europe and America, and an increase of wars fought in Asia, Africa and the Middle East.[65] The use of the military is usually restricted to a parade, or to the transportation of troops to the frontier, as an adequate warning gesture; while on many occasions there has been an appeal to the International Court of Justice for arbitration and mediation, to find a peaceful solution to frontier problems. Diplomatic rights, i.e. diplomatic immunity and political asylum — violations of which have been the cause of several conflicts in Afro-Asia — have in Latin America been generally adhered to.

The use of diplomatic means in the new countries of Afro-Asia has yet to be integrated into their political structures, and the insecurity of not knowing the possible reaction of other countries has been a contributing cause of increased tension. Rumours, such as an expected political assassination in a neighbouring country are not unusual in Africa and the Middle East. In certain areas, the use of armed force is the accepted form of relationship between countries. This is seen in South East Asia in the inter-reaction between Vietnam, Laos and Cambodia; or in the Middle East between Israel and the surrounding Arab countries.

In conclusion, we can accept Cantori and Spiegel's view, when analysing a sample of six subsystems according to the level and type of interaction, from non-conflict to conflict: the order was Western Europe, Latin America, Western Africa, Maritime South East Asia, Middle East and Mainland South East Asia.[66] We have stressed the existing differences between Latin America and Afro-Asia, but it is also relevant to point out similarities and common interests. In making a projection of the comparative situation in the future, the trend seems to be that on an economic developmental level, Latin America will more closely resemble Asia-Africa, and the gap between them and the developed countries will widen.[67] This process is illustrated in Table 12: the Latin American countries rank lower by 1975 than in 1950, with European countries and Japan taking their place in the second and third groupings. Table 12 shows that it is in the Latin American common interest to tackle the economic problems of the three continents on a common basis and in co-operation with each other; and in international conferences it is in Latin America's interest to identify with those countries in need of aid, and not with those who supply it.

Foreign aid figures also show a greater sum allocated to Africa

Table 12: GNP Per Capita

1950		1975 (projected)	
United States	$2300	United States	$3550
Canada	1750	West Germany	2900
Britain	1200	Canada	2600
Belgium	1000	Czechoslovakia	1950
France	750	Belgium	1875
Netherlands	675	Britain	1800
West Germany	600	France	1750
Argentina	500	USSR	1625
Venezuela	480	Netherlands	1475
Czechoslovakia	450	Venezuela	1400
USSR	400	Italy	1330
Italy	350	Poland	1300
Chile	340	Japan	1140
Poland	320	Yugoslavia	925
Spain	290	Spain	700
Brazil	235	Brazil	500
Mexico	225	Chile	480
Colombia	220	Argentina	455
Turkey	200	Mexico	395
Japan	190	Colombia	390
Philippines	185	Philippines	335
Yugoslavia	165	Turkey	305
Egypt	135	Egypt	285
Indonesia	120	China	190
Thailand	85	Indonesia	170
Nigeria	70	Thailand	130
Pakistan	70	Burma	115
India	70	Nigeria	95
China	50	India	85
Burma	45	Pakistan	75

Source: Bruce M. Russett, *et al., World Handbrook of Political and Social Indicators* (Yale University Press, New Haven, Conn., 1964).

than to Latin America, even larger if considered according to their total population. This can be seen in Table 13, together with a no less crucial fact, the diversification of sources of aid. In Latin America, a median of 94.9 per cent of foreign aid (excluding Cuba and Argentina) originates from the United States.[68]

A further factor linking these regions is their population growth rates; higher in Latin America with an annual average of 2.9 per cent, while for Africa it is 2.3 per cent, and for Asia it is 2.2 per cent. Latin

Table 13: Net Bilateral Aid by Major Donors, 1960-1967 (millions of U.S. dollars)

Region	Belgium	Canada	France	Germany	Italy	Sino-Soviet	United Kingdom	United States	Totals Without Sino-Soviet	Totals With Sino-Soviet	% Increase or Decrease (without Sino-Soviet)
AFRICA											
1950	$ 86.0		$ 307.5	$ 5.3	$ 16.6	90.0	$ 123.6	$ 39.0	$ 578.7	$ 668.7	
1961	70.5		304.0	13.4	18.5	310.0	228.0	75.0	710.8	1,020.8	22.8
1962	63.4		325.9	59.2	12.5	35.0	172.5	197.0	833.4	864.4	17.2
1963	75.8		337.3	54.1	22.5	66.0	163.5	159.0	816.3	882.3	− 2.1
1964	76.5		345.6	41.4	16.4	212.0	211.3	161.0	863.7	1,075.7	5.8
1965	96.0		319.2	61.2	26.8	78.0	210.0	248.0	984.2	1,062.2	13.9
1966	59.7		327.0	95.8	22.9	46.0	191.6	276.0	1,008.1	1,054.1	9.7
1967	63.1		386.0	74.2	57.5	119.0	176.6	221.0	1,028.4	1,147.4	2.0
Total	$591.0		$2,652.5	$404.6	$193.7	$957.0	$1,477.0	$1,376.0	$6,823.6	$7,780.6	
Average	$ 73.8		$ 331.5	$ 50.5	$ 24.2	$119.6	$ 184.6	$ 172.0	$ 852.9	$ 972.5	9.9
Source as % of total bilateral aid	8.6%[b] (7.5%)[c]		38.8% (34.0%)	5.9% (5.2%)	2.8% (2.4%)	— (12.2%)	21.6% (18.9%)	20.1% (17.6%)	100.0%[a]	— (100.0%)[a]	
LATIN AMERICA											
1960		$ 4.8		$ 23.3				$ 184.0	$ 206.3		
1961		3.8		30.6				702.0	735.0		256.2
1962		20.7		37.6				578.0	673.1		− 8.5
1963		34.9		36.4				560.0	649.5		− 5.6
1964		33.8		6.2				452.0	490.3		−24.6
1965		6.2		45.4				613.5	720.8		47.0
1966		3.6		46.0				723.0	762.8		5.8
1967		3.4		57.2				604.0	676.4		−11.4
Total		$111.1		$282.7				$4,416.5	$4,914.2		
Average		$ 13.8		$ 35.3				$ 552.0	$ 614.2		37.0
Source as % of total bilateral aid		2.2%		5.7%				89.8%	100.0%		

Source: Calculated from OECD, Geographical Distribution of Financial Flow to Less-Developed Countries, 1960-64, 1965, 1966-67 (for OECD countries); UN, International Flow of Long-Term Capital and Official Donations, 1960-62, 1961-65, 1962-66, 1964-68 (for Sino-Soviet countries).

[a] Taken from J. Stallings, op. cit., pp. 16, 17.
[b] Percentages for major donors do not add to 100 per cent because of minor donors
[c] Percentage including Sino-Soviet aid
[d] Excludes Soviet aid to Cuba because of lack of data (the commonly used figures is $365 million per year)

America has on many occasions found itself in a period of economic stagnation which has created a depressive atmosphere. The Second World War years are remembered as the high point of economic development and wealth for South America, and ever since they have been attempting to regain such levels, but unsuccessfully. This is the situation and feeling in wide circles in Argentina, Chile and Uruguay; countries have now endured continuing economic crises for many years. A report by CEPAL draws attention to this fact, as it shows that the participation of Latin America in world commerce is smaller today than it was 20 years ago, as shown in oil, food, beverages, tobacco and raw material.[69]

When analysing statistics from Latin America and Afro-Asia, not in any given year, but over a period of time, so as to identify trends in the fields of industrial production and exports, the annual growth rate is larger in Afro-Asia than in Latin America. In Latin America only 5 per cent of the population is to be found in the highest quartile, surpassing the Afro-Asian level:

Table 14: Manufacturing Production: Rate of Increase, by Region 1960-68

Region	Distribution					
	First quartile (percentage per annum)	Population in countries at or below the first quartile (millions)	Median (percentage per annum)	Population in countries between first and third quartile (millions)	Third quartile (percentage per annum)	Population in countries at or above third quartile (millions)
Developing countries	4.6	85.5	7.6	987.3	11.2	215.0
Western hemisphere	4.7	123.5	7.3	110.3	11.5	12.7
Africa	3.8	20.7	8.8	119.4	11.4	46.1
Asia	5.9	571.3	10.1	128.6	11.2	156.2
Rest of world	5.3	197.5	6.3	378.3	8.3	496.4

Source: Yearbook of National Account Statistics, op. cit., p. 24.

The statistics in themselves emphasise this trend, Latin American politicians and statesmen have not failed to realise the existing situation. This is reflected in a growing frustration due to the gap between aspirations and actual achievements: one can measure it by evaluating the

economic plans proposed, and the success of those plans in achieving
the stated goals in the time period forecasted.

As a result of the differences between Latin America and Afro-Asia,
the former subsystem in reality is at a different level in all spheres to
the latter subsystems, and as such, needs to be categorised at an intermediate level between the developing Third World and the developed
countries. The reason for this intermediate role can perhaps be explained by the fact that the countries of Latin America gained their
independence at a time somewhere between that of the Old European
nations, and the recently constituted post-war states. Similarly, the
ethnic composition of Latin America, with a high percentage of people
of European origin, represents a medium position between that of the
European countries and Afro-Asia. The Catholic religion — although its
values are less concerned with personal achievements than are the
values of Anglo-Saxon Protestant ethos — has created pressures stimu-
lating economic development, similar to that of the Latin countries in
Europe, and perhaps with better results than certain of the Eastern
religions. Williams mentions the possibility of Latin America being a
bridge between Europe and Afro-Asia, and suggests that Latin America
be considered the 'Fourth World'.[70]

4 Eastern Europe and Western Europe

The ideal of a 'United Europe' in the future should not be interpreted
as an attempt to revert to the situation that existed before the establishment of the bipolar system of the superpowers. Europe, until the end of
the last century, was *the* international system, with all alliances and
conflicts being European in dimension. Even though it was not politically foreseeable that the continent would be divided in two, economic
differentials already existed, with the Eastern zone being more agrarian
and enjoying a lower standard of living, and more monarchist and fragmented than the Western zone. Similar criteria separated Catholic
Southern Europe or the Mediterranean countries from the Northern
tier, which was more advanced at all levels. The actual division of 'East'
and 'West' in the international system is the result of the cold war.
Because of this, before comparing the two subsystems (East and West
Europe) according to the framework of this study, it is necessary to
establish the premises accompanying this comparison.

Firstly, although the creation of both subsystems resulted from the
intervention of the superpowers on which they both became dependent
to varying degrees, the United States is physically separated from
Western Europe by a natural geographic barrier, while the USSR is a

territorial extension of Eastern Europe. The 'political frontier' between
the USSR and the adjacent countries is of minimum importance, as the
USSR's neighbours increasingly resemble the metropolis politically.
With the economic reconstruction of Western Europe after the Second
World War, by mutual agreement this region became increasingly more
independent of the US, as both shared similar value systems, and the
same basic goals. In Eastern Europe the USSR not only forms an integral part of the subsystem, it is also the initiator and controller of its
functioning.

Secondly, a system that is not based on a wide consensus lacks an
important element of power. This premise, as applied to the relations
among the various countries of the COMECON, and of the citizens of
those countries towards the ruling groups, is a point of weakness in the
common front *vis à vis* the West European system. There, affiliation to
the regional framework is voluntary, the governments are more representative and have received the legitimisation of the voters.

Undoubtedly, there will be those who disagree with these premises.
However, the need to expound them before comparing the two subsystems derives from the fact that they represent the major differences
between the two subsystems. It is the difference in participation between the superpowers in the subsystems, the contrasts in the functioning of the regional organs, the degree of voluntarism in participation, and the degree of national consensus in respect to the governments in general, and to the inter-regional relations in particular, which
are indicators enabling us to differentiate between Eastern and Western
Europe.

The *level of cohesion.* In Eastern Europe every regional institution
includes the Soviet Union, while in Western Europe, with the exception of military co-operation (NATO), the majority of the institutions
exclude US participation. Geographically, the lack of legitimisation of
borders, such as with Poland, creates certain regional problems: the
existence of the minority of a neighbouring country within one's borders is still a source of friction. The West European countries have in a
majority of cases enjoyed national independence and unity for many
centuries (exceptions being Italy and Germany — where the national
unity process was accentuated and intensified by the violence of Nazi
and Fascist nationalism — and the present struggle in Ireland). In Eastern Europe in some countries formed since The First World War,
national consciousness of different ethnic groups, though existent, does
not overlap state boundaries, and is a source of weakness in their inter-
relation within the subsystem and *vis-à-vis* the superpower. However,

the degree of interaction between the East European countries tends to be higher in all fields than that in the West. Of importance in increasing regional cohesion is the greater similarity in the political systems among the regimes of East Europe, making for greater political integration. In spite of this, though, taking into consideration the already mentioned premises, it would seem to be in Western Europe that one witnesses more authentic unity. This is observable when making an analytical comparison of COMECON with the EEC, in which the core countries of the subsystems are represented. For such a comparison, the articles by Bergthum and Nielsen and by Pinder are an excellent basis.[71]

The member countries of the EEC have a higher level of development in all economic indexes, and also greater homogeneity; the differential between the GNP in the major and minor members in the EEC is in a ratio of 1 to 1.8, while in the COMECON it is 1 to 2.2. The higher level of development and economic homogeneity in the EEC has led to a greater degree of integration. On the other hand, it is important to emphasise that, in its functioning, the centralised and monopolistic character of the economies of the East European countries hinders any better adaption to regional fixed prices and tariffs, and does not encourage the distribution of economic facilities on a regional basis, on the criterion of rentability. The greater intensity and scope of activity in the EEC can be seen in the larger permanent organisational staff maintained compared to the COMECON, by the more numerous formal sessions held and the greater decentralisation of departments and staff.[72]

Perhaps the best way of showing the different relationships that have resulted between the regions is in the progress made toward supranational organisations, as shown by Pinder, who compared the functioning of the two. 'While the nations of the West, and particularly those of the Community, have been in the process of moving beyond national soveriegnty, those of Eastern Europe have been either standing pat on that concept or moving in the reverse direction.'[73]

The *level of communications,* a significant factor when comparing subsystems that show a basic unity in fundamental premises, is not one which is relevant in this case, because of the basic differences between the regions. There is not an acute difference between the two subsystems. The educational substructure, the low percentage of illiteracy, the number of newspapers per inhabitant, are all similar, when taking into consideration not only the countries of the EEC, but of all Western Europe.

Inter-regional tourism is high in both European subsystems; in

Eastern Europe regional tourism is stimulated by the limitations on it
by those countries to extra-regional areas. Means of transportation,
especially in commercial aviation, are much more developed in Western
Europe. Exchanges of elites, scientific conferences, athletic meets, etc.,
have contributed to a higher interaction among the countries of Eastern
Europe, which are restricted in their movement outside the area. Linguistic problems — important in regional mass media communication —
are found in both subsystems; the Russian language is no less common
at the elite level in the Communist countries than English and French
in Western Europe. The basic limitations of mass media communications as an integrative force in Eastern Europe are the inherent characteristics of the subsystem. As a result of official censorship enforced
in all countries, those who seek to extend their information beyond
official levels are brought by circumstances to rely on extra-regional
sources. This limitation is also relevant to the use of personal means of
communication (letter, telephone, telegram, etc.).

The *degree of power* has been discussed partly in the analysis of
said regions. Table 15 presents significant differences in the socio-
economic level, the consumer market and the level of technological
development.

The economic links of Eastern Europe with the Soviet Union are of
paramount importance. Since the Second World War, variations of
Soviet foreign trade with the region have remained within the range of
70 per cent to 83 per cent of her total. It is also the same in reverse;
irrespective of the desire of East European countries to diversify their
markets, the regional market has remained the major purchaser and
supplier.

From the military aspect, the armies of Western Europe linked with
NATO are more autonomous than those of the 'popular democracies'
(except Yugoslavia); they are highly dependent, both materially and in
centralised command structure on the Supreme Soviet Command of the
Warsaw Pact,[74] and dominated by the superior numbers and direct
presence of Soviet troops in East Europe. The marked disproportion
between the size of the military forces in favour of the Western troops
is balanced by the massive presence of the Soviet Union in the Warsaw
Pact countries, particularly if compared with the undersized American
presence in the Western part. This aspect is of fundamental importance
in understanding the restrictions upon the freedom of action of the
'satellites' in Eastern Europe and in observing that the few cases where
independent moves away were taken from the superpower (Yugoslavia,
Romania), the Soviets were militarily absent.

Table 15: Comparative Figures of Eastern European States with Selected Western European States

Country	Passenger Cars x inhabitant	Population Urban	Population Rural	Telephone x 100 inhabitants	Income per capita in $US	Higher Education x 100	Newspaper Circulation x 1,000	Life expectancy years	Illiteracy	Hospital bed per inhabitant	Physician per inhabitant
Albania	1 x 2300	35	65	0.31	$ 300	0.1	45	65-67	N.A.	210	1300
Belgium	1 x 5	62	38	18.26	$1408	0.8	285	71	0-37	220	692
Bulgaria	1 x 857	48	52	4.5	$ 620	1.0	172	70	10-15	158	560
Czechoslovakia	1 x 30	48	52	11.71	$1010	1.02	280	71	0-5	128	546
East Germany	1 x 92	70	30	10.42	$1500	0.66	475	71	0-1	80	750
France	1 x 5	63	37	13.96	$1436	0.85	238	71	0-3	86	900
Hungary	1 x 80	40	60	6.2	$ 800	0.9	178	70	3	129	509
Italy	1 x 7	52	48	13.44	$1300	0.76	100	70	6	110	610
Luxemburg	1 x 5	62	38	0.19[a]	$1648	1.33	418	68	0-3	90	1030
Mongolia	N.A.	25	75	1.0	$ 390	0.79	103	64	25	117	800
Poland	1 x 118	50	50	2.5	$ 730	0.80	167	68	5	168	786
Romania	1 x 1288	39	61	1.6	$ 650	0.68	110	68	11	130	682
Sweden	1 x 4	77	23	49	$2860	1.20	541	77	–	62	890
United Kingdom	1 x 5	75	25	21.87	$1358	0.4	488	70	–	101	977
West Germany	1 x 5	79	21	17.21	$1753	0.2	417	71	0-1	93	650
Yugoslavia	1 x 80	41	59	2.2	$ 510	0.95	90	65	20	227	1336

N.A.: figures not available.

Source: The data were compiled by the author from *The New York Times Encyclopedia Almanac 1970*, section on individual 'World Nations'.

[a]The figure mentioned here has been included by the author despite certain doubts as to its validity. 1964 statistics given by another source provide the rate of 2.58 telephones per 100 inhabitants. *Oxford Economic Atlas of the World*, 4th Edition (1972), Statistical Development.

The evaluation of intangible elements, such as 'national morale', the quality of diplomacy and the type of government and degree of consensus of the population toward it, is complicated. As far as type of government and degree of consensus are concerned, the West European regimes are strengthened by their greater pluralism and by a more representative character. In regard to nationalism as a unifying force, even in Eastern Europe this is a powerful element, as seen by the anti-Soviet demonstrations that periodically surface, to the detriment of subsystem unity and strength. In Western Europe the 'national interest' is of primary importance, and this establishes the order of priority for the goals of the governments; 'European integration' is one of the goals of 'national interest' to most of the countries. In Eastern Europe 'national interest' is indivisible from the 'defense of socialism', which is reflected in the need to strengthen the source and centre of World Socialism, the Soviet Union, before all else.

As far as diplomatic capacity is concerned, the Romanian experience has demonstrated that there is nothing inherent in the 'diplomatic technique' that may limit the quality of East European representation. The main element curtailing freedom of diplomacy is superpower limitation, in this case by the USSR, placed on the regional governments.

Finally, the *structural relationships* at the formal level express themselves in Eastern Europe in a 'bloc' system, while in the case of Western Europe, they are based on functional interactions expressed by an 'alliance' or 'co-operation' system. In reality, as shown by the need of the Soviet Union to intervene militarily on several occasions in order to maintain 'bloc' unity, in spite of the formal structure of the Eastern bloc, it suffers from serious distintegrative tendencies.[75]

The variety of relations in both subsystems is diffuse, and relates to nearly every field. Bearing in mind that, for a period of 30 to 50 years, conflict relations existed, the present lack of tension within the two subsystems is surprising, with the past not being an impediment — exceptions do occur between certain countries of the Eastern bloc, mainly over territorial disputes with neighbours, including the Soviet Union.

In conclusion, the major differentiating factor between these two subsystems is the dominant, active, intrusive presence of a superpower in one of them.

Notes

1. Louis J. Cantori and Steven L. Spiegel, (eds.), *The International Politics of Regions: A Comparative Approach* (Prentice-Hall, New Jersey, 1970). While the theoretical scheme of the authors presents a remarkable continuity, the expositions by the contributors on the regional cases, much to our regret, do not usually apply the analytical method of the authors. The present work, however, will attempt to use their analytical framework.
2. For the purpose of this work Latin America does not include the following countries: Trinidad and Tobago, Jamaica, Barbados, Guayana and the French, British and Dutch colonies. Located on the periphery, their inclusion would impair the unitary character of the region. This distinction is a result of different historical tradition and experience, and the linguistic, ethnic, religious and cultural differences of these countries.
3. It is assumed that there is a high correlation between the degree of complementarity of the countries of the subsystem and their level of cohesion. According to many researchers, cultural homogeneity is a factor that increases interaction (Lidgren, Russet, Deutsch and others), as well as similar historical experience between two or more countries. These hypotheses are presented in the text together with hypotheses which do not consider the affinity relevant. In our case the empirical evidence seems to corroborate the proposition. See Roger W. Cobb and Charles Elder, *International Community* (Holt, Rinehardt and Winston, New York, 1970), pp. 39-43.
4. Hans Morgenthau, *Politics Among Nations,* 4th edition (Knopf, 1966), Chap. 9.
5. Charles O. Lerche Jr. and Abdul A. Said, *Concepts of International Politics,* 2nd edition (Prentice-Hall, New Jersey, 1970), pp. 59-76.
6. L.J. Cantori and S.L. Spiegel, ibid, p. 388.
7. Ibid, p. 387.
8. These characteristics are analysed in detail in the comparison of Latin America and Afro-Asia (Chapter 3, Section 3, p. 84).
9. Martin C. Needler, *Political Development in Latin America. Instability, Violence and Evolutionary Change* (Random House, New York, 1968).
10. Alba summarises this point by stating that 'Latin American unity is first of all the result of human action, it is a social product. Latin American diversity is a product of nature, of geographic and climatic factors that man cannot influence even with the most modern technique'. Victor Alba, *The Latin Americans* (Praeger, New York, 1969), p. 5.
11. *Europe's Trade,* a study of the trade of Eastern European countries with each other and the rest of the world; by the League of Nations, Geneva, 1941, p. 51. In 1928, Austria, Germany and Czechoslovakia accounted for 42 per cent of the imports and 40 per cent of the exports of the total foreign trade of Bulgaria, Greece, Hungary, Romania, Turkey and Yugoslavia; in 1938 the figures increased to 47 per cent for both imports and exports, with Soviet participation being minimal.
12. Felipe Herrera, *Nacionalism Latinamericano* (Editorial Universitaria, Santiago de Chile, 1967), p. 79.
13. Felipe Herrera, ibid, p. 21.
14. Louis J. Cantori and Steven L. Spiegel, *International Politics of Regions,* p. 385.
15. Hugh Seton-Watson, *Eastern Europe Between the Wars* (Cambridge University Press, Cambridge, 1946), pp. 268-277.
16. Hugh Seton-Watson, *The East European Revolution* 2nd edition (Methuen & Co., London, 1952), p. 19.

17. *Listy,* Rome.
18. Broadcast quoted by Stuart S. Smith, 'Russia, China and the Balkans', *Midstream* (New York, December, 1971), p. 13.
19. A well-known phrase of Simon Bolivar's was: 'The United States seems destined by the Providence to plague America with misery in the name of liberty.'
20. David Bronheim, 'Relations between the United States and Latin America', *International Affairs* (London, July 1970), p. 502.
21. William J. Fulbright, *The Arrogance of Power* (Pelican Books, Middlesex, England, 1970), pp. 104-5.
22. *Le Monde Diplomatique,* Paris, December 1969, p. 13.
23. Letter published in *The Times* on 1 November 1974, reproduced in 'Index on Censorship', London, vol 4, No. 1, Spring 1975, pp. 74-5.
24. Louis Mercier Vega, *Autopsie de Peron* (Duculot, Gembloux, 1974), p. 203.
25. Jose Luis de Imaz, 'Adios a la Teoria de la Dependencia'.
26. Generalising from his studies on Latin American under-development, Gunder Frank suggests the following hypothesis: 'That within this world-embracing metropolis-satellite structure the metropoles tend to develop and the satellites underdeveloped . . . that in contrast to the development of the world metropolis which is no one's satellite the development of the national and other subordinate metropoles is limited by their satellite status.' Andre Gunder Frank, 'The Development of Underdevelopment' (published in *Monthly Review,* September 1966) reprinted by *Bay Area Radical Education Project,* San Francisco, p. 7.
27. 'Pentagonism has established a governmental schizophrenia, a double power in the United States: that of the civil government and that of pentagonism. The American armed forces obey the latter. Latin American armed forces – with only rare exception – will also obey the pentagonist power rather than their national governments.' Juan Bosch, *Pentagonism: A Substitute for Imperialism* (Grove Press, New York, 1968), p. 121.
28. 'With the exception of Albania, Yugoslavia and to an extent Romania, the foreign policy makers (of Eastern Europe) also share a similar communist world outlook which includes the acceptance of a pre-eminent role for the USSR in certain areas of foreign policy and military planning.' R.B. Farrell, 'Foreign Policy Formation in Communist Countries', *East European Quarterly,* vol. I, No. 1, (March 1967), p. 70.
29. J.W. Fulbright, *The Arrogance of Power,* p. 99.
30. Hugh Seton-Watson, ibid., p. 385.
31. G. Almond, 'Comparative Political Systems', *Journal of Politics,* no. 18 (3 August 1956), pp. 391-409; I.L. Horowitz, *Three Worlds of Development* (Oxford University Press, New York, 1972).
32. 'Although many of the Latin American countries could perhaps be fitted into the more detailed typology, the differences between the two major areas are such that the inclusion of these countries in the following analysis of functional profiles would tend to dilute the distinctiveness of these categories – hence the focus here will be only upon the African-Asian System.' G. Almond, and J.S. Coleman, *The Politics of the Developing Areas* (Princeton University Press, New Jersey, 1960), p. 56.
33. The general declaration of the *First Conference on the Solidarity of the African, Asian and Latin American Peoples* held in Havana from the 3rd to the 15th of January 1966 established an ideological parallel in the analysis of all the themes related to those three continents. Already in the first sentences we find such expressions as: 'The imperialism will not re-

nounce by its own will, its politics of exploitation, oppression, looting, aggression and interference'; 'The people of Africa, Asia and Latin America know, by their own experience, that the main strength of colonial oppression and international reaction make up the Yanqui imperialism, implacable enemy of all the people of the world.' Tricontinental, 'Declaration generale de la premiere Conference', Paris, no. 1, January-February 1968, p. 102.

34. 'The Soviets have long taken the position that Latin America is considerably more advanced than the countries of Africa, Asia and the Middle East, most of which are considered still to be in the pre-capitalist state. Latin America, on the other hand, is said to stand midway between the advanced industrialized countries and the bloc of developing nations.' Wayne S. Smith, 'Soviet Policy and Ideological Formulations for Latin America', *Orbis*, vol. XI (Winger 1972), p. 1134.

35. '. . . it is absolutely impossible to classify the wars of national liberation in Latin America within the same category of those taking place in Asia and Africa,' Robin Blackburn (ed.), *Regis Debray: Strategy for Revolution* (J. Cape, London, 1970), p. 78.

36. John D. Martz, 'The Place of Latin America in the Study of Comparative Politics', *Journal of Politics,* no. 28 (Fall, 1966), pp. 57-80; and Edward Williams, 'Comparative Political Development: Latin America and Afro-Asia', *Comparative Studies in Society and History* vol. II (Cambridge University Press, 1969), pp. 342-53. In both cases, the authors point out the differences existing between Latin America and the 'underdeveloped Afro-Asia', stressing as well certain similarities between Latin America and Europe.

37. See Table 6, p. 86.

38. The World Bank now divides the developing countries (average income per capita GNP: $115.90) in three categories. On the 'lower income level' we find nations such as Tanzania, Afghanistan, India, Burma, Sri Lanka, Laos and Pakistan. The 'middle-income poor' (average income per capita GNP: $347.30) includes such countries as Angola, Bolivia, South Korea, Philippines, Egypt, Zambia, Rhodesia and Tunisia. The greater part of Latin America falls into the third category, the upper income developing countries (average income per capita GNP: $1,033.10), together with Israel, Turkey, Spain, Taiwan and Lebanaon. (See the article by Leonard Silk, 'The Poor as Activists', *New York Times,* 14 January 1976). The overrepresentation of Latin America within 'the aristocrats among the poor' and its absence from the lowest category is indicative of its differences with the other parts of the Third World.

39. Marshall R. Singer, *Weak States in a World of Powers* (The Free Press, New York, 1972).

40. Joseph S. Nye Jr., (ed.), *International Regionalism* (Little, Brown & Co., Canada, 1968), Introduction, p.

41. Robert W. Gregg, 'The UN Regional Economic Commissions and Integration in the Underdeveloiped Regions', in J.S. Nye, op. cit., p. 318.

42. Robert W. Gregg, ibid., p. 328.

43. Such as the former Brazaville and Casablanca.

44. Separatist trends can be represented by the division of the continent into smaller units; Spiegel and Cantori mention five subsystems in the African continent (Northern, Western, Eastern, Central and Southern), and five in Asia (Eastern Communist, Southern, Southeastern Continental, Southeastern Asiatic Maritime and Middle Eastern).

45. *Yearbook of National Accounts Statistics,* op. cit., Table 10a, 'Educational

status of the populations at the beginning of the 1960s (primary, second-ary and tertiary level)', p. 203-4. Data from the general cadre.

46. This statistical data has been taken from Tables 6 and 7.

47. See chapter dealing with intra-continental migration in Georges Rocheau, 'Migration Movements in Latin America', *Migration News,* International Catholic Migration Commission, Geneva, no. 176, Jan-March 1976, pp. 4-7.

48. This validates the hypothesis that 'the much-publicized view that maximi-zation of power, defined as military and economic probability, is the chief motivating factor in state behavior is invalid for middle powers'. M. Brecher, B. Steinberg, J. Stein, 'A framework for research in foreign policy behaviour', *The Journal of Conflict Resolution,* XIII (1 March 1969), p. p. 92.

49. These points were elaborated before the outbreak of the world energy crisis. Certainly, oil production and reserves in the Arab countries have drastically altered their level of power. It would therefore be more con-venient to separate the Middle East subsystem.

50. Edward J. Williams, op. cit., p. 343.

51. Yearbook of National Accounts Statistics, op. cit., p. 38.

52. Data of UN experts, reproduced in *Haaretz,* Tel Aviv, 31 October 1974.

53. *Clarin,* Buenos Aires, 11 December 1972, p. 24. Data compiled by the author.

54. T. La Palombara, and M. Weiner, 'The Origin and Development of Political Parties', in La Palombara T. and Winer M. (eds.) *Political Parties and Political Political Development* (Princeton University Press, 1966), pp. 3-42. 'The political party is both a manifestation and a condition of the trust to modernity; it is unlikely that we shall find it in societies where all other attributes of modernity are almost utterly lacking.' (p. 30).

55. Frank Bonilla, 'The Urban Worker', in John J. Johnson, (ed.), *Continuity and Change in Latin America* Stanford University Press, 1968), pp. 186-205.

56. 'Today these groups (the middle sectors) hold a prominent position in the social-political amalgams that control Argentina, Brazil, Chile, Mexico and Uruguay. These five countries contain two thirds of the land, two thirds of the population, and produce more than two thirds of the gross product of the twenty Latin American Republics.' John Johnson, 'The Emergence of the Middle Sectors', in Robert D. Tomasek, (ed.) *Latin American Politics* (Anchor Books, New York, 1966), pp. 169-96.

57. Eric D. Nordlinger, 'Soldiers in Myth: The Impact of Military Rule Upon Economic and Social Change in the Non-Western States', *American Political Science Review,* 64:4 (Dec. 1970) p. 1146.

58. The argument is far from being exhausted whether the price for develop-ment is an unavoidable increase in the socio-economic gap. In the partic-ular case of Latin America, according to Stallings, the main effect of a de-pendent development 'has been to promote economic growth at the same time that inequality was intensified'. Ann Stallings, *Economic Dependence in African and Latin America* (Sage Publications, Beverly Hills, California, 1972), p. 39.

59. *Ranchos, cinturones de miseria, poblaciones cayampas, cantegrilles, favellas, villas miseria, etc.*

60. Data compiled from the New York Times Encyclopedia Almanac, op. cit.

61. *Yearbook of National Accounts Statistics,* op. cit., p. 44.

62. Carlos A. Astiz, (ed.), *Latin American International Politics* (University of Notre Dame Press, 1970), p. 14.

63. David Wood, *Conflict in the Twentieth Century,* Adelphi Paper no. 48

(International Institute of Strategic Studies, London), p. 18.

64. In the extreme case of Bolivia's demand for an outlet to the ocean, she severed diplomatic ties with Chile, but nevertheless, consular, trade and official contact continued.

65. Alan Dowty and Ran Kochan, *Recurrent Patterns in the History of International Villence: The Constraints of the Past on the Future of Violence,* Jerusalem, paper submitted to the AAAS Washington Meeting, December 26-31, 1973.

66. Louis J. Cantori and Steven L. Spiegel, op. cit., p. 60.

67. This proposition has also remained controversial, figures being provided to show that the rate of growth for Africa and Asia is lower than for Latin America (see A. Stallings, op cit.). As will be mentioned later, it is important to stress that a narrowing gap with other developing countries has been persistently forseen by Latin American decision-makers and has repercussions in their increased involvement in Third World forums.

68. J. Stallings, op. cit., p. 21.

69. *La Opinion,* Buenos Aires, 29 March 1972.

70. E.J. Williams, op. cit., p. 353.

71. John Pinder, 'EEC and COMECON', in Joseph S. Nye, op. cit., pp. 22-42; Olav Lorents Bergthum and Terkel Troels Nielsen, 'COMECON and EEC – A Comparative Analysis', in *Republica,* no. 3, (Brussels, 1968), pp. 407-32.

72. 'While about 70 per cent of the employees in the COMECON Secretariat were Soviet citizens and 15 per cent Polish, a clear Soviet predominance, 28 per cent of the officials of the Community were from the Benelux countries and those countries constitute only 12 per cent of the total population of the EEC,' Bergthum and Nielsen, op. cit., p. 417.

73. In its statues, 'The members of the EEC were "determined to establish the foundations of an even closer union among European peoples," while COMECON is established on the basis of the principle of the sovereign equality of all member countries of the Council', J. Pinder, op. cit., p. 23.

74. The Warsaw Treaty Organisation '. . . constitutes the single most important formal commitment binding the European Communist States to the USSR, officially limiting their scope for independent action by precluding their participation in other alliance systems'. Zbigniew K. Brzezinski, *The Soviet Bloc: Unity and Conflict,* rev. ed. (New York, Praeger, 1961), p. 447.

75. See an excellent article about the USSR and Europe by Adam B. Ulam, 'The Destiny of Eastern Europe', *Probems of Communism,* XXIII, Jan-Feb. 1974.

4 THE EXCEPTIONS: PERIPHERAL AND SEMI-PERIPHERAL COUNTRIES

1 General Characteristics

In examining the relevance of the hypothesis that regards the Eastern European and Latin American subsystems as spheres of direct influence of the superpowers, one has unavoidably to discuss the cases of certain states exhibiting, to a greater or lesser degree, independence of action. Though still numerically exceptions to the general rule, their role in the subsystem appears to be different from the majority; further explanations related to the foreign policy behaviour of those countries are required bearing in mind the position of the determinants external to the subsystem that have already been mentioned.

Every country that participates in a subsystem can be categorised according to its degree of participation in the system, either to the 'core' or 'peripheral' sector; countries that do not belong to the region but which are important and affect its internal relations belong to what is classified as the'intrusive system.' States belonging to the 'core' or centre of a region are the focus of the politics of that region, and maintain a high rate of interaction with the actors of the subsystem. Countries belonging to the 'peripheral' sector are usually alienated from the core states to a certain degree, but still play a role in the politics of that region. In some cases a country belonging to the periphery may belong to the periphery of more than one subsystem. In Latin America, the mainland countries (Argentina, Brazil, Mexico, etc.), form the core sector, while the periphery consists of some of those countries geographically separated from the mainland, i.e. the Caribbean Islands, Cuba and the Antilles, which as a result of international political orientation of a different cultural heritage belong to alternative subsystems (the Socialist bloc, the British Commonwealth, French and Dutch dependencies). The major powers play the role of the intrusive system, penetrating both the core and periphery, and as a result exert an influence on the character, behaviour and orientation of the subsystem. Some countries can be classified in an intermediary position; they neither belong to the core sector nor to the periphery, but fall somewhere in between. They may at times belong to either one or the other, but neither position need be stable, and their identification with the subsystem is not clear and absolute.

Taking these criteria as a basis, we can consider the characteristics of the exceptions within the spheres of influence. Selecting six countries – Cuba, Peru, Yugoslavia, Romania and Albania (as well as the recently crushed regime in Chile) – as exceptions, is based on the fact that apart from the last one, *at present,* they maintain policies different from the majority of countries in their respective subsystems. In the case of Cuba and Yugoslavia, the continuous maintenance of such a position for an extended period of time has permitted a stabilisation of their independence and the acceptance of it almost as a recognised *status quo.* In the other cases, i.e. Peru, recognition and acceptance of deviant behaviour by the superpower has not been consolidated because of the short existence of the phenomenon.

The fragility of such exceptions is shown by the ease with which Chile's Popular Unity government was overthrown. We could have included in a similar category the 1968 Czechoslovakian regime, but the short duration of the 'Prague Spring' limits considerably the possibility of analysing it as an exception. In both cases, the attempt to define it as an innovatory 'pluralistic socialism' or 'humanitarian socialism' were ended by the covert or open action of both superpowers.

Other attempts to follow such a line of action, besides the aforementioned six (Bolivia in 1970, Brazil in 1962 and Poland and Hungary in 1956, etc.), were monitored successfully by the respective superpower in a similar and effective manner. By limiting the present discussion to six countries, there is no implication that they were the *only* deviationist examples from the general model, but they have been, relatively, the most successful cases, although Chile is no longer one of them.

There is a further difficulty in deciding whether a country belongs to a periphery or not. A continuous spectrum exists from the core to the periphery, and a country can change its position along this. Of the five successful exceptions, only Yugoslavia, Albania and Cuba are sufficiently marginal to be classified as periphery states. All three are also associated with alternative subsystems: the neutralist, the East Asian (Popular Republic of China), and the Soviet Union. The two other cases (Peru and Romania), can be classified as in an intermediary position or with a semi-peripheral status. Their peculiar position is due to their ability to manoeuvre the core countries close to the superpowers, and also the peripheral countries, without being excluded or excluding themselves from their respective subsystems. Peru associates with Cuba, yet maintains diplomatic relations with the United States and membership of the Organisation of American States. Romania has friendly relations with Communist China, and has continued to keep its close connections with the rest of Eastern Europe, fulfilling many economic and military obligations to the Soviet Union.

To a lesser extent other countries also exercise some autonomy of action (on a decreasing scale): Ecuador, Panama and Argentina in Latin America, Poland and possibly also Hungary in Eastern Europe. In the case of the first three, the relative lack of change in the internal structure, as well as a more controlled foreign policy (as for instance Ecuador's not re-establishing diplomatic relations with Cuba after many years of nationalist government, and Panama's lack of relations with the USSR), leaves them basically within the core of the subsystem.[1] Poland and Hungary, more concerned with internal reforms, have not shown any signs of following an independent foreign policy, in contrast with Romania.

The cases of Mexico and Finland are examples[2] which show similarities; in both cases they fought bitter wars with their neighbouring superpower, lost part of their territories, and now have self-imposed limitations on foreign policy so as to align themselves with the neighbouring superpower. In regard to Mexico and the United States,

> geography has placed them together, and that resulted in a confrontation with Mexico, losing large parts of its territory; this cannot be forgotten in Mexico and provokes an attitude of justified resentment against the United States, thus blaming on the "Yanki" everything that goes wrong in Mexico or in the rest of the Latin American countries. But geography forces Mexico to take into consideration the long frontier that it has with the United States, and obliges it not to push too hard its anti-Yanki feelings. Of course there are other considerations of an economic character that bring Mexico closer to the United States: the USA investments are necessary (more than that, they are vital) for the economic development of Mexico; besides, a sector of the Mexican bourgeoisie feels more secure with the presence of the United States and thus is interested in getting near to that country.[3]

This policy of 'self-restraint' has been maintained with different variations but with great continuity by the PRI (Institutional Revolutionary Party) regime. Despite having undergone a great social revolution during the second decade of this century Mexico is a country which, notwithstanding a tradition of relative independence in foreign policy, form of government and economic structure, remains an undetachable ally of the 'West' and the United States. Left-wing and protest movements have been inexorably crushed and US investments are powerful.

Finland differs on this point. On one hand, it maintains a cautious foreign policy, carefully avoiding antagonising the Soviet Union, and forsaking all alliances which may undermine its neutral position.[4] On the other hand, its political, economic and social internal structure is that of a country belonging to the 'capitalist' world, and cannot be considered part of the periphery of the Soviet-controlled system.

Observing the processes of the peripheral and semi-peripheral states, in both spheres of direct influence, we can make some generalisations leading to the six following propositions about the factors allowing the exercise of independent action. The first two have been advanced by David Vital,[5] while discussing small/large power confrontations:

(a) 'The maximilization of intrinsic military potential up to, but not beyond, the divide between conventional and nuclear weapons.'[6] The avoidance of a situation where a powerful opponent is driven to unmanageable reactions, sometimes of a pre-emptive nature against the increasing atomic capacity of the small state, yet, hand in hand with increasing the cost of conventional military conflict to a maximal level.

(b) 'The determined, but careful use of diplomatic and, where necessary military capabilities in an effort to make the major opponent fully and continually conscious of the high costs of conflict and of the refusal of the small state to be deflected from its objectives — provided the latter are, on other grounds, attainable.'[7] The superpowers' perception of the difficulties of intervention have to be made clear, mainly through political and diplomatic channels.

To these two propositions we can add an additional four related to the superpower-satellite relationship:

(c) Independence of action by a determined country in a sphere of influence of a superpower is achieved without the participation or help of the rival superpower. The Soviet Union does not plan or extend help for the preparation of socialist revolutions or subversive activities in Latin America. Neither does the United States guide the East European countries on how to liberate themselves from the Soviet yoke. The absence of this strategy is emphasised by the fact that it has often been used by both superpowers in other subsystems (Angola, Greece, Cambodia, Indonesia, Sudan, Iraq).

(d) Only after a specific stage is reached in the consolidation of independence by the 'satellite' from the superpower will the rival superpower extend the required economic, political and military assistance necessary to maintain itself facing the hostile dominant superpower. Once such a situation has been established, neither the Soviet Union nor the United States will pass over the opportunity of taking advantage of the new reality.[8] In spite of not having participated in the process of political emancipation by the satellite, the rival superpower will, however, attempt to strengthen and protect that independence once gained. This was seen in the case of Soviet support to Cuba, and United States aid to Yugoslavia.

(e) 'Having achieved a state independence from the superpower controlling the subsystem to which it belongs does not mean that it will enter into a similar new dependency relationship with the rival superpower.' Even if the new relationship entails a high degree of agreement, its position will remain more independent than that of the countries at the core of the region of the sphere of influence of that superpower. Even in the extreme case of Cuba, the pattern and closeness of relations with the Soviet Union still remain more vague and less well-defined than is the case with the countries which comprise the East European bloc.

(f) 'A country seeking greater freedom from the influence of a superpower, and which has already achieved this purpose to a degree, will attempt to play a role in the international system above its expected status inside its own subsystem.' It will seek co-operation from and alliances with countries from varying regions and subsystems, in order to strengthen and consolidate its newly achieved position. This shift from *seeking* support to that of *offering* support is operationalised by its involvement in the problems of other subsystems, and the attempt to formulate and implement an international policy, in contrast to a regional one. This has been the case with five out of the six peripheral and semi-peripheral countries. Albania, in its diplomatic endeavours and propaganda efforts was associated solely with Communist China, and again, far above its national potential.

One could go on to elaborate other possible propositions related to the domestic structure: massive support, national characteristics, economic resources and other tangible and intangible components. But it was felt that in the first stage it would be worthwhile to concentrate on external attributes directly related to foreign policy decision-making. Having stated the above principles, it is possible to analyse the specific cases and try to validate the above-mentioned hypotheses.

2 Yugoslavia

Tito's rise to power in Yugoslavia was the fruit of the struggle by his partisan forces against Nazi occupation of his country, and with the subsequent withdrawal of the Germans, his was the only force left receiving wide national support. Between 1945 and 1948 Yugoslavia was voluntarily within the Soviet orbit and continually attacked both capitalism and the West. However, in 1948 internal differences appeared between the two resulting in irreparable differences. No extra-subsystem interference sparked off the controversy: the differences were inherent in the varying world outlooks of the two countries, a direct result of Yugoslavia gaining power on its own, in contrast to the rest of Eastern Europe.

Firstly, during the war period, Tito's forces received minimal aid from the Soviet Union with resent of this being fuelled further by Molotov's compromising attitude toward Yugoslavia's clash with Italy and the Allies over the future of Trieste. Secondly, Yugoslavia's Balkan outlook, and the primary importance placed on that region by Tito, was disapproved of by Stalin; it was said in the post-1953 revelations that Stalin and Molotov personally vetoed plans for a Balkan federation in January 1948.[9] Thirdly, Soviet attempts to penetrate both the economy and political structure of Yugoslavia were successfully resisted by Tito and his supporters. A further difference between the two countries was their diverging concept of what the internal structure of a socialist country should be — with regard to the organisation of armed forces and the economic system.

The principal cause, though, was basically Yugoslavian resistance to Soviet hegemony; Stalin was used to ruling all other Eastern European countries with an iron hand. In order to implement this control over Yugoslavia, the Soviet Union attempted to strengthen the loyal pro-Soviet elements within all levels of the Yugoslavian administrative framework, up to the highest level of the Central Committee of the Communist Party and the High Command of the Armed Forces. Tito, however, succeeded in effectively eliminating those subversive elements from within his regime. Khrushchev reports that Stalin's reaction at the beginning of the dispute was to say 'I shall shake my little finger and there will be no more Tito.'[10] However, the development of events belied this boast.

With the rapid escalation of the 'differences of opinion', the Soviets came to use every means, short of military force, to topple Tito's regime — propaganda, subversion, economic blackmail, politics, etc. When in February 1948 Tito turned down an invitation to visit Moscow, the Kremlin refused to renew a vital commercial agreement with the country. This created serious problems for Belgrade, considering the extent of Yugoslavia's trade with the Communist Bloc — 95 per cent of all imports and 50 per cent of all exports were with that region. In an exchange of correspondence between Stalin and Tito, Tito was reviled as a Trotskyist, Revisionist, spy for the imperialists, etc.[11] In June 1948, the Yugoslavs, out of fear for their lives, declined an invitation to attend a Politburo meeting in Moscow to review Soviet-Yugoslavian relations, and as a result were expelled from the World Communist Movement, and refused to participate in a Cominform meeting in Bucharest. With Tito now an 'enemy of the Soviet Union', Moscow inaugurated a propaganda drive to foster nationalistic feelings amongst the minorities within Yugoslavia, calling on them to overthrow and replace the country's leadership. Internal terrorism, border skirmishes and the threat of military invasion by Romania, Hungary and Bulgaria failed to produce the desired result. Instead of undermining Tito, all these efforts had the opposite result; internally his position became stronger.

The reason for this unforeseen result — unforeseen by the Soviets, that is — were firstly, the degree and strength of Yugoslavian military preparedness, and even more their willingness to resist, based on their wartime experience. Secondly, the geographical location of Yugoslavia made it difficult for Soviet troops to attempt to carry out an invasion of that country. Thirdly, both the government and Tito received widespread mass support within Yugoslavia. Soviet military action was temporarily forestalled, but the economic effects of the blockade were creating serious internal difficulties.

Although Tito's situation was desperate, he was reluctant to seek aid from the only possible source, the 'imperialist' West. Throughout his life, he had been accustomed to look upon the capitalist world as an enemy, and he could not discard these ideas overnight. That the Soviet Union was now recognized to be evil did not, from the Yugoslav point of view, make the Western countries good. Furthermore, Tito did not wish to lend credence to Cominform charges that he had deserted the socialist camp and become a 'hired lackey of Wall Street'.[12]

This view is further supported by Ulam who considers that, during the first stage of the conflict, when challenging the leadership of the USSR in the communist world, Tito 'literally did not have a single friend'.[13] Confrontation was unavoidable when it became quite clear to Tito, himself one of the few survivors of previous Soviet purges, that the minimal price that Stalin would demand for 'forgiveness' was the liquidation of the entire leadership, and first of all, himself. It was out of despair, perhaps, that the Yugoslavian leadership committed themselves to such a high-risk situation.

However, it was undoubtedly impossible to resist economic strangulation without outside help. At this stage in the conflict, the West intervened to support Tito and uphold his power.[14] In December 1948, Yugoslavia signed a Commercial Treaty with Great Britain and later with the United States in which they provided $47 million immediate aid. In 1949 the rejection of Yugoslavia's application for membership in the COMECON, although it could have been foreseen, provided a further legitimation for its appeal to the West. Between 1951 and 1955, Yugoslavia received half a billion dollars in economic aid and also US military aid to the value of half a billion dollars. Without doubt this American support enabled the Yugoslav regime to stand up to Soviet hostility, but at the price of temporary dependency on the rival superpower. Following Stalin's death in 1953, Yugoslavia adopted a neutral stance, started to re-establish its relations with the USSR (in July 1953, diplomatic relations were re-established), and with world communism. The final legitimisation of the Yugoslav position was endorsed by Bulganin and Khrushchev's visit to that country and the subsequent joint Soviet-Yugoslavian Declaration, signed on 2 June 1955, setting forth the principle of mutual non-interference in the internal affairs of either country.[15]

The crises of 1956 in Poland and Hungary, a possible consequence of Soviet recognition of Yugoslavia's right to an independent position within the Socialist Bloc, and the direct Soviet accusations about Yugoslavia's support for Hungary, rekindled Yugoslav-Soviet friction. But this period lasted only briefly, co-existence again received official backing a year later. This policy was further reaffirmed, after a decade, in the joint Soviet Yugoslavian Declaration signed in Belgrade in 1971 in which each was to respect the other's different views on the development of socialism, and in which emphasis was placed on the principles of equality for all countries and non-intervention.[16]

The independence of manoeuvrability shown by Yugoslavia is exemplified in its ability, and the use of that ability, to criticise both superpowers. This trend could already be traced in 1950 when the war in Korea was viewed by them as a struggle between two rival superpowers unconcerned with the Korean people.[17] Later, the United States was strongly condemned for its action in Vietnam, the Middle East and other regions, while the Soviet Union was condemned for its military intervention in Czechoslovakia. Yugoslavia has called on both superpowers to abandon the armaments race, and instead to increase the aid given to developing countries. The Yugoslavian position is summarised by them when they point out that

taking into consideration the fact that the antagonism between the blocs of the great powers represent a great danger for the world peace, [Yugoslavia] has developed its foreign policy activity during the last years, and has tried to orient the efforts of the smaller countries, particularly those that have not compromised themselves with the blocs, to obtain the place they deserve in the UNO and in the international life, in general.[18]

Most of its criticism is aimed at the West, with the Soviet Union only rarely receiving its share. Of importance, though, is that the portion that the USSR does receive asserts the Yugoslav independent position, and sets an example for the rest of the East European subsystem. This is one of the main reasons why Yugoslavia should be considered by the American State Department as a positive element in the international arena:

Yugoslavia not only defied Stalin but stopped supporting the guerilla aggression against Greece, reached an agreement with Italy on Trieste, and increased its economic, political and cultural ties with the West. It is not a member of the Warsaw Pact. As a non-aligned state, it has gained influence among uncommitted nations of the world. Sometimes it agrees with the Soviet Union in particular points of foreign policy, sometimes not. In brief, Yugoslavia is not shipping arms to be used against the democratic government in Venezuela, and it is not trying to destroy non-Communist governments in South Vietnam and Laos.[19]

Yugoslavia cemented its independent position with the international policies which it followed. In the intial   post-war period Yugoslavia played a leading role in Balkan politics, with ambitions to become the region's leader — following the break with the USSR, Yugoslavia re-

paired its relations with the remaining neighbouring countries, Greece
and Turkey. From the early 1950s she played a vital and central role in
the formation of the non-aligned nations and the doctrine of 'positive
neutralism'. Tito established, on a personal level, close relations with
many of the Afro-Asian leaders, e.g. Nehru, Sukarno, U-Nu, Nasser and
Nkrumah. Excellent relations existed with both Western Europe, and
with Romania and Czechoslovakia during the 'spring of 1968'. The role
played by Yugoslavia and its importance in the international system, is
far in excess of both its strategic capabilities and of its economic
potential.

All six propositions seem to be confirmed in the present case study,
but the first one appears to play an extremely important role in
Yugoslavia's independence. The fact that this was the only country
where the Communists gained power through domestic revolution and
not through force imposed from outside, strengthened the military
capability with a formidable high national morale.

3 Cuba

From the *Sierra Maestra*, at the beginning of Castro's *26 of July*
Movement's guerilla war, to its eventual success, the revolution was
made without PSP (Cuban Communist Party) support. The line
adopted by the Cuban Communist Party – the once 'loyal defendants'
of governmental measures taken by Batista[20] – was to consider the
guerilleros as 'adventurist' and 'childish'. Up to a few weeks before the
revolutionary forces entered Havana, the Cuban communists still
believed that the only viable way to overthrow Batista's dictatorship
was by the formation of a 'national unity' movement which 'would
prepare the road to a coalition democratic government'.[21]

It is important to realise that during this period (the revolutionary
stage), Fidel Castro did not appear as a communist, and neither was he
during the first two years following the revolution. He could be defined
at this stage as being a 'Christian radical'. In the speeches Castro made
during his first year of government in 1959, he criticised both capitalism
and socialism since in his opinion neither system cared primarily for
man, the human personality'.[22] A critic of Washington's policy considers that 'the accusations of communism have preceded the "com-
munization" of Cuba'.[23]

The period 1959-61 was of crucial importance to Cuba. During this
period Castro went through a transformation resulting in the regime
being defined as 'socialist', and after the Bay of Pigs invasion as
'marxist-leninist'. The US policy of retaliating with economic reprisals

after the nationalisation of American interests in Cuba helped thrust Castro into this new stance. Castro's *anti-Yanki* personality, his rebellious temper, and the general feeling that from a historical point of view the United States simply replaced Spanish domination over Cuba by American domination, evoked within him an antagonism that culminated in a growing disparity between the policies of the two countries and in mutual aversion. Castro was eventually faced with either going back on his enacted policies, or becoming dependent on the USSR; he chose the latter. It could be said that Castro 'forced the Soviet Union to become his ally against his will'.[24]

The Bay of Pigs invasion of 1961 by Cuban exiles, organised and supported by the US government, was a disaster which ended in a crushing defeat for the US. Soviet military help had little bearing on the successful defeat of the invasion attempt; of greater importance was the lack of preparation and the ignoring of strategic considerations by the CIA. In the past, expeditionary groups with fewer men and poorer equipment were sufficient to overthrow other regimes in the Caribbean and Central American area. There was the successful example of Castillo Armas' insurrection in 1954 against the radical regime installed in Guatemala by President Arbenz.

In order to understand the ambivalence of the Soviet interest in Cuba it is necessary to assess the value of the Cuban connection. The advantages accuring to the USSR are:

(a) Cuba is the first country to declare itself a member of the Communist bloc without the existence of geographical continuity, either direct or indirect, with the USSR.
(b) With the exception of the South East Asian regimes, Cuba is the only state to have aligned itself with the Communist bloc, as a Communist country. With the disappearance, from the international scene, of Sukarno, Nkrumah, Ben Bella and Nasser, Castro became even more important
(c) Cuba is used as a psychological pressure in the bipolar relations with the United States. Even without nuclear weapons, and a Soviet military base 90 miles from the United States, Cuba can serve, to a certain extent, as an instrument of bargaining and disssuasion in the hands of Moscow.

In spite of the advantages accuring to the USSR, the relationship also entails disadvantages:

(a) The high price of economic aid to Cuba (calculated at between 400-600 million dollars a year).
(b) The existence of strong ideological reservations about the Soviet Union among Cuba's new Communists. The differences are basically over the character of the new socialist society (for instance, criticism by Che Guevara of the 'bourgeois parliamentary regime' which the Soviet Union has copied from the West), the transitional process towards socialism (and even to communism according to certain Cuban ideologists), which does not necessarily demand intermediary stages towards national liberation, and the means to be used in order to implement the social revolution (armed struggle or pacific evolution).
(c) The decline in the popularity of pro-Soviet communism in Latin America resulting from public criticism by Fidel Castro.
(d) By providing the 'rebel' Cuba with massive assistance the Soviet Union is unwillingly encouraging further independist trends in other member states of the Communist bloc, i.e. North Korea and Vietnam — with whom Cuba maintains the most friendly relations. It legitimates the existence of a semi-autonomous bloc of countries inside the Soviet orbit but with allegiances and close ties with other 'suns' such as China.

Cuba has recurrently demonstrated relative independence from the Soviet Union and its model of socialism. Internally, the political structure developed independently (with no constitution, parliament, or national elections), and in its economy with the reliance on variant methods (use of moral incentives, free services, etc.).

At different times, the Cuban revolutionary regime has carried out purges of 'sectarian' communists, attacking them for their blind obedience to Moscow. The old syndicalist communist leader, Anibal Escalante was expelled (exiled to one of the East European countries), for attempting to manoeuvre members of the original PSP into positons of power. Afterwards, Castro revealed the existence of the so-called 'micro-faction', and the veteran communists Juan Marinello and Favio Grobart were ousted from directing the University of Havana; leading Cuban economic figures such as Ramon Calcines and Escalona were sent to plant trees on the 'Youth Island'.

Signs of political independence can also be seen in Cuba's failure, over a long period, to side with Moscow in the Sino-Soviet conflict; in their refusal to sign the pact for the 'Non-Proliferation of Nuclear Weapons', in their abstention from joining the international condemnation (practically unanimous), of aerial piracy, until September 1973; in the maintenance, at variance with the Soviet position, of diplomatic relations till 1973 with Israel, together with supporting most Arab extremist states (Syria, Libya and Algiers), in anti-Israeli resolutions at the United Nations and not those moved by Egypt and the Soviet Union, in its absence from the Economic Conference at Budapest in 1968, etc.

This is a list of the most outstanding exceptions, but it should also be mentioned that while in reference to global issues, Cuban policy has become more aligned with that of the Soviet Union, on matters of special significance to Cuba, for example the future of the Latin American revolution, she has usually adopted an independent position openly in conflict with the Soviet line, and with that of the majority of Latin American communist parties, i.e. Cuban preference for guerilla movements and armed struggle in general. During the international Conference of Communist Parties in Moscow, 1969, the Cuban delegate delegate, Carlos Rafael Rodriguez, attacked the proposed resolution for Latin America. He even opposed the line adopted by the Congress when denying itself to be the 'vanguard' in the struggle for national liberation, and against imperialism.[25] This position was maintained even with the triumph of the Popular Front in Chile, with Rodriguez, who represented the Cuban government at the inauguration ceremony of Allende's regime, presenting at a press conference in Santiago the theory that armed struggle is the only way to achieve national liberation in Latin America, with Chile being the only exception to the rule.[26]

Within the last few years, there has been a *rapprochement* between Cuba and the USSR, with a de-emphasis on apparent differences. Cuba's economic problems brought home its dependence on Soviet aid;[27] and the lack of success of the guerilla movements during the decade of the sixties in Latin America has led Castro to re-evaluate and adopt a more pragmatic approach in regard to leftist electoral movements and parties. With this change, one of the major points of disagreement with Moscow has been removed, or at least minimised. Castro's visit to Chile, and the possibility of the re-acceptance of Cuba within the Latin American family of nations, has moderated the *Lider Maximo's* extremism, the cause for its total isolation on the continent.

Communist Cuba attempted to become the revolutionary centre, not just of Latin America, but of the Third World. In 1965, Cuba organised and directed the Tri-Continental Conference, with its Permanent Secretariat being established in Havana (OSPAAAL), but out of disappointment at the lack of revolutionary zeal amongst the Afro-Asian leadership, she diverted her attention to the developments amongst the New Left in Europe and the US (International Cultural Conference in Havana in 1968), with a re-emphasis on Latin America. The guerilla movements of the continent were represented in Havana in 1967 at the Conference for the Organisation of Latin American Solidarity (OLAS), where it was decided to emulate Che Guevara. With the weakening of the guerilla movements there has been a corresponding reduction in the OLAS functions, but the aspiration to create, in Cuba, the centre of the 'Fifth International' remains.[28]

Finally, the event which aroused controversy and complicated Cuban-Soviet relations, and Soviet influence within Latin America, is without doubt the Cuban Missile Crisis of 1962. Many have attempted to explain Soviet behaviour and motives. What is an accepted outcome is that as a reaction to the US stand, the USSR agreed to remove the missiles from Cuba. The Soviet attempt has been attributed to Moscow's inferiour nuclear position resulting from what became known as the Soviet Missile Gap,[29] and her desire to guarantee and protect Cuban independence from new aggression. What the truth may be, we still do not know, but it is clear that the position taken by President Kennedy forced a Soviet retreat and loss in prestige. Castro's opposition to the withdrawal of the missiles failed to influence the Soviet decision, and therefore, fortified Cuban belief that the only ultimate guarantee of security was their own power sources.

With the crisis escalating to potential nuclear conflict, Cuba became a tool of negotiation in the cold war, together with Berlin and the issue of US missile bases in Turkey. The crisis, and its developments, increasingly emphasised the inability of the Soviet Union to provide unlimited security guarantees to a country within the US sphere of influence — the Western Hemisphere — seeking to extend its independence.

When Cuba became, briefly, a Soviet military base, the potential bipolar system suddenly became actual; in the naked confrontation between the two powers, the United States won because of its overall strategic superiority and because it had turned the tables superbly. What prevented the confrontation from escalating was, at heart, the fear of nuclear war. Now it is this new rational recoil before the use of force that explains why, when faced with a hostile Cuba acting *on its own,* the United States has hesitated to apply heavy pressure and why it has failed when it has done so. The Soviet Goliath defied the

American Goliath and lost; the Cuban David continues to defy the American Goliath.[30]

The American military base at Guantanamo, Cuba, still symbolically represents Soviet recognition of Latin America as belonging to, and being under US power. In Libya, for instance, the USA was willing to evacuate the Wheelus Air Force Base following the petition of the new nationalist government; in Cuba, despite more than ten years of socialist government, the US presence remains.

The overthrow of the Allende regime was a serious blow to Castro's policy and perhaps a warning of the necessity of moderating even more his attitude towards the Western Hemisphere. Vice-President Rafael Rodriguez admitted that although objective conditions for socialism do exist in Latin America, he did not see any immediate possibility of its installation in other countries, and stressed that Latin America is living in an era of 'strong nationalism' but no longer of 'imminent revolution'.[31]

The new and more realistic line now includes accommodation with the United States. Basically it stands as a Cuban initiative with a rather cool and passive response from the State Department.[32] Although formally indicating that the United States was responsible for severing relations and had declared a blockade and consequently that the diplomatic first step should be undertaken by them, Cuba has made approaches a number of times. Most indicative is the withdrawl of the idea of 'exporting' the Cuban revolutionary ideas to other countries, now accepting that 'each country has to undertake its own revolution'.[33] However, Cuban military involvement in the Angolan civil war and the support extended to Puerto Rican independentist elements seem to express a dissatisfaction with the American lack of responsiveness to previous 'openings'.

By 1975 the first fruits of Cuba's growing acceptance in the Latin American subsystem on a continental level can be witnessed. After being welcomed back as a participant with the Latin American caucus at the UN, this process has been formally legitimised by the San Jose resolution of the OAS lifting the recommendation that all countries should sever bilateral relations with the island. Other Latin American states followed in re-establishing diplomatic relations, air links were reassumed and the visits of Mexican President Echeverria and Panama's ruler Omar Torrijos provided further emphasis of the importance with which Cuba has been considered by the main statesmen of the continent. At the same time, Cuba is attempting to diversify her sources of foreign aid, particularly in relation to the 1976-80 Five Year Plan, as stated by Rafael Rodriguez during his official visit to France.[34]

The massive Cuban military involvement in the Angolan civil war has to be interpreted as a desertion from previous signals about a possible normalisation of relations with Washington. One could locate Cuba in 1976 as a country combining both the elements of a submissive policy towards the Soviet Union with a gradual opening to Western secondary powers. Viewed from a perspective covering the entire period of the Cuban Revolution one can conclude that in this case study the six propositions underlined in our study appear to be largely confirmed.

5 Romania

Romania is perhaps the classic case of a country slowly and cautiously emancipating itself successfully from a superpower without having to pass through a violent upheaval. Romania's policy was orientated towards achieving an intermediary position between the two major Communist powers — in order to maintain an independent stand in its relations within the socialist camp and the world. The reasons why Bucharest was interested in gaining independence from the USSR were: a traditional nationalist anti-Russian feeling intensified by the loss of territories to the USSR (Bessarabia and Northern Bukovina); a desire to resist the process of military unification under Soviet central control; and opposition to a regional economic plan proposed in the COMECON in which there would be 'specialisation of labour' in the socialist camp, which would have retarded Romanian plans for industrialisation; and last but not least, the desire to resist de-Stalinisation.[35]

Until Stalin's death in 1953, Romania remained completely subservient to Kremlin dictates.[36] A series of purges served to unify and homogenise the Party apparatus under the strong direction of Gheorgiu-dej. In 1953 Soviet criticism was voiced that rapid industrialisation should not be at the expense of the agricultural sector or at the expense of the standard of living of the population. All the same, it has been made very clear that Romania does not intend to remain at a low economic level and restrain its industrial development, in fact industrial development is central to Romanian economic plans. The reduction of military expenditure, replaced by guarantees of its sovereignty, the diversification of potential sources for economic aid, and the increase of trade with the West were all aimed at enabling Romania to hasten its industrial development programme. From there onwards Larrabee divides the Romanian relations with the USSR into four phases: Phase I

— latent conflict, 1955-61; phase 2 — emerging conflict, 1961-64; Phase 3 — expanded conflict, 1966-67; phase 4 — institutionalised conflict, 1968 onwards.[37]

Despite the economic differences that developed with the USSR following the rise to power of Khrushchev, in the political sphere Romania exhibited a conservative attitude in line with the Soviet Union. Bucharest supports the policy of pacific co-existence,[38] renewed its relations with Yugoslavia; and supported the need for the 1956 Soviet invasion of Hungary with the declaration that 'the Romanian delegation agreed that the Soviet government's assistance to the Hungarian government had been in discharge of its "international duty to the working people of Hungary and of the other socialist countries" '.[39] In accordance with the principle of collective leadership, Gheorgiu-dej resigned from his post as Secretary General of the Party in 1954, and only retained the position of head of government. The Secretariat was divided on a functional basis into the Secretary and three assistants, among whom was Ceausescu. In 1958 Khrushchev ordered the withdrawal and evacuation of Soviet troops from Romanian territory, a decision criticised later in the Kremlin as it enabled Bucharest to follow a more autonomous policy *vis-a-vis* the USSR without the immediate fear of Soviet military intervention. Till 1961, Romania greatly emulated the Soviet Union and its political guidelines.[40] At that time the Moscow leadership had to face many crisis situations such as Berlin and Cuba, and perhaps the most menacing from Peking.

In the second phase, by exploiting the deterioration in Sino-Soviet relations from 1961, Romania emerged in the role of mediator and arbitrator, and solidified her gains up to then. In contrast to Albania, Bucharest managed to maintain, simultaneously, a dialogue with Moscow and Peking without serious repercussions. From February to March 1964, Romanian delegations travelled back and forth from Moscow to Peking, finally proposing a joint Russian-Romanian-Chinese *communique,* unsuccessfully. The way in which Romania exploited the position in which she found herself enhanced her prestige in both the socialist camp and in other regions.

By tackling the economic development problems before her, Romania expanded her trade and commercial contacts with the West. Between the years 1958 and 1962 the West's share in Romania's total trade expanded from 22 per cent to 33 per cent.[41] Firstly by getting an Austrian and a British-French consortium to invest 20 and 40 million dollars respectively in the Galati furnaces[42] and later with larger

American investments in the petroleum and rubber industries; she established growing links with the US culminating in 1964 in the decision by both countries to raise the diplomatic representation to ambassadorial level. By 1963, many of the Western European countries (e.g. Great Britain), had already decided to elevate the legations to embassies.

What was still considered in the second phase to be mostly a strong divergence of views on economic matters emerged in the third stage as a political controversy. In 1963 Romania introduced reforms in the educational system making Russian an optional language, a direct challenge to the symbolic importance of the Soviet Union, and the beginning of a new phase in which the USSR was both directly and indirectly criticised. Radio exchanges between Moscow and Bucharest commentators became mutually aggressive and the celebrated Romanian polemical talents were shown at their best. In 1964, in a declaration by the Central Committee of the Rumanian CP, one hears of 'equal independence' for all socialist countries, and that the supranational character of the Warsaw Pact is incompatible with the principle of national sovereignty. Romanian leaders visited Peking and Paris in 1965 and also received Chou-En-Lai in a State visit. In 1966, Ceausescu called for the abolition of all military blocs and this newly felt independence was openly expressed during the Budapest Conference. On 31 January 1967, the Romanians established diplomatic relations with West Germany, becoming the only Communist country besides the USSR to enjoy such status, in opposition to a Soviet dictat to the Eastern bloc against such an action. In April of that year Romania boycotted the meeting of European Communist Parties at Karlovy Vary in Czechoslovakia, opposed the Soviet nominee to the post of Commanding Officer of the Warsaw Pact, and in June 1967, following the Six Day War, refused to sever diplomatic relations with Israel.

Moscow's increasing concern over developments in Romania did not crystallise in a firm policy due to the internal changes of leadership that occurred with Khrushchev's dismissal. A year later, during his visit to Bucharest in 1965, Brezhnev attempted to clarify the 'margins of political security' acceptable by Russia. It was around 1968 that the conflict became institutionalised so that both sides could realise the limits of their mutual expectations. The events in Prague were, in this respect, the catalyst. During 1968 the Romania regime maintained friendly relations with the Czechoslovakian government during its 'Spring' period – following the invasion by Soviet troops Romania openly condemned the Russian action. The invasion, all the same, acted as an uncomfortable reminder to Bucharest of what can happen to a country deviating too much from the accepted line. In the aftermath of Czechoslovakia, the USSR increased its economic control over Romania and suggested the carrying out of military manoeuvres within that country's borders by Warsaw Pact troops. Romania quickly modified its position, but not totally, as it still continues in its attempts to achieve its basic goals.

A strong supporter of the European Security Conference, Romania combines in its declarations the principle that 'the close alliance and the collaboration with the socialist countries constitute the foundation stone of Romanian foreign policy', in its efforts to 'reinforce the unity of the socialist countries.[43] At the same time, 'in our opinion, to implement European security, it first needs to be established among all the countries of the continent, relations based on the principles of equality of rights, of independence and national sovereignty, the non-intervention in their internal affairs, all to mutual advantage'.[44]

From this analysis, it appears quite clear that Romania's first step towards national independence was undertaken without any involvement of the rival superpower. All the diplomatic manoeuvres were conducted inside the Communist Bloc. Furthermore, in the second phase, even though the United States stabilised, by its support, Romanian independence *vis-à-vis* the Soviet Union, at no stage did it involve implications of a dependency relationship towards the Western superpower. On the contrary, Bucharest has not failed to criticise Washington on a variety of issues, i.e. US involvement in Vietnam. Romania has continually shown the ability to maintain a position of non-alignment on a multitude of problems in the international arena, and continues to pursue a flexible and independent policy. It supports peaceful co-existence, while at the same time opposing the Treaty on the Non-Proliferation of Nuclear Weapons. Both in the economic and political fields, Romania has improved relations with West Germany without suffering any serious complications in dealings with Pankow. In remaining neutral in the Sino-Soviet conflict, it benefits from friendly relations with both countries. In spite of maintaining diplomatic ties with Israel, it usually votes with the Arab States, including the recognition of the PLO and attempted to play, in 1971, the role of mediator in the conflict, inviting leaders of all the countries to visit Bucharest. In Lima (1975) it also asked to be admitted as an observer for the non-aligned countries. In the United Nations it achieved distinctive recognition, with the election of its delegate as Chairman of the General Assembly. Romania's case is one with a feedback effect, its active international role strengthening its independence *vis-à-vis* the Soviet Union — while its independence is reflected in its active international role, which is, in itself, in excess of Romania's given power capabilities.

The principal reasons for Romanian ability to safeguard its independence *vis-a-vis* the USSR can be listed as follows:

(a) the absence of either a rapid escalation in the process, or a severe crisis which might have called forth Soviet military action, providing the necessary time lag for Kremlin leaders to think through all the implications involved in such an action. As the whole process was one of slow evolution, the Soviets were always faced with the question: what would be the 'price' of such an intervention, and how convenient would it be to postpone it to a later stage?

(b) Along the same lines, the Soviet Union was continually confronted with more pressing and dangerous cases (the theory of 'Alternative Cost' in economics) — Communist China from the beginning of the 1960s, and Czechoslovakia in 1968. One result of 1968, all the same, was its use by Moscow as a warning to Romania.

(c) No challenge was made to the Soviet communist model, leaving Romania even more conservative than Russia where some patterns were slowly changing.

(d) The relative economic independent position of Romania due to restricted potential Soviet action (economic sanction, for instance, was not a feasible weapon), may have contributed, or intensified the desire to step up relations with the West and Yugoslavia.

(e) From the Soviet Union's point of view there was always the nagging fear that a military conflict in the West would be exploited by China in the East, intensifying border hostilities.[45]

(f) Romania received tacit American support — though not in the realm of direct intervention — and thereby any hostile Soviet actions against Romania could have repercussions in the field of economic co-operation for the Soviet Union in its dealings with the West, and might even have scuttled the whole *detente* policy between the superpowers.

The first of the six propositions is not truly represented in the Romanian case. Rather than speaking of its military capability as a significant deterrent, the emphasis should be placed on the lack of direct threat from the Red Army after it withdrew in 1958. But such a decision by Moscow was reached mainly because of the capability displayed by

Romania on the political-diplomatic front. It therefore emphasises the importance of the second proposition. A final comment relates to the difficulties in presenting clear-cut points of transition from one phase to another. Several experts would provide different time dimensions for the various phases.[46] It is precisely through this slow escalating process that Romania's deviationist trend could become an accepted fact by Moscow.

5 Peru

Peru is a marginal case of a semi-peripheral country which, when included amongst the exceptions, creates problems. The nationalisation of American enterprises, i.e. the IPC; the extensive agrarian reform; and the 'social control' of industry (worker and state participation in private enterprises), reflects an internal structure different from the rest of the countries of the subsystem. The regime is developing along the path of a planned and centralised economy residing in public entities such as 'Petroperu' (oil state monopoly) or 'Mineroperu' (mines state monopoly) and a control over foreign trade. At the same time, emphasis has been placed on the decentralisation of the administration and on co-operative initiatives. These lines do not suggest, however, the following of a socialist or communist model.[47] Furthermore, Peru has not associated itself with any other subsystem and cannot be considered as depending on Soviet support.

General Juan Velasco Alvarado came to power, with wide backing from the armed forces, in a *coup d'etat* in October 1968. At the time of the *coup*, diplomatic relations did not exist between Peru and the Soviet Union, and the country's Communist Party was too involved in its own struggle for survival amidst the fragmented left — the guerilla groups being more popular — to have taken any part in national revolution. The new military government quickly and effectively repressed the guerilla movements, and the pro-Soviet Communist Party supported most government actions so as to strengthen their own position *vis-a-vis* the now weakened left and to place themselves near the centre of power. The military junta formed a cabinet consisting exclusively of members from the upper echelons of the armed forces and devoid of any communist participation at all levels of the government machinery. All the same, from 1971 they did recognise the pro-communist CGTP (General Confederation of Peruvian Workers), as the sole representative of the trade unions and workers.[48] In all declarations and speeches by ministers of the new government, at no time did they refer to themselves as Communists, or even 'socialist', and in fact were careful to avoid labelling themselves as such.[49]

The government efforts to disassociate themselves from communism were evidenced when the Foreign Minister, Miguel Angel de la Flor del Valle, rejected the motion 'that Peru encourages the armaments race with equipment bought in the Soviet Union and maintains a Communist government',[50] as an attempt to undermine the prestige of the Peruvian government. The need for Peru to diversify its sources of military hardware and training was necessitated when the US invoked the 'Pelly Amendment' and stopped the sale of further military equipment to Peru in retaliation for the dispute over Peru's interpretation of the territorial sea limit.[51] As a result, Peru not only approached the Soviet Union as an alternative supplier, but also Canada, Israel and France.

Only in February 1969 were diplomatic relations at the Ambassadorial level re-established between Peru and the Soviet Union. This step was justified on the grounds of the Peruvian desire to widen the whole framework of their international relations. They declared, 'the Peruvian Government believes that the best way of serving the international society is by affirming the liberty of States, and consequently, projecting the diplomatic ties towards new perspectives which will recognize in the dialogue the civilized procedure of living together', adding at the time, 'that in this sense we consider not only desirable but profitable for Peru, whose roots are nourished by the legacy of our indigenous cultures and in the thoughts of Christian civilization, to establish friendly relations with a great country as the one H.E. represents [the Soviet Union] beyond the different ideologies which inspire them or the political regimes that govern them.'[52]

The following of an independent foreign policy was emphasised by the regime's recognition of Communist China, and later in the establishment of diplomatic relations with it. In 1971, in conjunction with its independence in the international arena, Peru re-established relations with Cuba. The Soviet aid extended to Peru at the time of her catastrophic earthquake achieved a propaganda success, but in reality the amount of assistance was not large, even by the standards of the poor Latin American countries.

In foreign policy Peru maintains a position close to neutralism. Her aspiration to play a central role among the non-aligned countries is reaffirmed by her hosting of this bloc's Conference in Lima in 1975. As a whole the revolutionary government has attempted to play an active role in international life, seeking recognition as an example of how a progressive military regime can tackle the problem of development amongst the countries of the Third World. In 1972 it organised the meeting of the '77' club to prepare and co-ordinate the policy to be followed by the developing countries before the UNCTAD meeting in Chile. Participating in the recent meetings of the non-aligned countries at Lusaka, Georgetown, Algiers, and by hosting in Lima the 1975 Conference, it has also brought Latin America closer to the other countries of Africa and Asia. Peru took the lead in the demand for a 200-mile territorial sea limit,[53] it plays a central role in the Andine Pact; and in furthering its friendly relations with Cuba, signed a joint declaration as 'revolutionary governments' opposed to the 'foreign domination and imperialist aggression', without mentioning a specific superpower. Referring to the inequality among states established by the veto system at the UN, President Velasco Alvarado appealed to the developing countries: 'We are still on our way to independence and therefore we the developing countries must unite to prevent these two imperialist countries imposing their dictates on us'.[54] When General Morales Bermundez displaced General Velasco from the Presidency in 1975, a purge of left-wing officers in top positions signalled a step back into the regional self-imposed restrictions, or in his own words 'to rectify the path of the Revolution to the "true channel"'.[55]

In briefly examining Peru in relation to its independent position within its subsystem, the six propositions are met. However, it is difficult to find a clear-cut transition between the emerging step and the consolidation of the 'deviant' case. No large crises are to be noted in her relations with the United States while on the other hand reliance on assistance from alternative sources of aid is spread among different countries of the East and West.

6 Albania

Before analysing Albania's role in the international arena it is important to understand the internal features of that country, which is so different from other European states. The population barely reaches 2 million, the economy is based on agricultural produce, and without doubt, it is the least developed country of Europe. The annual per capita income is approximately $300, approximately half that of the other poverty cases of Europe (Bulgaria and Yugoslavia). The population is approximately 70 per cent Moslem, differentiating it from the rest of Europe, both in regard to religion and family structure — which in Albania's case was autocratic and feudal.

Albanian independence from the First World War up to 1948, was basically a continuation of the dependency status which it has suffered since the fifteenth century — controlled by either Greece, Yugoslavia or Italy. Ethnically, the country was split into the Ghegs (Northerners, semi-barbarian mountain dwellers), and the Tosks (Southerners, coastal-dwellers, more modernised), both competing against the other for power. This ethnic struggle is stressed by the fact that 'from its birth to the present the history of Albanian Communism provides a classic example of ideology serving a mask for ancient historical factors, geographical conditions and local pressures'.[56]

From the time of the creation of the Albanian Labour Party (communist) in 1941, until the deterioration in Soviet-Yugoslavian relations, Yugoslavia exerted direct political control over Enver Hoxha, Albania's leader, and reduced Albania to a total dependency on Yugoslavia. Belgrade's ideas of a 'Balkanian federation' were feared by the Albanian communists as annexation, for all practical purposes. Albania quickly took advantage of the developments of 1948, supporting Moscow in order to gain independence from Yugoslavia. The Albanian Labour Party's Central Committee declared that the Yugoslavian leaders 'have tried to destroy the independence of our country and our Party'.[57] This development freed Albania from the fear of Yugoslavian expansionist ambitions, and also provided the Albanian Tosk leadership with an excuse for purging the Party of Gheg elements in 1948 by accusing them of 'Titoism'. The latter, as exiles in Yugoslavia, formed within that country an Albanian minority (750,000 inhabitants), an opposition base for the Ghegs. This aggravated the already tense situation caused by the irredentist nationalistic aspirations of the Albanians, in considering the territory of Kossovo-Metchifa as an integral part of their country.

However, the *rapprochement* between Moscow and Belgrade in 1955 resulted in the present Albanian international position.[58] 'The major cause of Hoxha's antagonism toward Khrushchev, namely his probably justified fear that the Soviet leader would sacrifice him for the sake of a *rapprochement* with Tito had already been present in 1956.'[59] Albania, with great caution, began to disassociate itself from the Soviet Union. Following the Twentieth Party Congress of the Communist Party in the USSR and the resultant attack on the personality cult created by Stalin, Albania diverged from Soviet leadership by maintaining its Stalinist system.[60] This reflected the attempt to achieve two aims; greater autonomy for Albania *vis-à-vis* Yugoslavia; and the maintenance of Hoxha's personal power which was in itself partly based on a cult of Stalinist outlook. Though he formally left the government and adopted the position of Secretary General of the Party, all the same, Hoxha remained the real power in Tirana. Khrushchev during his short visit to

Albania in 1959 did not fail to criticise this situation.

From 1959 the differences came out into the open and relations between the two countries quickly deteriorated – coinciding with a similar deterioration in Sino-Soviet relations – and China became Albania's natural ally. At the Twenty-second Congress of the CPSU (Communist Party of the USSR), Albania was attacked:

> Our Party's policy aimed at eliminating the harmful consequences of the personality cult did not . . . meet with the understanding from the leaders of the Albanian Party of Labour . . . This stand of the Albanian leaders is due to the fact that, to our deep regret, they are themselves using the same methods as were current in our country at the time of the personality cult.[61]

In 1961 the USSR broke off diplomatic relations with Albania, and the rest of the East European countries recalled their representatives. However, the break with Albania was not made final, with certain connections being left intact. This attitude was in contrast to the US policy of forcing all its satellites to isolate Cuba totally, and to include the Western countries in the economic boycott, and also in contrast to the previous total segregation of Yugoslavia in the era of monolithic rule in the Communist Bloc. The Soviet Union maintained communication links with Albania by permitting her satellites to continue commercial intercourse – Poland, Hungary and Czechoslovakia followed Communist China as the principal trade partners of Albania.

As indicated above, Albania has enjoyed a relatively independent position in the communist world. Geographically, she is isolated from both the Soviet Union and its closest allies (Yugoslavia being the only geographical threat), and this in conjunction with the relative unimportance placed on Tirana by Moscow, enabled the Albanian regime to maintain an independent policy position from 1955 to 1960, without being militarily attacked. That it eventually became a Chinese satellite, was a voluntary move on Albania's part as an insurance policy for the future to avoid being exploited by China. This was a rather unique opportunity for Peking to incorporate in its orbit a former sector of the Soviet sphere of influence, a chance it could not miss. According to Landuai, 'as far as Albania's over-all position is concerned, the country has for the first time in its history an almost ideal protector, powerful but at a safe distance, that even if it wished to, could not restrain Tirana in a possible search for political and economic alternative'.[62] However, the distance factor can also be regarded as a drawback should the Soviet Union decide to intervene physically.[63]

The role played by the United States, and its importance as far as Albania is concerned, was practically non-existent during the whole process.[64] With Albania's position strengthened and consolidated, it came to play a role (minor as it was) in the international arena far above its real power potential. Until 1972, Albania acted as the voice and representative of Communist China in the United Nations and all other international bodies to which it belonged. In the period of the deterioration of relations between China and the Soviet Union, the USSR condemned Albania as deviationist, while at the same time Yugoslavia was condemned by China — both these countries were used as indirect targets for mutual accusations by the major Communist powers.

Albania, being a Moslem country, maintains both good trade and political relations with the more extremist Arab countries, and with the recent improvement in Sino-Yugoslavian relations, the Albanian attitude towards Belgrade has become more moderate. This is still very much a forced attitude and a result of having relied on only one source of support, China. Timidly Albania is nodding to other countries, notably Italy.

It is very hard to find a reasonable explanation for why the Soviet Union has not crushed this minute deviant regime. The analogy of an elephant failing to kill a mosquito might well be used. The idea of an intervention by a strong superpower in a tiny and backward yet challenging country was repeatedly put aside until it was finally accommodated by ignoring it. The six propositions are confirmed though the absurd disporportion between the rivals stresses the inherent weakness of the propositions in extreme cases. The fifth proposition in this case refers not to the relationship with the rival superpower but to the contending intra-bloc power, China. Still the basic assumption — that the new dependence ties are looser than the previously maintained links with the regional superpower — is likewise met.

7 Chile

The achievement of power by the government of popular unity in 1970 seemed to mark a further increased in the number of exceptions to the rule of superpower domination in Latin America. Its overthrow on 11 September 1973, and the replacement of the leftist regime by a right-wing military dictatorship, restored Chile to 'dependentist' normality. All the same, despite the regime's short life, it is still interesting to apply to it the already formulated principles, in order to test its internal validity.

Allende's election as President on 24 October 1970 was no major surprise, and his success was not dependent on any foreign sources or influence. The persistence of the left-wing front, strengthened by support from splinter groups of the Radical and Christian Democratic parties, gained for 'Popular Unity' 36 per cent of the total votes, ensuring their candidate first place, with the largest share of the popular vote. Under Chilean parliamentarian tradition, this was sufficient for the mobilisation of the support of the majority of Congressmen in order to elect Allende as President. The Christian Democrats, still led by the moderate Tomic, turned the ballot in his favour. This vote for the 'popular front' was not a new phenomenon in Chile; in 1938 they attained power there for the first time (also for Latin America), with the Radical, Aguirre Cerda being appointed President. The last previous occasion of a Radical administration was in 1946, when for a short time the cabinet also included three Communist ministers. The left-wing front was reformed into a socialist-communist front, with the FRAP (Popular Action Front) in 1958, when the Socialist Salvador Allende was its candidate; following two unsuccessful attempts in 1958 and 1964, he achieved power in 1970.

It is important to bear in mind that the Communist Party in Chile for many years did not reflect the revolutionary image, preferring the role of a respectable electoral force. Furthermore, 'hostile to the armed struggle policy defined at Havanna in the 1967 OLAS (Organization of Latin American Solidarity) Conference, the Communist Party, loyal to the policy of peaceful coexistence maintained by the Soviet Union, and facing the great electoral confrontation of 1969 and 1970, was closer to the points of view of certain radicals (the Chilean centrists) than to certain "allies" from the extreme left'.[65]

Allende, in spite of the fact that — as the opposition were quick to point out — he defined himself as a Marxist, had committed himself to the 'Constitutional Charter of Guarantees' given to the Christian Democrats before his election, promising to respect the democratic institutions, the pluralistic political system and the inviolability of civil rights.

The Soviet Union played no direct or prominent role in Allende's electoral achievement. It could be that they had sympathy for the left-wing coalition, and may even have provided some financial assistance, but in order to avoid creating the image of a 'communist plot', the Soviet Union minimised its support so as not to frighten the middle-class electors. Moscow's relations with the preceding Christian Democratic President Frei were friendly and provide parallels with the close relations between the Soviet Union and the Gaullist regime, even during elections, and with those of the French Communist-Socialist front.

On gaining power, the Soviet Union extended economic assistance to the new regime, but did not fulfil the needs and expectations of the Chilean left.[66] The 'invisible' economic boycott applied by the United States in conjunction with their refusal to renew the credit line until the payment of all foreign debts, brought Chile to economic bankruptcy. Moscow's efforts to supply material support were smaller than those provided in the case of Cuba.[67] It is reported that during the first year of Allende's regime, only $50 million in foreign aid was forthcoming from the Soviet Union. In 1972, facing a catastrophic economic situation, during a trip to Moscow Allende managed to secure credit of $335 million ($185 million in local currency), to buy indispensable consumer goods from Western countries,[68] while Foreign Minister Almeyda, during his tour of Eastern European countries in the same year, managed to mobilise an additional $100 million.[69] This amount, in relation to the annual debt payments of $400 million to Western creditors (principally the United States), was totally insufficient, especially when taking into account the loans provided to past governments, especially that of President Frei. China's supplementary assistance of $26 million in 1972 was purely symbolic, being of little real value.

The spirit of resignation in which the Soviet Union accepted the *coup d'etat* in 1973 in also noteworthy. It is true that the USSR severed relations with the new regime, but it did very little to prevent its gaining legitimacy immediately after Allende's fall. Many of the official commentaries avoided blaming the United States directly,[70] referring only to the 'fascist and reactionary forces' within Chile, and foreign imperialism outside — the foreign powers involved or accused of being involved, were not specifically named. For the sake of *detente* the name of the United States was deleted for a long time, until the press and the Congress in the United States revealed the massive involvement of the Executive branch a year later.

In the case of Chile, there was no question of the establishment of a dependency relation with the Soviet Union, as with Cuba. The Popular Unity government itself reflected a plurality of socialist beliefs, supporting nearly all socialist countries and their varying ideologies. Chile's foreign policy was situated somewhere midway between that of the neutralists and that of the Communist Bloc, with many official state-

ments aimed at the Third World — supporting the 'defense of the interest of the underdeveloped countries facing the Great Powers'.[71] Chile
endorsed the claim by the developing countries for a 200-mile patrimonial sea, adopted a uncommitted position over the Sino-Soviet conflict, maintained full and cordial diplomatic relations with Israel, and
generally showed many similarities in foreign policy outlook to that of
Yugoslavia.

In three years of power, Allende attempted to play an increasingly
active role in the international system. The close links established by
the Christian Democratic movement in Latin America with Western
Europe during Frei's presidency were expanded and built upon by
Allende, and Santiago itself was transformed into a centre of international gatherings. In 1972 she hosted the meeting of the Bureau of
the Social Democratic Socialist International, and the Conference of
UNCTAD (United Nations Conference on Trade and Development),
with 3,000 participants. Chile remained active in the regional
'Andean Pact', and also in Latin America as a whole. Cuban support
was overwhelming, Castro personally doing whatever he could to
appease the demands of the extreme revolutionary left in Chile and
extending economic assistance. Diplomatic relations were established
with Arab and Asian Communist countries, and even with Albania. All
these efforts though, failed to gain sufficient world support or relevant
substantial support to prevent the dramatic end of the regime. The
lack of control over the internal forces became evident when the army
— the same group that had previously agreed to share temporal power
with Allende — assumed the role of the executioner of the aims of the
centre and right-wing forces, the economic circles and the governmental agencies of the United States.[72]

When analysing the validity of the six general propositions, the
failure to fulfil some of the more important ones might be considered
as a source of the fall of Allende's regime. The first is notably absent;
the Chilean Army retained close ties with the Pentagon and the Popular
Unity government failed to control its actions, the military potential
turning against the elected regime. The criteria of the second proposition are also not fully met. Diplomatic capabilities were not displayed
by the Chilean regime in all its dimensions. The possibilities of raising
support from important social-democratic regimes in Western Europe
(West Germany, the Scandinavian countries), were far from being exhausted, while the Chilean Radical Party belonged to this International
movement; on the contrary, the 'domino' theory of the White House
considered the success of the Socialist-Communist alliance as a danger-

ous precedent for the strengthening of similar coalitions in France and perhaps Italy.[73]

Finally, the fourth criterion is not satisfied, since the Soviet Union appeared unwilling to extend a high level of commitment towards the preservation of the Socialist regime in Chile. Its assistance seems insignificant when compared with the economic boycott declared by Washington, and the intricate and intensive covert operation carried out by the CIA in Chile.[74]

NOTES

1. Furthermore, Panama's ruler, General Torrijos, is considered: 'Despite his fiery anti-American rhetoric and his flirt with the left, he has long been seen by the USA as the only person capable of accepting a new treaty containing Panamanian concessions and remaining in power long enough afterwards to lend legitimacy to the agreement' (*Financial Times,* London, 9 October 1975). Washington has extended more economic aid since his takeover than in the sixty-five years since independence. This view is shared by the extreme left which argues that Torrijos is 'a favorite of the Pentagon', a drugs trafficker. (Statement by the *Comando de Liberacion de Panama,* published in *El Mundo,* Caracas, 24 September 1975.)

2. This proposition is developed by 'Espartaco'; 'The "Latin American Crisis" and Its External Framework', in Carlos A. Astiz, op. cit., p. 40.

3. Modesto Seara Vazquez, *La Politica Exterior de Mexico* (ed. Esfringe, Mexico City, 1969), p. 105.

4. 'Finnish neutrality is unmistakably neutrality against the enemies of the Soviet Union.' David Vital, *The Survival of Small States* (Oxford University Press, New York, 1971), p. 111.

5. David Vital, ibid., p. 129. He also formulates a third criterion. 'The still more careful and judicious exploitation of all available contingent attributes, political as well as strategic, in an effort to lever the greatest possible auxiliary counterpressures from outside the immediate small/great power conflict system.' This recommendation is much more difficult to evaluate than the remaining propositions, and was therefore deleted from the list suggested for corroboration of the six case studies.

6. David Vital, op. cit.

7. Ibid.

8. Smith considers correctly that 'The Soviets have sensed new opportunities as the entire political spectrum in Latin America shifts to the left. Essentially, *this radicalization process is a function of Latin America's search for political identity and economic well being, not of communist (and certainly not of Soviet) machinations or presence.'* Wayne S. Smith, 'Soviet Policy and Ideological Formulations for Latin America', in *Orbis* (Winter 1971), pp. 1123, 1124. Author's italics.

9. Adam B. Ulam, *The History of Soviet Foreign Policy* (Praeger, 1968), p. 463.

10. Thomas T. Hammond, 'Foreign Relations Since 1945', in Robert F. Byrned, (ed.), *Yugoslavia* (Atlantic Books, Praeger, New York, 1957), p. 23.

11. A valuable source of documentation on the Soviet-Yugoslavia conflict can

be found in Buss and Marbuty, (eds.), *The Soviet-Yugoslav Controversy 1948-1958. A Documentary Record* (Prospect Books, New York, 1959).

12. Thomas T. Hammond, op. cit., p. 26.

13. The capitalist powers were not likely to support a communist regime, at least not without attaching certain conditions to their help; and, on the other hand, the Communist leaders of Yugoslavia in their 1948 frame of mind could not and would not ask for help from the side which they considered diametrically opposed to their social and political philosophy and whose assistance at this early stage of the conflict would have alienated from them a considerable body of supporters, whose allegiance to the principles of Marxism was almost as strong as their loyalty to Tito and his 'lieutenants'. Adam B. Ulam, *Titoism and the Cominform* (Harvard University Press, Cambridge, 1952), pp. 98-9.

14. 'Considering Yugoslavia's economic dependency on the Soviet Bloc, Communist economic punishments and rewards should have succeeded; they failed simply because Yugoslavia turned to the West and found alternative supply and market sources.' K.J. Holsti, *International Politics — A Framework for Analysis* (Prentice-Hall, New Jersey, 1972), p. 247.

15. In the document it is stressed: ' . . . compliance with the principle of mutual respect for, and non-interference in, internal affairs for any reason whatsoever, whether of an economic, political or ideological nature, because questions of internal organization, or difference in social systems and of different forms of Socialist development are solely the concern of the individual countries. 'Z. Brezezinski, *The Soviet Bloc: Unity and Conflict* (Harvard University Press, Cambridge, Mass., 1967), p. 57.

16. 'The methods of the edification of socialism, reflecting the experience and specification of the development of the different countries are the affair of the people and of the working classes of that country and do not have to oppose the one to the others.' *Bulletin d'Information,* editions 'Paix et Socialisme', no. 20 (204) (Prague, 1971), IX annee, 'Declaration-Soviete-Yugoslave' *(Pravda,* 26 September 1971), p. 10.

17. Adam Ulam, *Titoism and the Cominform,* p. 221.

18. Information Services, *Actitud de Yugoslavia frente a los Problemas Internacionales* (Ediciones Jugoslavija, Belgrade, 1961), p. 39.

19. Dean Rusk, 'Why we treat Different Communist Countries differently', *Department of State Bulletin,* vol. L., no. 1920 (March 1964), p. 395.

20. Text of a letter sent by Juan Marinello, President, and Blas Roca, Secretary General of PSP in 1944. Document reprinted in Aguilar, Luis (ed.), *Marxism in Latin America* (A Knopf, New York, 1968), p. 153. Although this document refers to Batista's first presidential period, the communists after the *coup d'etat* in 1952, while not supporting the dictator, also did not seek co-operation with the guerilla movement. There are many examples of a hostile communist attitude, such as the denunciation by 'Marquitos' Rodriguez of the three participants in Batista's attempted assassination on 13 March 1957, with the purpose of detaching the student revolutionary movement from 'anti-communist elements'. This, as well as other stories, appears in K.S. Karol, *Les Guerilleros au Pouvoir* (Robert Laffont, Paris, 1970).

21. Test of a message of the PSP to the Chilean Communist Party a month before Batista was ousted. Aguilar, op. cit., p. 43.

22. Silva Luis Santiesteban, *Review of International Affairs,* no. 491 (Belgrade 1970), p. 44.

23. Albert Samuel, *Castrisme, Communisme, Democratie Cretienne en Amerique Latine* (Chronique Sociale de France, Paris, 1965), p. 73. This

observation is followed by more convincing quotations of Castro's neutrality. 'Between the two political and economic ideologies, actually debated in the world, we have our own position . . . neither bread without liberty, nor liberty without bread. Neither dictatorship by one man nor dictatorship of a class, neither a dictatorship of a group or a cast . . . Liberty with bread and without terror. This is humanism . . . Our Revolution is an autonomous Cuban revolution.' op. cit., p. 79.

24. H.S. Dinerstein, 'Soviet Policy in Latin America' in *American Political Science Review,* I (March, 1967), p. 84.

25. *Granma International,* 'Speech of Carlos R. Rodriguez at the Communist Parties'. *La Habana,* weekly edition, 27 April 1969.

26. *El Mercurio,* international edition, 3-5 November 1970, p. 4.

27. As a result of this economic dependence, the Soviet Union is in a position of exerting pressure on Cuba. In March 1968 (it is asserted), Moscow delayed its signature on a new economic agreement with Cuba. (News published in *Granma,* Cuba, 23 March 1968, reproduced in Stephen Clissold, (ed.), *Soviet Relations with Latin America – A Documentary Survey* (Oxford University Press, London, 1970), p. 304.) According to another version based on the testimony of a deserter from the Cuban Secret Service, the Soviet Union promised to increase its technical aid, in both raw materials and agricultural machinery, to Cuba, in return for the cessation of Cuba's criticism of pro-Soviet Communist parties in Latin America. *Christian Science Monitor,* 'Castro Hidalgo's Testimony', 16 July 1969.

28. The term 'Fifth International' is suggested by John Gerassi who specifies his geographic and ideological limitations in the documents gathered in his work *Towards Revolution,* vols. I and II (Weidenfeld and Nicolson, London, 1971).

29. See R. Hilsman, 'The Missile Gap', in R. Hilsman, *To Move a Nation* (Garden City, 1967), and A. Horelick, 'The Soviet Gamble' in A. Horelick, 'The Cuban Missile Crisis', *World Politics* (April 1964), pp. 363-77.

30. Stanley Hoffman, 'The International System Toady', in Sondermann, Olson, and McLelland, *The Theory and Practice of International Relations* 3rd edition (Prentice Hall, New Jersey, 1970), p. 64.

31. *Le Monde,* 15 January 1975.

32. See 'Cuban Official's Effort to Visit U.S. Blocked', in *Washington Post,* 26 July 1975.

33. Declarations of Prime Minister Castro to Mexican journalists, *La Opinion,* 12 January 1975.

34. Op. cit., 18 January 1972. The French private banks were requested to participate and invest in an ambitious 15,000 million dollar scheme.

35. For a more comprehensive analysis see Kenneth Jowitt, *Revolutionary Break-throughs and National Revolutions: The case of Rumania* (University of California Press, Berkeley, 1971).

36. In the Romanian Constitution, approved by the Parliament on 24 September 1952, there is a declaration stressing that 'friendship and alliance with the great Soviet Union, its support, and its disinterested and fraternal aid, assure the independence, sovereignty, development, and progress of the Romanian People's Republic'. *Keesings Contemporary Archives,* 1952-54, p. 12703.

37. F.Stephen Larrabee, 'The Rumanian Challenge to Soviet Hegemony', *ORBIS, vol.* XVIII, no. 1 (Spring 1973), p. 227.

38. On 26 June 1956 the declaration announcing Tito's visit points out that Romania agrees that 'the policy of active peaceful co-existence between

all States, irrespective of their social and political systems, is the only way
to strengthen and develop international cooperation'. *Keesings Contemporary Archives,* op. cit., 14954 D.

39. Declaration announcing Tito's visit. Ibid., 1955-56, 15283 C.
40. Kenneth Jowitt, op. cit., p. 176. Romania's commitment to industrialisation appeared to be a 'routine' conflict with Moscow. Many other principles were still automatically followed, and on the specific issue at stake, Bucharest could defend herself by overstating positive Russian references to industrialisation.
41. Richard V. Burks, 'Perspectives for Eastern Europe' in *Problems of Communism* no. 2 (March-April 1964), pp. 73-81.
42. David Floyd, *Rumania-Russia's Dissident Ally* (Pall Mall Press, London, 1965).
43. Ion George Maurer, Rumanian Minister for Foreign Affairs, in *Le Monde,* 'Une Politique etrangere au service de la paix', 19-20 November 1972.
44. Ibid.
45. Stuart S. Smith, 'Russia, China and the Balkans', in *Midstream* vol. XVII, no. 10 (December 1971), p. 10.
46. The second stage for Jowitt covers the period of 1962-5 while Larrabee refers to 1961-64.
47. For a description of the reforms carried out by the military regime see Juan Aguilar Derpich, *Peru: Socialism or Militarism* (Fuentes ed., Caracas, 1972).
48. Without taking into consideration the more powerful Confederation of Workers of Peru, of Aprist direction (populist). Hugo M. Sacchi, (ed.) *Chile, Peru, Bolivia – documentos de tres procesos latinamericanos* (Centro Editor de America Latina, Buenos Aires, 1972), p. 70.
49. 'Our revolution, to be consequent with its unrenounceable political option of non-capitalist character as well as non-communist must build up the future economic development of Peru through the enterprisal forms that will translate the facts into that fundamental option.' Ibid., p. 71.
50. *Clarin,* Buenos Aires, 17 June 1974.
51. Daniel A. Sharp (ed.), *Estados Unidos y La Revolucion Peruana* (Sudamericana, Buenos Aires, 1972), pp. 72-96.
52. Ministry for Foreign Affairs, *El Peru y su Politica Exterior,* Lima, Peru, 1971. Speech delivered by the Chancellor General E.P. Edgardo Mercado Jarrin in the Ceremony of the Establishment of Diplomatic Relations with the USSR, 1 February 1969, pp. 33-4.
53. At the Conference of the Rights of the Sea in Caracas, the President characterised the superpowers as 'two countries opposed ideologically but united by economic interests . . . to claim to be the owners of the waters that belong to the poor countries'. *La Opinion,* 28 June 1974.
54. Ibid.
55. *Latin American Newsletter* vol. IX, no. 14 (London, 7 November 1975).
56. P. Lendvai, *Eagles in Cobwebs – Nationalism and Communism in the Balkans* (Macdonald, London, 1969), p. 182.
57. Stavro Skendi, (ed.), *Albania* (Atlantic Press, London, 1975), p. 25.
58. B.S. Morris, op. cit., p. 58.
59. Ibiã.
60. *Keesings Contemporary Archives,* 1961-1962, p. 18477.
61. 'From Enver Hoxha's point of view, Comrad Khrushchev was setting the wrong example by deviating from the path of Stalin.' T. Zavalani, 'The Importance of Being Albania', in *Problems of Communism,* vol. 10, no. 4 (1961), p. 3.

62. P. Landuai, op. cit., pp. 204-5.

63. See analysis of both aspects in William E. Griffith, *Albania and the Sino-Soviet conflict* (MIT Press, Cambridge, Mass., 1963).

64. 'There are, however, no indications of any Albanian overtures for a *rapprochement* with Washington, and in view of Communist China's implacable hostility, at least in the foreseeable future.' W.E. Griffith, 'Albania – an Outcast's Defiance', in *Problems of Communism,* vol. XI, no. 3, 5-6 (1962), p. 5. The recent *rapprochement* between China and America has not yet found expression in a similar change in regard to Albania, although the beginning of limited Western tourism enables us perhaps, to forecast a similar development with Albania.

65. Marcel Niedergang, *Les vingt Amériques latines,* vol. II, (Editions du Seuil, Paris, 1969), p. 29. Another source considers that, 'A few parties rooted more deeply in society – the Chilean for example, 25,000 to 30,000 strong, represented in the national legislature, regarded as a legitimate party, not merely as an alien offshoot of Moscow – could conceivably go their own way; yet they maintain their Soviet line.' B.S. Morris, *International Communism and American Policy,* (Altherton Press, New York, 1968), p. 91.

66. The *Guardian,* London, 27 September 1973.

67. 'The limits of Soviet sympathy for the young regime in Chile are however rather clear, and a difference is drawn in Moscow between Cuba, where the revolution has already succeeded, and Chile, where the revolutionary process is now in its course but not yet considered as being achieved.' *Le Monde,* Paris, 7 December 1971.

68. *Keesings Contemporary Archives,* October 9-16, 1971, p. 24873.

69. Ibid.

70. Commentary by Yuri Zukhov, mentioned in *La Opinion,* 6 October 1973.

71. Speech of Foreign Minister Almeyda, mentioned in *La Opinion,* Buenos Aires, 4 April 1972.

72. See Armando Uribe, *Le livre noir de l'intervention americaine au Chili* (Cobats, Seuil, Paris, 1974).

73. *U.S. Chilean Relations.* Hearings before the Subcommittee of Inter-American Affairs of the Committee on Foreign Affairs. House of Representatives. Ninety-third Congress, 6 March 1973; and *Multinational Corporations and United States Foreign Policy.* Hearings before the Subcommittee on Foreign Relations. United States Senate. Ninety-third Congress, 1973.

74. See the discussion of the motivation for American intervention in the excellent article by Richard R. Fagen, 'The United States and Chile: Roots and Branches', *Foreign Affairs,* vol. 53 no. 2, 1975. The failure of the Popular Front in Chile does not imply automatically that the same strategy cannot be carried out in other European countries, but simply underlines the limitations facing a country in the sphere of direct influence of a superpower.

PART 2

5 THE OPTIONS FACING THE SUPERPOWERS

1 Theoretical Options

Taking as a basic premise the theory that the policy of the superpowers is aimed at the maximisation of power, we can understand that this concept is also applied, with varying degrees of intensity, to both their own and their rival's spheres of direct influence. It is difficult to differentiate between the various options available to the superpowers as policy alternatives are ranged along a continuum, rather than presenting themselves as clear alternatives. Of importance in regard to the decisions adopted, is the position of the observer in relation to the time sequence curve — an event such as military intervention is viewed differently a week before, or a week after its actually taking place. Nevertheless, it could prove beneficial to identify recurrent patterns of superpower behaviour. The choice between possible theoretical alternatives — presented as parallels for both superpowers — does not imply that both are simultaneously following the same option; only empirical findings can elucidate their real policy. The intensity and constancy with which the option is followed should also be taken into consideration. What is sometimes regarded as a moderate attitude can be explained by the low ranking of the sphere of direct influence in the superpowers' priorities. Furthermore, it is sometimes confusing that in spite of a general policy formulated by the superpowers in regard to the spheres of influence, an alternative line may be adopted towards one or a few countries of the area depending on the type of regime existing in the 'satellite' country, the regularity of an independent line being taken *vis-à-vis* the superpower, etc.

    I. The first pair of alternatives refers to the options available to the superpowers in the rival's adjacent sphere of influence; namely the Soviet Union in Latin America and the United States in Eastern Europe.[1] The three following options are considered:

(a) The ability of superpower Y to obtain a decisive influence in the subsystem controlled by superpower X through subversive activities, i.e. encouraging the overthrow of the existing regimes. Faced with a situation in which there is nothing to lose, and lacking the opportunity for and viability of direct military action, all other means become serious options for changing the reality (one that is condemned on ideological grounds by the official ideology of superpower Y). The disadvantage of opting for this alternative action is that the possibilities for success are restricted from a strategic point of view, and at the same time, it can result in a similar action being undertaken by the adversary superpower X in Y's sphere of influence. Finally, the general repercussions could be to the detriment of the existing bipolar relations within the international system.

(b) All efforts are oriented to improving the bilateral relations between Y and the governments in the sphere of direct influence of X while weakening Xs control over its adjacent subsystem. The policy means used are not primarily political, but rather economic, cultural, technical co-operation instruments based on the assumption that a constant and persevering drive will enable the satellite country to achieve greater autonomy from its contiguous superpower. The difficulty involved in embarking on such a policy is that the superpower X has sufficient power and capability to intervene and stop such an emancipatory process — it can result in the imposition on the satellite of direct control, and the replacement of the governing elite by a more loyal and obedient one. Furthermore, there is no guarantee that extensive aid from superpower Y will lead to a deviationist policy by the satellite country, and to a change from its traditional policy of obedience to the neighbouring superpower.

(c) Y attempts to reach an understanding or tacit agreement with X, by which a greater freedom of action is permitted to Y in Xs sphere of influence in exchange for concessions by Y to X in other strategic, political, or economic fields, or for the granting of a similar freedom in Ys sphere of influence, or a change in the existing *status quo* in another part of the world in Xs favour. The prevailing climate of bipolar relations in the international system may provide a foundation for an understanding based on mutual acknowledgement of the need to grant slightly more liberalisation within the spheres of influence; as a symbolic gesture to relax global tension. At the same time it could be convenient for the superpower X to permit rival Y to participate in the economic development of the satellites; this aid, of course, being restricted so as not to undermine Xs primacy in his sphere of influence

II. The second pair of alternatives cover the options available to the superpowers in their own spheres of influence, that is to say, the Soviet

Union in Eastern Europe and the United States in Latin America. We
can consider a spectrum existing from great/small freedom of action for
the countries situated in the spheres of influence; what was called in a
previous chapter 'margins of political security'. The continuity of the
spectrum can also be divided into three broad options:

(a) Increasing the margins of political security to the quasi-total limit-
    ation of freedom of action for the states in the spheres of direct
    influence: with means ranging from the control of the states' inter-
    nal affairs; the reversing of decisions and the overthrow of leaders;
    and if necessary, direct military intervention. The major disadvantage
    of the use of this option is that when military force is constantly
    used, instead of being a potential threat, it loses its potency and can
    result in active rebellion or in a passive boycott by the local popu-
    lation, and an increase in nationalistic feelings. The development of
    such a situation might lead to a need to use the coercive methods
    which jeopardise the image of the superpower in the world. But
    failure to apply such a policy may also result in a loss of prestige for
    the superpower. The growth of nationalism in a certain country in
    the sphere of influence may force upon the superpower the need for
    direct or covert intervention in order to prevent this phenomen from
    spreading to other countries of the subsystem.
(b) The maintenance of an intermediate situation in which the margins
    of political security are not forced to any of the extremes. Generally,
    this would be a position in defence of the *status quo,* provided there
    is no considerable threat from the rival superpower or from internal
    forces in the subsystem. Such a policy can often be attributed to a
    lack of consensus amongst the decision-makers of the controlling
    superpower or to a lower degree of interest in the sphere of influ-
    ence; in such a case, the leaders of the 'satellite' states may attempt
    to exploit the situation to adopt a more autonomous position in
    relation to the dominating superpower.
(c) Reducing the margins of political security to a minimum, and ac-
    quiring, likewise, a flexible approach, may enable the superpower to
    include in its sphere of influence all, or nearly all, of the proximate
    countries. States considered peripheral or semi-peripheral can there-
    fore return to the subsystem and gradually accept traditional rules
    of behaviour, but on the other hand the risk is entailed that other
    subservient regimes will be encouraged to follow a more independent
    line, assuming that no threat of intervention by the superpowers is
    present. The superpower exercising this option may take into con-

sideration the fact that in the long run, control of the sphere of influence is preferably based on the formation of a large and positive consensus from the peoples involved; that there is mutual benefit for both the small and the major members of the subsystem from such developments. The dilemma for the superpower is how to reach a maximal level of voluntarism within the subsystem without losing the ultimate power of intervention in any case where this relaxation is exploited by hostile internal or external elements. A further danger of liberalisation is that once begun it is a process that may surpass the dependency limits fixed by the superpower as ultimate and necessary.

The decision on which option to adopt determines for the superpower, to a great extent, the image assigned to the leadership of the countries: 'Liberal' or 'Conservative', 'Hawk' or 'Dove', 'co-existential' or 'aggressive'. Labels are applied to different administrations which do not always fit the same policy-makers in internal affairs. Furthermore, there is not usually a situation in which all actors in the administration favour an identical option. Particularly, in no-crisis situations the divergence as far as preferences are concerned can be traced to both superpower's decision-makers. This fact, together with the fluctuations from one option to another in different chronoligical situations makes it even more difficult to single out stages with a clear-cut differentiation. Having registered these reservations, it now remains to proceed to an analysis of the two pairs of options available to the United States and the Soviet Union; firstly, the options existing within the rival power's sphere of influence, and then within their own.

2 The Soviet Union in Latin America

A brief historical perspective can help clarify the options open to the Soviet Union in Latin America.[2] Immediately after the Bolshevik Revolution, the principal objective was to assure the survival of Soviet Russia, encircled as it was by national and foreign insurgent troops. Sporadic attempts to pursue plans for a world revolution were abandoned after its failure in Europe and the dismantling of foreign communist agent networks in other continents. Outside its national frontiers, the Communists' main interest remained in Europe; at the beginning it restricted itself to encouraging what was at the time considered to be the imminent social revolution in countries such as Hungary and Germany. Later the Soviet Union concentrated her efforts on trying to break down the chains of economic and political isolation in

which they were bound by the West; the Rapallo Agreement with
Germany was the first breakthrough. The search for allies in Europe
was intensified with the rise of the Third Reich. Stalin feared the irredentist intentions of Hitler's Germany, and concentrated Soviet efforts
on military and political preparations for war; European coalitions,
alliances and treaties, including the Molotov-Ribbentrop Pact signed in
1939, failed to keep the USSR from becoming involved in the Second
World War.

With the end of the war, and with survival no longer the sole pre-
occupation of Soviet foreign policy, she tried to consolidate her position in different regions of the world. Her varying interests were co-
ordinated in the various areas according to a set of priorities and the
prevailing international conditions. The first priority of the Soviet
Union in the post-war period was to take advantage of the Allied victory and to encircle herself with a periphery of socialist regimes under
her direct control. By 1948 she had already satellitised and subdued
Bulgaria, Poland, Hungary, Romania, Czechoslovakia, East Germany,
Albania and Yugoslavia, with some areas, such as Austria and Berlin,
remaining points of friction and tension with the other main powers.
With the attainment of nearly total domination over this area, the
Soviet Union could turn more of her interest to areas where local developments were raising hopes for the establishment of Communist
regimes. Communist China's control of a greater part of the Asiatic
continent from 1949 became the basis for further expansion towards
the south. The importance of this for Russia's foreign policy is shown
by the struggles that took place in Korea, the Philippines and Indochina
in the late 1940s and in the 1950s. But it was not till after Stalin's
death that the two-camps theory was relinquished, a theory which
completely ignored potential new allies in the developing world. After
1955 the Soviet interest in the Middle East increased, taking advantage
of the vacuum of power left by Great Britain and of the deterioration
of Egyptian-North American relations. In order to penetrate the system
she became a source of military and economic aid, supporting the new
nationalistic and military elite of the Arab countries. Independent
Africa became in the early 1960s a new area of interest for the Soviets,
especially after the process of decolonisation, with the Kremlin exerting its influence on the more radical regimes and playing a role in the
civil wars of the Congo, Nigeria and Angola by siding openly with one
of the parties involved.

Many observers believe that Latin America ranks far behind all other
subsystems in Soviet foreign policy priorities. It is presumed that the

unexpected success of the Cuban Revolution and the subsequent deterioration of relations with the United States led the Soviet Union to venture into the Western hemisphere, a region in which she was not yet willing to expend any great efforts. The leadership in Moscow have traditionally been wary of involvement in Latin America; not only because they considered it the sphere of influence of the United States, but also because of a sort of fatalistic geo-political perception of the impossibility of establishing a socialist regime in a Latin American country, due to its vulnerability from US pressures and intervention.

The first option was rarely used by the Soviet Union in Latin America. Support for revolutionary activity can be related to the various positions of the Comintern and Soviet interests. During the Sixth Party Congress in 1928, the importance of revolutionary activity was stressed, only as a product of Stalin's internal power struggle against the 'rightist elements'; Communist activity in Latin America was applauded, appeals were made for rebellion and revolution in the different countries, appeals distinguishable from those of the other left-wing forces by their intransigent and militaristic attitude. Although in most cases the expression never passed beyond the vocal, in 1932 an Indian rebellion in El Salvador against the landowners was crushed, and within four days suffered thousands of casualties, among them urban Communist militants; in Brazil a national uprising of young military officers headed by Carlos Prestes (later to become the Communist Party Leader), was only finally controlled in 1935. From then on — with a short interruption during the duration of the Molotov-Ribbentrop Pact — the general policy line was the formation of the 'Popular Front' or 'Democratic Front', the search for unity with other political forces; and during World War II, with any anti-Nazi group, even from the right, under the framework of so-called 'National', 'Patriotic', or 'Anti-Nazi' Unity Fronts.

With the beginning of the cold war, Stalin did not see any benefit deriving from the establishment of relations with Latin American governments. In a superficial generalisation, he considered all 20 countries as 'a war instrument of the United States . . . acting in favor of the demands of the American aggressors'.[3] This policy was not accompanied by any encouragement of the use of violence by the Communists on the continent — they were trying to maintain the privileges obtained as a result of their legal activity during the period of the Second World War, a luxury considered as essential for a normal framework of activity. With the advancement of the period of peaceful coexistence, the Soviet Union became openly opposed to the use of subversive methods, a policy which could jeopardise its diplomatic efforts:

> The Soviet Union is accused of fictitious 'subversive activities' and
> blamed for the political demonstrations, strikes, peasant unrest,
> student riots, and *even armed struggle* [italics added to stress the
> extent of the efforts to dissociate the USSR from revolutionary
> activities]. The absurdity of such 'exposées' is self-evident . . .
> American propaganda hastened to accuse the Soviet Union of
> 'fomenting guerilla warfare.' Although such fabrications are obvious
> nonsense, they are repeated day in, day out by US propaganda, and
> this inevitably poisons the minds of certain elements of public
> opinon.[4]

While local Communists helped in trying to reform the equation
'USSR=Communist subversion', a new political force placed Moscow in
a delicate position in Latin America. All over the continent during the
decade of the sixties, the Castroists adhered to the path of armed
struggle, and demanded the assistance of the pro-Soviet Communist
parties. Castro himself involved his country in training, propaganda and
supplying economic and military assistance to the guerillas, putting the
Soviet Union into the position where it has had to manoeuvre to maintain a position which supports the friendly Cuban revolutionary regime,
and at the same time takes into account the need to avoid upsetting its
relations with the 'capitalist' regimes in the countries of the continent,
even advancing the establishment of diplomatic relations. A compromise was achieved at the Latin American Communist Parties Congress in Havana in 1964 through Soviet initiative. In the official
document issued by the Congress, it was stated that objective conditions favoured the path of armed struggle in Paraguay, Haiti, Honduras,
Guatemala and Colombia, with Venezuela mentioned separately. This
meant that guerilla activity was considered as legitimate in six countries
only, while for the rest of the continent the preferred way was one of
peaceful participation in the electoral process. In all six countries open
to guerilla activity, there were no diplomatic relations with the Soviet
Union, and/or the local Communist parties were outlawed.

The second alternative consists of a *rapprochement* by the Soviet
Union with the governments of Latin America, regardless of the poli-
tical colouring and orientations of the regimes; this has become the
guiding line since the beginning of the 'peaceful coexistence' period.
This was stated by Bulganin in 1956, when he said that the Soviet
Union desired to strengthen its economic, cultural and other ties with

the Latin American countries, and pledged Soviet support to the principle of non-interference in the internal affairs of other states.[5] By
following this policy the Soviet Union has been quite successful in expanding a diplomatic network, restricted in 1956 to three countries
(Argentina, Uruguay and Mexico), with the establishment at ambassadorial level of relations with twelve countries, by 1972 representing
nearly 90 per cent of the continent's population and land.

This alternative promotes the increase in commercial relations
shown in Table 16. Nevertheless, the trade figures of the Communist
countries (including Eastern Europe), with Latin America, by the beginning of the 1970s, did not exceed 5 per cent of the total foreign
trade of those Latin American countries (excluding Cuba).

Table 16: Soviet Union: Imports from the Developing Countries
by Major Source, 1960-1969

Source	Value of imports, f.o.b. (millions of roubles)			Percentage share		
	1960	1965	1969	1960	1965	1969
Developing countries, total	569.8	1,025.1	1,173.7	100.0	100.0	100.0
Africa	177.8	223.5	357.2	31.2	21.8	30.4
United Arab Republic	109.2	147.1	205.3	19.2	14.3	17.5
Asia	259.9	349.9	496.6	45.6	38.5	42.3
Iran	17.1	16.3	50.8	3.0	1.6	4.3
India	61.6	169.4	199.3	10.8	16.5	17.0
Malaysia	100.4	101.4	109.6	17.6	9.9	9.3
Latin America	125.5	405.0	302.4	22.0	39.5	25.8
Cuba	93.4	308.0	208.5	16.4	30.0	17.8

Source: Vneshnaya Torgovyla, SSSR 1959-1963, 1968, 1969 (Moscow).
Quoted in Raymond W. Duncan, (ed.), *Soviet Policy in Developing
Countries* (Ginn-Blaisdell, Waltham, Massachusetts, 1970).

Within the commercial framework, Brazil is of particular importance,
not only because of its share of the total Latin American trade with the
Soviet Union (50 per cent of the total, excluding Cuba), but also
because of the facilities and terms granted by the USSR, in spite of the
right-wing orientation of the military regime; it was stipulated that at
least 25 per cent of the Brazilian exports to the Soviet Union would be
industrial or semi-industrial products. In the period January-September
1972, Brazilian exports to all of Eastern Europe reached $173 million,
representing an 88 per cent increase compared with the same period for
the preceding year.[6]

Moscow is mainly interested in selling machinery, tools and raw materials for heavy industry in Latin America, in this way making the basic industries of those states dependent in the long term for supplies of spare parts and equipment. Buses, agricultural equipment, tools, television sets, etc. are sold on a 20 to 30-year credit basis at an annual 4 per cent interest rate, making the Russian offer very attractive.

Changes of regime do not usually affect the continuity of the Soviet policy or connection. According to Dinerstein, 'the Soviet Union, for one, is quite willing to be used in this way, and the political color of the regime with which it is so dealing makes little difference. Thus, the Soviets were prepared to go along with Goulart, and are now willing to arrange trade agreements with his successor, Castello Branco.'[7]

The Soviet Union has begun to prize connections with certain interest groups, previously considered to form a part of the 'oligarchy' and 'reactionaries', e.g. the Church and the military. Mentioning the example of the army regime in Peru, a Soviet commentator stated that 'without overestimating the role of the military in the anti-imperialist process in Latin America, the continent's revolutionary forces neverthe-less believe that the increasingly radical mood of the military is of ob-jective help in furthering these processes'.[8] However, when taking into account the amount of economic aid dispensed by the Soviet Union in other regions, and to other developing countries, the Russian effort in Latin America can be considered of a low level and of low intensity. Table 17 provides a general picture; one should bear in mind, though, that of the figures for Latin America, nearly all the aid granted is for Cuba.

Cultural relations and propaganda received a strong impetus in the 1960s. The great scientific achievements and progress in fields like education have created, generally, an image of a powerful Soviet Union able to contribute to the progress of the Latin American nations. Along-side the direct contacts between the governments, the Soviet Union has succeeded in forming groups of intellectuals, artists, labour leaders and students, and placing them in front organisations dealing with a precise field or sector of the public. Among them we have the World Peace Council, the International Union of Students, the Women's World Union, Democratic Lawyers, Teachers, Trade Unions, Human Right Leagues, Peasant Leagues, Youth Federations, Committees for the Defence of Natural Resources, etc. While many of them are indepen-dent and not even left wing, the control remains in the hands of the more involved Communist members. Their function is important, not only in legitimating the Soviet Union in the struggle against 'imperialism,

colonialism and neo-colonialism', but also in combating the deviationist
accusations from elements instigated by Communist China. There are
also societies of bilateral friendship between Latin America and Communist countries, e.g. the Soviet-Argentinian Institute for Cultural
Relations, the Hungarian Cultural Centre in Uruguay, etc. Their role is
not directly political, but aims at the promotion of bilateral relations in
all fields and in publicising the achievements of the Soviet Union in
that country. They can play an important role in maintaining contacts
with opposition elements in countries where the Embassy is restricted
in its relations with the government, and in countries where there is no
permanent Soviet diplomatic representation; such associations may
work as a pressure group for the formalisation of bilateral relations. In
countries where Soviet ideological and cultural publications in the
Spanish language are not banned, they are distributed in great numbers
at nominal prices; Soviet broadcasts in Spanish increased from 15–17
hours weekly in 1948 to 30–31 in 1953 (with the participation of
Czechoslovakia and Hungary), and by 1967 it exceeded 250 hours
weekly. Latin American students receive scholarships to study in the
Soviet Union, special visitors and delegates are invited to conferences
and mass gatherings (several thousand a year), and where diplomatic
relations exist so does tourism.

Table 17: Soviet Economic Aid Extended to Less Developed
          Countries by Area 1955-67
                (In million U.S. dollars)

	Total	Africa	Asia	Latin America	Middle East
Total	5,989	858	2,802	185	2,144
Year					
1955	126	0	126	0	0
1956	243	0	223	0	20
1957	260	0	147	0	113
1958	345	0	37	30	278
1959	855	137	577	0	141
1960	594	69	255	0	270
1961	547	193	354	0	0
1962	53	24	27	0	2
1963	236	100	53	0	83
1964	998	206	262	0	530
1965	419	43	76	15	285
1966	1,244	77	660	85	422
1967	69	9	5	55	—

Source: Raymond W. Duncan (ed.), op. cit., p. 5.[9]

Finally, at the internal political level, the general line followed is the formation of 'Popular Fronts', with the Communists playing an important role, but not publicly appearing as the central force. The outstanding example was the 'Popular Unity' in Chile, which existed in one form or another from the late thirties, and under the leadership of Salvador Allende from 1958. His election as President, in the 1970 elections, served as a strong incentive for the formation of similar fronts in other countries where an electoral system functions. The *Frente Amplio* (Wide Front), in Uruguay, received 19 per cent of the popular vote in the 1972 election, an increase on previous elctions, but disappointing considering the high expectations of the left wing. In Argentina the *Encuentro Nacional de los Argentinos* (ENA – National Reunion of Argentinians), tried to capitalise on Peronist feeling, but was dissolved before the 1973 elections: the 'Popular Revolutionary Alliance' (Communist-dissident Christians, socialists and radicals), received a mere 8 per cent against the Peronist majority candidate. In Venezuela, the *Neuva Fuerza* Front suffered a serious loss when the third national party – the *Union Republicana Democratica* (URD – Democratic Republican Union – left its ranks, and received only 5 per cent of the vote during the 1973 elections. It should nevertheless be emphasised that it is only under 'democratic' conditions that the Communists have any chance of receiving some form of popular support – hence their consistent electoralist character.

The third option is the acceptance by the Soviet Union of the limits delineated by the United States on its activity in Latin America, but with the hope that as a result of common agreement, Moscow's role would be enlarged. Since the missile crisis, Moscow has repeatedly transmitted clear signs to the United States that she does not seek military-strategic advantages in that region and wishes to avoid provoking nuclear escalation; both in the vulnerable Caribbean area and in the continent in general. The denials of subversive activities are intended to reassure the United States that the establishment of a Soviet embassy in a Latin American country will not be followed by clandestine insurrectional activity inspired by the USSR.

Washington may eventually be interested in sharing the economic burden of providing aid assistance for the development of Latin America with the Soviet Union, especially in some of the more expensive projects in those countries in which there is no fear of change in the political orientation of the pro-American regime (Brazil, Colombia, Uruguay). At the same time the Soviet Union would be willing to permit the United States to relieve her of the heavy costs of financing

the Cuban economy and régime.[10] This development towards greater
co-operation is reflected in a change in Soviet tactics *vis-á-vis* the
Organisation of American States; while still considering it as a tool of
North America, more and more importance is now attached to internal
developments in the organisation.[11] The Kremlin supports the campaign for the reintegration of Cuba into the OAS, even though Cuba
still maintains (officially) a hostile line towards the inter-American
organisation. More importantly, the Soviet Union has come to consider
the possiblity of joining the OAS in the capacity of a permanent observer, offering on behalf of herself and the other Eastern European
countries, aid or technical assistance for projects.[12]

The selection of one or another of the alternatives is a dynamic
process. They are not necessarily self-excluding, but some limitations
exist on the simultaneous use of differing options. The support of
guerilla activity in some Latin American countries failed to satisfy
either the extremist viewpoint represented by Fidel Castro or the
demands of the other Latin American governments. Castro understood
that the selection of only six countries for revolutionary action considerably restricted the possibility of the spread of armed insurrection
to other countries (in Haiti, for instance, no guerilla groups whatsoever
operated). In Paraguay, the former Communist Party leader, O. Credyt,
was expelled from the Party because of its co-operation in an unsuccessful attempt to start guerilla activity in a neighbouring territory. In
Venezuela and Guatemala, in 1966 and 1968 respectively, the leaders
of the majority faction of the Communist Party decided to abandon the
use of violence and military means and opted for an electoral strategy,
working within the system; the guerillas condemned their abandonment of the armed struggle. In Colombia, the extermination of the pro-
Communist guerilla groups operating in the Marquetalia area led to a
re-evaluation of the role of the Communist Party and the means to be
used, resulting in its participation in the 1974 elections and the use of
legitimate methods.

However, the Latin American governments were not willing to maintain normal relations with the Soviet Union if in neighbouring countries
where the Communist Parties were banned and diplomatic relations
with the USSR did not exist, Moscow supported those elements attempting to overthrow the regime. They realised that keeping silent
today, on such a question, could entail dangers tomorrow for their own
regimes; guerilla movements could grow and spread to their own country. In 1966 four Soviet diplomats were declared *persona non grata* in
Montevideo. It was charged that at the 'Tricontinental Conference' that

had just taken place in Havana, the speech by the head of the Soviet delegation was considered, by the Uruguayan government, as an appeal for subversion on the continent.[13] In order not to damage further its incipient relations with Latin American countries, the Soviet Union insisted that Rachidov, the Head of the delegation at the Conference stressed that he was speaking in a personal capacity,[14] and was not an official representative of the USSR government, but simply a representative of a 'Soviet social organisation' (the Trade Unions). The gradual abandonment of those guerilla movements supported by the pro-Soviet Communist Parties provoked an irreparable rupture with Cuba in 1967; however the general failure of guerilla movements on the continent, and Soviet economic pressure, forced Cuba from 1968 to re-appraise its political line in Latin America and adopt a more moderate line of co-operation with various regimes. The pro-Soviet Communist Parties advocated that it was up to the political forces in each country to decide which way to follow, the decision being based on the prevailing objective conditions;[15] this provides a freedom of action for the various movements, resulting in the majority of cases in the adoption of an electoral strategy. The fall of the Allende regime and the fore-closure of the electoral strategy in most countries, either by military *coups* (Uruguay) or by the victory of the right-wing or centre parties, has placed the use of electoral means in considerable doubt. This does not imply that armed struggle is a more useful strategy, but the feeling of frustration resulting from the failure of legitimate means has brought into doubt the possibility of the establishment of left-wing regimes.

Over the last twenty years, the Soviet Union has generally followed the second alternative, and rejected, orally and in practice, the first option (insurrection and subversive activities).[16] While following the second line, she included certain aspects from the third one, namely the attempt to prise from the United States acceptance of USSR activities in Latin America in exchange for the renunciation of all attempts to use subversion, or challenge the military-strategic supremacy of Washington on the Continent. Concessions to the United States in other parts of the world are not necessarily tied to Soviet activity in Latin America, but the compliance of the US can help create a more relaxed atmosphere of *detente* with repercussions in other continents.

Finally, it is necessary to judge the level of intensity of Soviet activity in Latin America. Smith considers Soviet efforts rather insignificant and categorically states that,

The primary Soviet objective is not to 'communize' Latin America but to undercut US influence in the area . . . Moscow's efforts to achieve this goal are essentially cautious and opportunistic. The Soviets prudently seek to take advantage of unrest and growing anti-Americanism, but they do not create these conditions. They have little capacity to do so . . . Soviet efforts are not likely to play a significant role in determining the outcome of events in Latin America. The Soviet presence may at times become a complicating factor in US-Latin American relations and occasionally even an irritant in US-Soviet relations, but in both cases it is apt to remain something of a side issue. The central equation in the hemisphere is and will be US-Latin America.[17]

A twenty-year perspective so far corroborates Smith's observation. Moscow has been following the second option rather passively, maintaining relations with different types of governments.[18] Only in the case of Cuba has this alternative been complemented with great means and careful planning. The present failure of the 'popular front' policy should perhaps indicate that pursuit of the second option is not an open way for the communists to reach power, but there is no indication that they are turning back to the first subversive option. On the contrary, if anything, the move is towards a wider understanding with the United States, the recent keeping of a 'low profile' by the Soviets corresponding to a similar policy from the other side. Such a policy leaves the Latin Americans, indeed, in a precarious situation. 'Despised by the Soviet Union and taken for granted by the US, their room for diplomatic maneuver was extremely narrow.'[19]

3 The United States in Eastern Europe

Eastern Europe has not been a region in which the United States had traditional interests: in Europe generally, according to Hans Morgenthau, the North American interests are confined to three minimalistic aims: the US should avoid involvement in European conflicts; keep European powers out of the Western Hemisphere; and help maintain the balance of power in Europe.[20] American involvement in the First World War was motivated to a great extent by the desire to maintain this balance, but as a result of intervention, the United States was propelled into European affairs, and was forced into becoming a partner in deciding the future of independent countries of Central and Eastern Europe. One of the consequences of the war was the creation of twelve new states, among them Czechoslovakia and Yugoslavia. Woodrow Wilson's fourteen points delineated Poland's new boundaries, provided a strong impetus to nationalism, and stressed the rights of minorities, especially in Eastern Europe. This involvement impressed upon the United States a greater awareness of European problems, but America's later decision not to participate in the League of Nations, and its subsequent return to isolationism, can be interpreted as a tacit acquiescence in the new developments within Europe, including the sacrifice of Czechoslovakia to the Nazis in 1938. With the end of the Second World War, the United States once again found itself the decisive factor in the destiny of Europe.

The US has been accused of failing in this task, as it permitted the Soviet Union to transform Eastern Europe into a satellite region at the Yalta Conference in 1945. In exchange for Soviet support for the United Nations, a promise to join the Far East War, non-intervention in Greece and an ambiguous undertaking from Stalin about the future character of 'democracy' in Eastern Europe, those countries were left to Soviet mercy. Already at Teheran, Poland has been recognised as being part of the Soviet orbit, and with the use of the Red Army and the local Communist Parties, this whole region was transformed by the Russians into an extension of the Soviet system. 'Later the Yalta agreement was to be compared with the Munich surrender, and it is true that Roosevelt deliberately conceded domination of eastern and central Europe to Stalin, as Chamberlain had conceded it to Hitler.'[21] However, there are those who say that the US had little choice but to recognise the reality of the situation, that in the post-war period, Eastern Europe and much of Central Europe would in any case be under Soviet military occupation, and as such, also under political control, there were no means, short of war, of stopping Soviet domination of this region.[22]

Following the War, the precarious situation of Western Europe and the growing hostility of the USSR led Washington to adopt a policy of protecting or taking responsibility for the economic reconstruction of Europe during the first years of the cold war. US policy became one of 'containment' of the Communist advance to the West, implying the acceptance of the situation in Eastern European 'Peoples' Democracies', but restricting it to its existing borders by a security belt curbing the expansion of international Communism — which was considered as a genuine threat to America's interests. The liberation of the 'captive nations' of Eastern Europe became a remote goal without any hope of short-term implementation.

The absence of a definite policy for recovering the lost territories in Eastern Europe, and the lack of interest in such a project provoked strong criticism of 'the thoughtless and inconsistent passivity toward the future development of Central and Eastern Europe'.[23] There was a feeling that the problem was not one of a *mistaken* policy, but rather that the United States lacked a policy altogether. Campbell considers that in the period of 'peaceful coexistence' there were three alternatives for North American policy in Eastern Europe, in accordance with the general outline proposed:

> The first alternative would be to regard the Eastern bloc and the Soviet Union as an integral unit and to intensify the Cold War, attempting to capitalize on the internal troubles and upheavals within the different countries. The aim would be to overthrow the satellite regimes.
>
> The second alternative would be recognizing the dependent relationship of Eastern European countries on the U.S.S.R., hoping that other Eastern European countries would follow the example of Yugoslavia.
>
> This alternative takes as real the possibilities of a determined change in the nature of the regime in the direction of liberalism (with the discreet assistance of the U.S.A.) and following the aspirations of the population.

The third line of policy — to quote Campbell — 'is directed to the USA as well as Eastern Europe, in fact, primarily to the USSR. It would not make a point of trying to split the satellites off from the Soviet bloc, on the ground that this would make the essential policy of *detente* with Moscow more difficult and probably impossible anyway. It is based on the assumption that things are changing in the Soviet Union as well as in the satellites.'[24] The first alternative has not been exploited by the United States. In spite of the fact that while the Soviet Union conducted repressive measures against nationalistic revolts in Eastern Europe, and at the same time denounced and exposed 'imperialist plots', and 'espionage networks', all guided by the United States, it is generally accepted that the United States has not been involved in extensive subversive activities in this region, yet its involvement in the preparation of putsches and *coups* in other parts of the world has been publicly admitted.[25] The case of Yugoslavia is an exception, but as already explained, the wide aid extended to the Tito regime was extended *after* the gaining of independence from the USSR, and not before; it is more the case of supporting the legitimate authority, and its maintenance of power, then encouraging the overthrow of a regime by a competing elite.

On the other hand, though, it should be remembered that the assistance came in the light of the cold war, a period in which there was no fear that such activity could damage the already deteriorating relationship of the two superpowers. During later events such as the uprising and emancipation in Hungary and Poland in 1956, and Czechoslovakia in 1968, the US did not hasten to provide any assistance or aid to strengthen those governments. Nor did the Americans persistently provoke debates at the United Nations on the right of self-determination of the East European nations. The American authorities specified their position in such situations time and again. Secretary of State Dean Rusk declared in 1966 that 'ours is not an effort to subvert the Eastern European governments nor to make those states hostile to the Soviet Union or to each other. No one would benefit from an Eastern Europe that is again balkanized.'[26]

In 1970 President Nixon reaffirmed this stand publicly.[27] At the same time he was willing to allow the United States to follow the second alternative; 'We are prepared to enter into negotiations with the nations of Eastern Europe, looking to a gradual normalization of relations. We will adjust ourselves to whatever pace and extent of normalization these countries are willing to sustain.'[28]

With the establishment of a polycentralist reality in the Communist world, the United States expects other countries to follow the Romanian example of departing from the Soviet Party line — but the change should be cautious and incremental. America can be expected to take advantage of the existence of several centres of power to increase the margins of activity available in the various countries establishing closer relations with the United States. This process will be facilitated by the use of economic, consular and cultural resources. Aimed primarily at granting the Eastern European countries a greater bargaining power, with the Soviet Union, this strategy could in the long run be translated into a larger political independence. Even under the present restrictions, one can witness a growing interest among the leadership of certain Eastern European countries in improving the relations with the West within the prevailing limitations. The visit to Poland in May 1972 by President Nixon was in response to a declaration by Premier Jaroszewicz in which he expressed satisfaction 'for the interest of the United States in expanding economic, scientific and technical relations with Poland'.[29] The decision to send Witold Trampoczynsky, one of the most important economists in Poland as Polish Ambassador to Washington in 1971, was complemented by the sending of high-ranking professional, scientific and industrial delegations. The visit of the First Secretary of the Polish Communist Party, Edward Gierek, to the United States in October 1974 was a further step in the direction of increasing the sources of credit and technology in the United States: 50 per cent of Polish trade is nowadays with Western countries and the ambitious plan of industrial expansion relies heavily on such sources.

To further the development of *rapprochement* between most of the Eastern European countries and the United States, Western Europe plays an important role as indirect link and action line. In its global policy, the Soviet Union supports, in certain fields, the bilateral co-operation between the Eastern and Western parts of the continent, opening up even further opportunities for interaction and involvement in Eastern Europe. Cultural links (e.g. scholarships in universities) are becoming more common and accepted (e.g. Poland and Sweden, or Romania and France).

It can be assumed that the *OestPolitik* of former Chancellor Brandt received Washington's approval and encouragement, as the reduction of tension with countries such as Czechoslovakia, Poland and East Germany would fall into the general trend of *detente.* However, there are reservations about the support of a further fragmentation of the Communist bloc, as Pinder considers,

> If a union of the East European countries apart from Russia is indeed possible, the West should welcome and encourage it. Polycentrism is an improvement on the hegemony that went before it; but if taken to its logical conclusion it is no more than balkanization. The geographical connotations of the term are too evocative for the instability of such a system — or rather non-system — to be ignored ... A United Eastern Europe, standing between Russia and the West and too strong to be dominated by either side, would be much more stable an arrangement; neither hegemony, nor polycentrism, but perhaps oligocentrism.[30]

The third alternative is to seek out an understanding with the Soviet Union which could lead to the acceptance of greater US activity in Eastern Europe. Whether emanating from agreements at global level or as a result of increasing transactions at bilateral level between the two superpowers, this relationship could come to be acceptable to the Kremlin leaders. The Romanian proposal for the dissolution of both Western and Eastern military alliances in Europe, the appeal for the institutionalisation of the European Conference on Security and the disarmament talks could be constructive steps providing benefits for all sides, while also creating further openings for Eastern Europe.

There has been a decrease in the hostile propaganda content of the 'Voice of America' broadcasts to Eastern Europe, with greater emphasis on providing factual information. The recent discussions on the possible closure of 'Radio Liberty' are an open indication of American readiness to help reduce tensions. On the commercial level, the wheat exports of the United States and Canada to the Soviet Union represent a willingness to alleviate certain serious Soviet economic problems. The Soviet Bloc has also requested Western assistance and co-operation in the financing of projects through the Investment Bank of the COMECON. Within this framework, Hungary was the first Communist country to issue bonds on the Western stock markets. Several major Western corporations have co-operated in the establishment and development of industries in Eastern Europe and the Soviet Union — including the French colour TV system (SECAM), Renault and Fiat. These developments show that the Soviet desire for economic help and assistance'has had repercussions in its 'satellite' countries.

The 'bridge-building' policy of Kennedy and Johnson was oriented more towards the use of the third alternative while taking advantage of possible non-contradictory aspects of the second option.

The key role of the Soviet Union in any future liberalisation of Eastern Europe is emphasised by the American partisans of the *detente* 'Any improvement in relations between the Soviet Union and the West . . . is likely to benefit the people of the Baltic and Eastern Europe ultimately.'[31] Rather than events in Eastern Europe influencing the Soviet political situation, the argument is reversed. An agreement with the Soviet Union about the reduction of troops in Central Europe — it is argued — will obviously strengthen the governments of Eastern Europe. More economic links with the Soviet Union and the Soviet-dominated COMECON will have repercussions in a further opening up of the Eastern European economies. The lower the level of violations of human rights in Russia, the more likely it is to be extended to all other nations in the orbit. This is perhaps a longer path to freedom for Eastern Europe, but a safer one without unnecessary crises. This is not the view of former leaders of those countries now in exile. The *emigré* groups angrily denounced the American position at the Helsinki Summit of 1975 as a total sell-out, the formal acquiescence in the absolute masterdom of the Kremlin over subject peoples. In the words of a 'hawkish' journalist: 'Once again the peoples of Eastern Europe learned

the lesson of Munich in 1938, Yalta in 1945, Czechoslovakia in 1948
and Hungary in 1956; that they had little to hope from the West'.[32]
Distressed by the anti-interventionist constraints of the American
Congress in relation to the post-independence Angolan crisis, Kissinger
declared: 'For the first time, we have not reacted against the Soviet
military involvement *outside* their orbit'.[33] On the other hand, the
'Sonnenfeld Doctrine' has been interpreted as a recognition of Soviet
hegemony in Eastern Europe. Furthermore, by advocating the widening
of what today is mainly a military control of this area to a more
'organic' type of relationship, his remarks were understood by many
commentators as suggesting that the Kremlin should further strengthen
its hold over Eastern Europe.[34] Such a permissive American attitude
should be related to the strong views put forward by the Secretary of
State about the threat of Communist involvement in Western European
governments through electoral means. To a large extent one has to
admit that 'Europe' in the popular conception of the United States
covers the Western sector only, since they perceive Eastern Europe as
being an integral part of the Soviet Commonwealth.

4 The Soviet Union in Eastern Europe

The interest of the Soviet Union in its neighbouring countries can be
traced historically to Tsarist ambitions in this region. According to
Renouvin[35] the foreign policy of the Russian Empire during the
second half of the nineteenth century was built on two pillars: firstly,
expansion in the Far East based on colonisation of the Siberian region
and the maritime provinces; and secondly, the acquisition and control
of an outlet to the Mediterranean, control over the Balkans and desire
for control over the Dardanelles. By 1878, the Russian military drive to
expel the Turkish presence from the Balkans brought Russia into open
competition with the Austro-Hungarian Empire. The establishment of a
Principality under Alexander von Battemberg, in Bulgaria, consolidated
Russian tutelage especially with the appointment of two Russian
generals as Ministers of War and Foreign Affairs in Bulgaria. Furthermore, there were the partially successful 'pan-Slavic' ventures, e.g.
Fedaief Danilevsky's 'Charter of Slavic Solidarity', and the neo-Slavic
Congress of Prague in 1908.

In the thirty years from the Bolshevik Revolution till the Communist takeover in Eastern Europe, the Soviet Union made no progress in
the furtherance of its ideology in that region. There was the short-lived
success in Hungary, where a Red Army organised by the ex-officer
Bela Kun grabbed power for a few weeks in 1919. But following the

imposition of the dictatorships of Horthy and Bethlen in Hungary in 1919, the Communists were consistently persecuted, a policy maintained by their successors, Count Karolyi and Premier Daranyi.

The Czechoslovakian Republic was the only new sovereign state to enjoy a stable democratic system, with the first government coming from the Social Democrats. From 1918-38, Masaryk was Prime Minister, and was succeeded by his Minister of Foreign Affairs, Eduard Benes. It was a country surrounded by states with territorial ambitions, therefore it was in Czechoslovakia's favour to maintain cordial relations with all its neighbours, to support the role of the League of Nations, and to establish commercial relations with the Soviet Union.

The Baltic countries, after reaching an agreement with the USSR in the early 1920s, in which their independence and sovereignty were recognised, moved to control the progress of Communism and to destroy it as an internal threat. Estonia established a dictatorship in 1934, with the Fatherland Party declaring its opposition to both Communism and Fascism. In Latvia in 1934 Prime Minister Ulmanis carried out a successful *coup d'etat,* dissolved parliament, and imposed restrictive legislation under the banner of combating right- and left-wing totalitarianism. Lithuania, except for a short period of rule by the Communist and anti-clerical Socialists in 1926, underwent a conservative regime which carried out a repressive policy against the left-wing forces.

Poland, a country which had enjoyed eight centuries of independence, and for 200 years was considered a great power, showed few signs of legislative activity in its Republican regime, following the re-establishment of its independence after World War I, and until 1930 General Pilsudski maintained a strong grip over the country. Pilsudski combined an external policy of territorial revisionism with dictatorial powers internally. On his death in 1935 the autocratic character of the regime continued. The non-aggression pact signed with the Soviet Union in 1931 was invalidated in spirit when Poland signed in 1934 a ten-year non-aggression pact with Germany.

The Balkans underwent a different experience. Greece changed from a monarchy to a republic, with regimes ranging from conservative pro-British to pro-Nazi orientations. After a short experiment with the monarchy in 1935, a pro-Nazi dictatorship was established by General Metaxas in 1936. In Yugoslavia the constitutional monarchy was unable to overcome internal ethnic strife, and in November 1928 King Alexander assumed dictatorial powers. His assassination in 1934 was a prelude to further dictatorial regimes. Bulgaria enjoyed four years of

government by the Agrarian Party; then more conservative forces came
to rule the country, with frequent Communist uprisings. In 1934 a dictatorship was established along Fascist lines. Albania, governed since
1925 by Zogu, became a monarchy in 1928 when he was crowned
King Zog I — and was then drawn into the orbit of Fascist Italy.
Finally, Romania suffered an unstable monarchy and underwent a
series of short-lived governments, varying in quick succession from
conservative to liberal to national-agrarian. In five of those countries
the collapse of democracy brought about the installation of dictatorships, and national aspirations did not crystallise in firm political institutions.

This was the general picture between the two World Wars, and when
one bears in mind the growing threat of Nazism for the Soviet Union,
it is easier to understand the Soviet fears, with a chain of hostile
countries in the West, and the Japanese threatening it from the East in
China. All the regional groupings of its European neighbours from the
proposed federation between Czechoslovakia and Poland, the 'Little
Entente', or the 'Baltic Entente', were considered as threats by Moscow,
and the Soviet Union continually accused the French 'imperialists' of
trying to erect a *cordon sanitaire* around it. It is therefore in many
ways understandable that the Russians maintained as a primary foreign
policy objective, the consolidation of a buffer zone which distanced the
threats of European powers.

Initially the Comintern adopted the revolutionary line of encouraging uprisings and socialist rebellions within Europe; but the failure to
achieve such aims brought about a reassessment of Soviet foreign
policy, as well as recognition of the importance of the Western countries and the need to maintain normal political and commercial relations
with them. During the 1928-35 period, internal factionalism and
Stalin's struggle for absolute power corresponded with a sectarian and
isolationist foreign policy. However, the growing strength of Hitler and
Nazi power forced the Soviet Union to seek closer relations with non-
Fascist regimes in Europe. Foreign Minister Litvinov consulted with his
French and American colleagues (Kellogg-Briand Pact), and signed a
series of non-aggression pacts with the adjacent countries: Finland,
Estonia, Latvia, Lithuania, Poland, Romania, Turkey, Persia, Afghan-
istan and also France. The successful Nazi offensive on the Eastern
front, followed later by the invasion deep into Russian territory,
strongly influenced the Kremlin in maintaining full military control
over the Eastern European states.

Following the German collapse in 1945, the Red Army occupied all

of this territory, up to the Oder/Neisse line, including Berlin. Mention
has already been made of both the direct and indirect concessions
granted by the Allies to Stalin at Yalta. In 1947 the *zhdanovischina*
was inaugurated, followed by the Sovietisation of Eastern Europe.
Except in Yugoslavia and Albania with the assistance of the Red Army
and with the acceptance (sometimes with internal dissenting factors
and lack of discipline), of the local Communist Party, absolute power
was consolidated in Communist hands; although in some cases the
formal aspect of a coalition with other political parties was maintained.
In 1948 the Soviet Union reinforced its control with bilateral military
and economic agreements, and in 1949 established the Comecon as an
answer to the Marshal Plan in Western Europe. Total control was
exercised over the satellite countries (Yugoslavia being an exception),
with the countries within the orbit suffering from a suffocating Soviet
hegemony with strong nationalist and revanchist overtones. During this
period only the first alternative could be applied, that is the maintenance of total control or the widening of the margin of political
security of the Soviet Union to the maximum.[36] No other alternative
was appropriate until 1956, as the three years following Stalin's death
still did not produce a clear change of policy towards the sphere of
influence. Khrushchev, after controlling the Hungarian and Polish up-
heavals of 1956, 'pursued policies and generated an atmosphere that
broke the rigid frame of Stalinist conformity in quest of a viability that
would make the communist system more operative and thus more
attractive to its own citizens and to those labouring under other
systems'.[37] This policy continued, basically till 1968, when the Soviet
intervention in Czechoslovakia came as a setback to the winds of
change. 'Counter-reform' was a huge step backwards: political docility
was again emphasised by the satellite leaders and planned changes in
economic structure were modified according to the new restrictions.

The first option was sporadically invoked when deemed necessary,
as in the case of Hungary in 1956 and Czechoslovakia in 1968, with the
use of military intervention; other ways of applying pressure have been
continually used. The forebearance shown toward the deviationist tendencies of Yugoslavia, Albania and Romania is evidence of a varying
order of priorities, with Central Europe and the Balkans[38] evaluated at
different levels; the countries of Central Europe suffer more stringent
control by the Soviet Union. It is arguable that one way of gaining
credibility for threats of force is the selective use of that force; therefore, immediate military intervention in Hungary should have been
expected, considering the leniency shown Tito's regime in Yugoslavia.

Similarly, the decision to intervene in Czechoslovakia can be also related amongst other reasons to the relative freedom in foreign policy allowed to Romania.

Such an alternative has been used after de-Stalinisation as a regulatory policy to deal with deviations by a country within its subsystem, and for ensuring the maintenance of discipline; this option is also being subjected to further consideration as to possible negative implications in global politics, bipolar relations with the United States, and trends within the international Communist movement.[39] Obviously the reason for using the weapon of military intervention has to be of extreme importance, or at least considered to be so. The peril of a growing nationalistic spirit in one country might provoke the disintegration of the entire Communist Bloc.[40] No less important are the possible implications of the Kremlin's policy in Eastern Europe for its own internal system.[41] The failure to carry out repressive measures against nationalistic trends or against a liberalisation process in its sphere of influence can have internal repercussions by encouraging similar demands within the USSR. The small demonstration by liberals in Moscow following the Soviet invasion of Czechoslovakia, and Tartar demands in conjunction with those of other minority groups, show the interdependence of this phenomenon and these processes.

When faced with a choice, what does Moscow consider to be the greater danger, the deviationist foreign policy of a satellite, or deviations in the domestic political structure of an Eastern European country? The decision to invade Czechoslovakia but not Romania, apart from the strategic calculations, might provide a partial answer to this question.

While the 'Prague Spring' was mainly a search for a new form of 'humanist' socialism, the Czechs did not deviate from the basic foreign policy line of the Soviet Union.[42] Romania, on the other hand, maintains a strong centralist regime with all the totalitarian restrictions, and carries on an independent policy and role in international relations with rival powers. The choice of Czechoslovakia as victim could be a result of the danger threatening Soviet society as a result of Prague's opening up a Pandora's box of liberalisation and freedom of expression – demands not heeded by the Kremlin in Russia.

The second alternative, that of seeking a medium 'margin of political security'', is related by Billington[43] to other causes, a result of the Soviet Union having imposed on it the role of a 'centrist power': (a) the USSR is accused by the West of being extreme in its Communism, while at the same time it is criticised by radical Castroists and

Maoists as being too conservative; (b) the collective leadership and the
continual need for compromise in the Kremlin has fragmented the
monolithic power, weakening the previous authoritarian power structure which enabled it to adopt extremist policies; (c) the fear of war on
two frontiers, the European and the Asiatic, has pressured Russia into
adopting a moderate line toward the Soviet neighbours to the West and
South.

After 1956 even in such cases as Czechsolovakia and East Germany
the Soviets had to force some satellite regimes to adopt a more liberal
policy, and economic exploitation by Russia within the Comecon
changed into a more equalitarian distribution. The approach accepted
by the Kremlin was the granting of a certain autonomy to the 'satellite'
countries particularly in the realm of administration and economic
systems. This so-called 'Goulash communism' permits Poland to change
parts of its bureaucratic system, and permits Hungary to experiment
with decentralisation of the economy, both in management and production through the 'New Economic Mechanism'; sociologists can now
refer to social problems in worker-state relations, criticise the lack of
housing, etc. All the same, the Eastern European countries are cautious,
being careful to maintain a level of self-control which does not risk
Soviet reprisals personally or collectively (measures as far-reaching as
the abolition of censorship, or the establishment of real political
pluralism, as in Dubceck's Czechoslovakia, are avoided).

A further reference to the influence of the character of Soviet
leadership as tending to a middle way policy is provided by Wolfe:

> Basically, the decline in the Soviet Union's once unquestioned
> dominance in East Europe during the past decade had left Khrush-
> chev's successors with the broad choice of either making the best of
> an unsatisfactory situation, with the attempt to reimpose the Soviet
> writ throughout the region. On the whole, they apparently accepted
> the former alternative in the first years of the new regime, when the
> Soviet Union followed a largely conciliatory and a fence-mending
> line in Eastern Europe, partly perhaps to ease fears and uncertainties
> that had arisen there after the change of leadership in Moscow.
> Eventually, of course, the Brezhnev-Kosygin regime reversed itself
> when it called upon trooops to restore Soviet authority in Czecho-
> slovakia.[44]

The margins of political security are set 'to create conditions in Eastern
Europe that will preclude the possibility, on both the national and

domestic levels, that divergences will assume the disruptive dimensions they have occasionally had in the past'.[45] Such a Soviet drive for uniformity does not only apply to the satellites but also to the deviant cases. After Ceausescu's visit to Peking in 1971, Romania had to improve her strained relations with Moscow by showing greater compliance with the participation of inter-bloc entities. In an attempt to guarantee that Tito's successor will belong to the pro-Soviet elements of the Yugoslav League of Communists, the Kremlin has intensified the activities of its loyal followers concentrated usually within the secret service. The arrest and court-martialling of such elements in Bucharest and Belgrade is intended as a warning to other countries that the threat of Soviet-inspired subversions is far from being over.

The third alternative could theoretically prove attractive to the Soviet Union. The possibility of closing the margins of security considerably could serve a number of important purposes to Moscow. First, for the sake of advancing the idea of European security and for the strengthening of economic and technical ties with the West, such a step would undoubtedly be considered as a positive gesture. Furthermore, Hartley believes that such a policy has three fundamental aims: '1) to hasten American withdrawal from Europe; 2) to gain formal acceptance of the *status quo* in Eastern Europe; and 3) once again, to inhibit further European integration, especially in the field of defense.'[46] But for most commentators, such a reaction from the West could not further liberalisation in Eastern Europe in any considerable way.[47] this being conditional only on a prior liberalisation inside the Soviet Union. 'The satellite regimes in Eastern Europe will not be unaffected. Indeed one would expect that a relaxation of Russian attention would leave very little remaining of the carefully constructed chain of people's democracies.'[48]

A further argument is that a continual policy of coercion by Moscow, may well in the long run provoke a cumulative increase in feelings of resentment which could explode in a general upheaval, therefore, it is preferable for Moscow to seek forms of voluntary adherence, even at the expense of relaxing the rigid controls over forms of political organisation, administration and economic activity. In other words, faced with the alternative of a possible 'Albanisation', the Soviet Union would prefer the lesser risk of the 'Finlandisation' of Eastern Europe.[49] Lukaszewski predicts categorically that,

however, the Soviet Union cannot continue forever to combat the unity and independence of Central Europe. Actually, the economic and political integration of the area would be profitable for it. A united and hence independent Central Europe would be much more likely to assure the Soviets stability on their western frontier than fragmented Central Europe can today. For behind the present official facade of friendship with the Soviets lurks dissatisfacton, dissent and even potential for violent disorder. Whereas such a Central Europe cannot be a secure partner for the Soviet Union, a united group of countries could well cooperate with their eastern neighbor out of genuine interest rather than coercion. It would also be a more useful link with the West than the present conglomerate of uncertain satellites.[50]

This prediction has not met with any repercussions among Soviet leadership. Geo-political considerations from the past, internal calculations in the present, and considerations of global policy, both in the world system and the international Communist movement, do not allow us to foresee the implementation of the third alternative.

The outcome of the European Security Conference in Helsinki does not, so far, point to any change which could lead to the enlargement of freedom of action in Eastern Europe. The 'Final Act' clauses that legitimate the maintenance of Soviet primacy in Eastern Europe are not balanced by guarantees preventing outside intervention. Moscow's interpretation is that such principles apply only when related to states with different social systems, while their invasions of Eastern European countries are to be regarded as 'military assistance' to brother members of the community, usually following a specific request for aid. It is hoped that the section called 'Basket Three' (civil liberties, travel, exchange of ideas and mass media), might compensate for the concessions made to the Soviet by the legitimation of the *status quo*. Indeed, even a very gradual implementation can produce a certain relaxation in the 'satellite' states. However, Yugoslavia and Romania (Albania was absent from Helsinki, being totally opposed to the Conference), fear that now Soviet presence in Eastern Europe has been ratified, their independence may be jeopardised.[51]

The present domestic 'conservatism' of the Soviet Union, extended to the Popular Democracies and increasing pressure on intellectuals, is considered by some sources to be a temporary reaction against expectations aroused by the conference, but in the long run, it is believed that the declaration may help in two ways:

First, its existence may raise the threshold of Soviet tolerance of

national independence in Eastern Europe — a decision to intervene
might be taken with more reluctance, both because of the more
adverse propaganda effect and also because of the danger to other
aspects of the detente package. Second, it may clear the way for
some progress towards a negotiated reduction of armed forces in
Europe in the Vienna talks. Reducing military tension would give a
better chance for liberalising the regimes of Eastern Europe and
their relations with Moscow, as well as helping both East and West
to solve their economic problems.[52]

In conclusion, one could say that the Soviet Union prefers, for the time
being, to pursue the second option, with the sporadic application of the
first option as a deterrent against possible misinterpretation of Soviet
intentions by her East European allies. Compared with previous regimes
this policy is based on a line of continuity — the extension of the
Russian ideas of domination in the area — with a line of change: the
extension of the socialist revolution to other countries. In other words
'the contents and aims of Soviet policy are different from those of
Imperial Russia, but the forms are often similar. And forms sometimes
even affect content.'[53]

5 The United States in Latin America

United States policy in Latin America and the Western Hemisphere for
more than 150 years, has been characterised by a consistency with the
formulations of the Monroe Doctrine — an outlook unchanged to this
day. The continuous adherence to the Monroe Doctrine by the changing
administrations is perhaps one of the few examples in the world where
a single foreign policy principle has been maintained for such an extended period of time. Therefore, in order to understand the present
policy of the White House towards Latin America it is necessary to
know and understand the basic percepts of its guiding doctrine. The
major elements of the doctrine were enunciated in a 'State of the
Nation' message by President James Monroe in 1823. They are: (a) any
attempt by European powers to extend their political power into the
Western Hemisphere would be considered a threat to the peace and
security of the United States; and (b) any intervention aimed at oppressing or controlling governments that have already obtained their independence would be considered as an unfriendly act towards the United
States.[54]

The American government sought to transform what was initially a
unilateral statement into a doctrine accepted internationally and

regionally by the other nations in the Western Hemisphere. In practice, the United States has applied this doctrine during different periods with varying interpretations and changing means. In the nineteenth century, the doctrine was used in a unilateral way with its application depending upon whether the United States considered its use to be convenient or efficient in specific cases. In this period the doctrine was amended, with corollaries added. The most important among them were the Polk corollary of 1845 (extending the enforcement of the doctrine to cases of transfer of territories without foreign intervention); the instructions sent by Richard Olney to the US Ambassador in London with regard to the boundary dispute between Venezuela and Great Britain (which stipulated that no reason — even foreign debts — is considered as justifying military intervention, and therefore forcing Britain to submit the case to arbitration); and the T. Roosevelt Corollary of 1904 giving the United States the right to use its troops as an 'international police force' (by which it justified the military intervention of the United States in other countries of the Western Hemisphere in order to force local governments to repay debts to foreign creditors and avoid the threat, therefore, of European intervention).

The attempt at converting the Monroe Doctrine into a principle acceptable to the rest of the world was seen at the First Hague Conference in 1889, and was presented as a *sine qua non* condition by the United States delegation to the Peace Conference of Paris in 1919. The League of Nations recognised the Monroe Doctrine, in Article 54 of its Charter, as a 'regional understanding' and Washington included a reservation in which 'the United States will not submit to arbitration or investigation of the Assembly or the Peace Council any of the questions that in the United States' judgement depend upon, or related to, its long term policy known as the Monroe Doctrine'.

In addition to the unilateral declaration, the *de facto* fulfilment and the *de jure* universal acceptance of the doctrine, the US also sought the legitimisation of the principle through its acceptance by the countries of Latin America. In spite of intensive criticism of the unilateral use of the doctrine, and the amendments and additional clauses, the Fourth Pan-American Conference meeting in Buenos Aires, in 1910, recognised the doctrine as 'a factor of international peace in the continent'. The suspension of all corollaries and additions — as proposed by Under Secretary of State Clark, in 1928 and accepted by President Hoover in 1930 — in the new policy of non-intervention by the United States, was instrumental in leading to a renewed acceptance by Latin American countries. Under the administration of Franklin D. Roosevelt the general stand against the Fascist ideology and German territorial ambitions strengthened continental consensus even more. In 1940 Germany was informed of the unanimous opposition to European interference within the America's political system ('common inter-American democratic ideal'). Following the Nazi conquest of Denmark, Norway, Holland and Belgium, the Second Conference of Foreign Ministers, meeting in Havana in 1940, adopted the principle of 'non-transfer' of European colonies of the former European powers to the new German occupying power.

Continental support or acknowledgement of the doctrine was also given at the Chapultepec Conference on Problems of Peace and War in Mexico in 1945, where the concept was expanded to include a military element, the creation of a Military Defence Alliance aimed not only against extra-continental aggression, but also against any country attacking another on the American continent. Subsequently the Inter-American Treaty of Reciprocal Assistance, Rio de Janeiro (1947), established the necessary measures to enforce collective security, define the framework to be adopted and the means to be used against an aggressor — ranging from the temporary withdrawal of diplomatic representation to the employment of force.

In the cold war period, the Monroe Doctrine was used not only against the Soviet Union in order to prevent its expansionist power, but also against Communism as an ideology, which was considered to be contrary to the democratic conception of the Western Hemisphere. This modification provided a convenient alibi when the US lacked — as it generally did — proof of Soviet intervention, direct or indirect. The threat and existence of a local Communist movement became sufficient justification for the application of the doctrine — which in turn provided an excuse for direct intervention. Prior to the invasion of Guatemala in 1954 a Pan-American Conference in Caracas was called providing the necessary declaration.[55]

The unexpected radicalisation of the Cuban revolution brought in its wake bilateral United States reprisal (economic boycott, sabotage and the mounting and assisting of the abortive 1961 invasion). Following the failure of these measures, efforts were enlarged to the continental scale by compelling Latin American countries to exclude Cuba from the continental framework (in 1962), and in 1964 (using the context of the Rio de Janeiro Treaty), to apply economic sanctions against Cuba, following the decision of the Ninth Foreign Ministers Pan-American Meeting. During the 1962 missile crisis, President John Kennedy declared, 'it shall be the policy of this nation to regard any

nuclear missile launched from Cuba against any nation within the
Western Hemisphere as an attack on the U.S.A.',[56] thereby imposing a
strategic corollary with US atomic superiority. Among the consequences of this crisis was a US commitment not to violate Cuba's
sovereignty. It could be argued that the doctrine did not become invalidated, but that by excluding Cuba from the inter-American family of
nations the doctrine became restricted to the remaining 19 countries as
an integral part of the Western Hemisphere.

It is important to note that the greatest progress towards the acceptance of the Monroe Doctrine on a continental basis was made during
F.D. Roosevelt's 'good neighbour' policy, committing Washington to
refrain from military intervention in the Southern Republics. During
the years 1933-65 no direct military intervention took place in the
region. The invasion of the Dominican Republic, by US troops in 1965,
was a unilateral act in violation of the principle of non-aggression
formulated and expressed in the Rio Treaty. The Resolutions of the
House of Representatives (Selden Resolution) passed by 321 to 52
votes, justified the unilateral intervention, considering that 'the subversive forces that form international Communism, operating openly
and secretly, directly or indirectly, threaten the sovereignty and
political independence of all nations in the Western Hemisphere'.

This brief historical description of the Monroe Doctrine, and its
applications, was introduced to emphasise that it is not a product of
the cold war, but a tradition inherent in American foreign policy. All
the same, the cold war and its consequences have not left this area
totally unaffected, so one can still investigate the alternatives of
American foreign policy facing Soviet strategy, and the existence of
peripheral countries such as Cuba and semi-peripheral ones such as
Peru and Argentina.

The Latin American social scientist Helio Jaguaribe, corroborates
the three alternatives, when he considers the US operations to be: (a)
the United States establishes a 'new Roman Empire', submitting the
Latin American countries to a rigorous control, which in his opinion
will inevitably lead to rebellion and in the long run to the establishment
of developmental or socialist systems; (b) the maintenance of the
status quo, which would become daily more difficult, considering the
existing major contradictions, and the need for a well-defined policy;
(c) the 'communitary' option, by which a more equitable system of
participation would be introduced, with the autonomy of the Latin
American countries *vis-à-vis* the United States being maintained, and
the relationship based on voluntary co-operation for the fulfilment of

common goals.[57]

The first operation is linked with the enlarging of the United States' margin of political security and the restricting of local governments to a minimum of freedom of action. The American ambassador plays in internal politics the role of an omnipotent Roman pro-consul, particularly in the capitals of the weak and smaller countries. Dissident groups within local elites are removed and replaced by elements unconditionally loyal and subordinate to Washington's dictates and to the detriment of the democratic experience, reinforcing technocratic military regimes. Rapoport projects the American policy-maker's image of what the latter considers as a 'legitimate' government in Latin America; not only do the Latin American elite have to prove themselves *non*-Communist, they also have to provide evidence of being *anti*-Communist.[58] In general terms, this was the policy maintained during the whole period of the cold war until 1961; President Kennedy decided to tackle the problem of US-Latin American relations from a different angle, and launched the Alliance for Progress programme, implanting a general feeling that the United States was in support of a 'community' approach. However, he did not hesitate to use force when Castro became unmanageable.[59] It should also be noted that until recently, Latin American governments, when colliding with a major American foreign policy arm, perceived the United States as a unitary actor. In matters such as the Panama Canal, Allende's Chile, Castro's Cuba and others, the contradictions between 'hawk' and 'dove' politicians or conflicting interest groups were not skilfully exploited. Senators such as William Fulbright and his successor in the Chair of the Foreign Relations Commission of the Senate, John J. Sparkman, or Latin American advisers to the White House or the State Department such as Charles Meyer, have not been sufficiently lobbied. The 1965 armed intervention in the Dominican Republic and lack of tolerance displayed by Nixon and Kissinger towards the Chilean socialist experience was a reaffirmation that when Washington perceives that national interests are at stake, it quickly reverts to the first option of intervention.[60]

The participation of varying and competing interest groups and administrative elements in the US decision-making process has helped to create the impression of a diffusion of policies, with the compromise and consensus solution closer to the second option. However, this diversity should not be exaggerated. Until a decision has to be made and implemented on a single important issue, the pluralistic approach enables optimists to point out at any stage the liberal aspects of official American foreign policy. The first reaction to information about the involvement of ITT in subversive activities in Chile, and the criticism in the press about the unofficial economic boycott and suspension of credit, helped to cause an over-estimation of the strength of moderate circles. Even the normal and close military relations maintained between the Pentagon and the Chilean army were often given a positive connotation. Nevertheless the overthrow of Allende's regime is sufficient evidence perhaps that in the post-Castroist era, when the United States is forced to take a risk in order to increase or even maintain existing margins of political security, the tendency is to rever to more conservative options.

In fact the southern part of the continent has never suffered from direct military intervention by the United States, but one must not forget that means of indirect intervention are available — subversions, the use of the CIA and other marginal agencies,[61] making the remote places of the continent vulnerable also. Furthermore, the pragmatic approach employed by the CIA in its covert operations has also been brought in to assist 'middle way' moderate political forces such as Christian Democrats in Chile or Socialist Democratic 'populists' like Jose Figueres in Costa Rica. What might be interpreted as sustaining the second option is often merely the choice of the lesser evil when faced with the threat of more radical forces from the left.

A further misleading conception is the North American acceptance of the second option in the military field. Since 1967 the United States has maintained a policy based on the 'Foreign Military Sales' law, which restricts to a maximum of $150 million the annual arms sales to Latin America, so as to encourage the Latin American countries to spend their monies in other fields. The result, though, was the turning of these countries to Western Europe, particularly the more developed and richer of the countries. As Table 18 shows, most of the money was expended on air forces and navies. In the field of internal security, in most Latin American countries the United States plays an important role.[62] Besides supplying equipment, training and logistic preparations for the maintenance of the armies in Latin America, they are dependent on the United States, as can be shown by the strict control exercised through the annual gathering of the branch commanders, and particularly through the Conferences of American Armies (CEA).[63]

At any rate, in a reappraisal of this policy, Secretary of State Kissinger considers it a failure, and has requested Congress to lift the former restrictions.[64] The second option consists in maintaining a precarious *status quo* in the continent; not actively seeking to overthrow the deviant regimes but rather to isolate them from other potential

Table 18: Selling of arms to Latin America 1967-1972
(millions of dollars)

Selling Countries	Navy	Air Forces	Army	Total
Western Europe	658	432	123	1213
United States	4	172	40	216
Canada	–	163	–	163
Australia	30	–	–	30
TOTAL	692	767	163	1622

Source: La Opinion, 23 November 1974.

followers in other countries. (So Adlai Stevenson reacted *vis-a-vis* Cuba:
'do not negotiate with Cuba, communism is not transferable',[65] not
necessarily attempting to demolish Castro's regime). For the rest of the
countries, dictatorships have to be accepted as allies and the few cases
of the non-deviant popular regimes warned against transgressing the
medium-range margins of political security. In the economic domain, it
implies not the mounting of a world-wide boycott but simply refraining
from the maintenance of bilateral relations with the deviant country, *per
se,* already a serious problem for the weaker counterpart. The Pelly
Amendment to the Fishermen's Protective Act was used to ban temporarily the sale of arms to Ecuador, during the dispute known as the Tuna
War. The Hickenlooper Amendment, calling for the suspension of
economic assistance to countries that nationalise American property
without adequate compensation, although discussed several times in the
case of Peru's nationalisation of the International Petroleum Company
(IPC), was never applied. No clear preference for democratically
elected governments can be traced, and even the pro-Western elements
in the continent would accuse Washington of conducting a 'low profile'
policy of apathy towards Latin America. While for any Latin American
country, relations with Washington are crucial, the general asymmetry
of the relationship from the other side, is even more strongly accentuated during these periods. Political and economic transactions with
other areas of the world assume an obvious priority and the treatment
of inter-American matters is left in the hands of lower echelon figures
in the Administration. Furthermore, the period of transition from one
option to another might be long and its undecided character might be
regarded as the continued existence of the second alternative.

The third option concerns the closing of the margins of political
security to a minimum, and finds an eloquent support in Senator
Fulbright:

I think further that it would be a fine thing if Latin American countries were to undertake a program of their own for 'building bridges' to the world beyond the Western Hemisphere — to Europe and Asia and Africa, and to the Communist countries if they wish. Such relationships, to be sure, would involve a loosening of ties to the United States in the immediate future, but in the long run, I feel sure, they would make for both happier and stronger bonds with the United States — happier because they would be free, stronger because they would be dignified and self-respecting as they have never been before.[66]

Under the third option, Cuba would be reincorporated, at least partially, into the inter-American system, just as Yugoslavia was from 1955 in the Communist Bloc. The nagging fear for the United States is that such leniency may indirectly provoke other Latin American countries to adopt a more independent stance. It is difficult to release Cuba from imposed isolation while there still exist on the continent other semi-peripheral countries, but with time and the widening of the margins of political security, the case of the re-integration of a single exception is simplified. A recent example of sustaining such a line can be found in the report compiled by former American Ambassador to the OAS, Sol Linowitz, which appeals to its government to finalise the signature of a new treaty with Panama, renew trade with Cuba, renunce the use of veto powers in the Inter-American Development Bank (BID) and put an end to the 'covert' operations in the continent.[67]

In more general terms, the option of supporting moderate social reformist governments on the continent as the best way to contain Communism has not been tried sufficiently to prove its validity. While President Kennedy was genuinely interested in such an option, other economic priorities and the emergence of the subversive activities of the guerillas prevented successful policy implementation; Chile, the sole instance of such a policy until 1970, turned out to be a failure for the ruling American circles. A further risk involved in the third option is a possible renewed attempt by the Soviet Union to change the post-1962 *status quo* that removed a Soviet nuclear presence from the continent. The news in 1969 of Soviet intentions to use the Cuban port Cienfuegos as a supply base for nuclear submarines produced a calm response from Foreign Minister Gromyko, who promised Dr Kissinger that they would withdraw any Soviet nuclear submarines from Cuban shores.[68]

It is possible to discard fear of Soviet military penetration, as an explanation for the United States' non-application of the third alternative; the answer, it seems, must lie elsewhere. It could be that economic interests in Latin America are too important to allow any process of nationalisation or unrestricted trade relations with other powers to move from the West and the East. However, general observation seems to point to a decrease over the last 20 years in US economic interest in Latin America. Once the major area of US foreign investment, it has declined from 30.5 per cent of the total to 14.7 per cent in 1969, with investments elsewhere having become more important — in Europe, Canada and other regions.[69] The increasing trade opportunities for the US in the Communist world, particularly with the Peoples' Republic of China and the Soviet Union, have added an extra dimension to US interests. Following the massive trade agreement with these countries in recent years, the US has become one of their most important trading partners. This has also led to a lowering of interest in Latin America, as expressed in the Plank report submitted to the White House in 1971, which emphasised the diminishing economic importance of the continent. One should not, though, under-estimate the enormous profits made by North America in Latin America. Among other examples, we may quote Gabriel Valdes, Under-Secretary of the United Nations for development programmes in Latin America, who affirmed that in 1968 USA firms sent $344 million into Latin America, and received in the same year $1,516 million as dividends, royalties and other benefits.[70] An American official source (see Table 19) presents an even more impressive disproportion.

Additionally, it should be mentioned that Latin America represents an important market for US products, creating a net profit in the balance of trade of a yearly $1.2 billion.[71]

The Nixon administration generally adopted the second option, while maintaining the threat of retaliatory punishment for attempts at far-reaching freedom of action on the continent. The Ford administration, through the presence of Kissinger, seems to assure a certain measure of continuity. During a long period, it maintained a 'low profile' policy towards Latin America.[72] But the reactions against US involvement in the overturn of Allende provoked an awareness in Washington of the need to present a better image. Kissinger's participation in the continent's Foreign Ministers' meeting in Tlatelolco, Mexico in 1974, was set to announce the opening of a 'new dialogue'. His presence was considered to be a guarantee for a renewed interest by Washington in her southern neighbours. However, soon afterwards his attention was diverted to other regions and other problems, and a frustrated Latin America commented sarcastically that the United States

seemed less interested in the OAS than the Latin Americans themselves.
The continuous postponements of announced trips by the Secretary of
State to the continent, the cancellation of the March 1975 consultative
meeting of Foreign Ministers in Buenos Aires, the coldness shown
towards Castro's openings, etc. are signs that the 'low profile' policy
was still being maintained at the beginning of 1976.

Table 19: United States Direct Investments in Latin America
(in Billions of Current Dollars)

Year	Book Value	Net Capital Outflows to Latin America	Earnings
1960	8.4	149	1.0
1961	9.2	219	1.1
1962	9.5	029	1.2
1963	9.9	235	1.1
1964	10.3	113	.2
1965	10.9	271	1.3
1966	11.5	307	1.5
1967	12.0	296	1.4
1968	13.1	677	1.6
1969	13.8	844	1.6
1970	14.7	559	1.5

Includes Caribbean countries. The book value of US direct investment in the 19
Latin American republics was $11.7 billion in 1969 as compared with $13.8
billion for the entire area.

Source: US Department of Commerce, 'Survey of Current Business, October
1970', p. 3, October 1971, p. 28 (quoted by H. Goldhamer, op. cit.,
p. 41).

With military and economic considerations showing a decrease in
American interest in Latin America over the same period, repercussions
in the continent could not fail to occur. The growing discontent of a
number of the Latin American countries, without expressing itself in
socialism or communism, became visibly and openly expressed from the
beginning of the 1970s. This dissatisfaction at their dependency
relationship brought about a change in the North American policy.
polarisation had taken place in the region; the 'Havana-Lima' axis,
inclusive of Chile, Argentina and Panama, openly criticised the United
States on a multiplicity of issues. They opposed the economic and
political interference of the multinational enterprises, such as ITT, in
their internal politics; supported the need to nationalise the Panama

Canal and the US oil companies; pressed for the re-acceptance of Cuba
in the inter-American system; criticised the selling of strategic mineral
reserves to the United States, and the rise in US custom duties; demanded the application of the principle of a 200-mile patrimonial sea;
wanted ideologic pluralism, opposed the use of economic boycott by
the United States against Latin American countries, etc. Countries
such as Venezuela, Mexico, Ecuador and Colombia shared many of the
'Havana-Lima' grievances. The opposite pole was represented by the
'Washington-Brasilia' axis, including most of the weaker and more
under-developed countries of Central America, and the dictatorships of
Paraguay and Bolivia; Costa Rica and Salvador supported Panama's
demands, with Costa Rica and Honduras carrying out a 'banana war'
against the American fruit corporations, as they wanted higher prices
than those fixed by the company. Even Uruguay — shortly before the
final military *autogolpe* — endorsed some of the reforms proposed for
the OAS structure. In an unprecedented situation, Washington was in a
minority position on most issues. A tour by Secretary of State Rogers,
in May 1973, when he visited Nicaragua, Mexico, Venezuela, Colombia,
Peru, Brazil and Argentina, brought home the point that USA prestige
had fallen very low in most countries. During some of the gatherings in
those years, the US found itself isolated. An ECLA meeting in Quito,
and a Security Council meeting in Panama on the Canal issue, saw the
United States alone in opposing the Latin American revisionist demands.
Following a suggestion by Venezuela, the OAS met to discuss the re-
structuring of the organisation. At a meeting in Lima in July 1973,
most countries supported either the separation of the Latin American
countries from the United States, or radical reforms in the OAS
structure in order to ensure equality;[73] rumours were spread forecas-
ting the imminent removal of the organisation's headquarters from
Washington to a Latin American capital.

The sudden shift to the right in the continent altered the whole situation in favour of the US. Allende's regime was overthrown in September 1973, and the military *autogolpe* of two months earlier took all
authority from the President in Uruguay and dissolved the Congress,
adopting a conformist attitude towards Washington. In Argentina, the
Peronist regime excluded the left-wing elements, and came to rely
heavily on the syndicalist and bureaucratic groups. Ecuador, Panama
and even Peru consequently lowered the tone of their criticism. The
only course left open for Cuba to avoid falling back into total isolation
was for it to moderate its policies towards the Latin American regimes,
especially old enemies such as the *Accion Democratica* regime in

Venezuela. With the re-establishment of its rule in Latin America, it
became easier for the United States to reconsider and inaugurate a
milder policy towards Cuba; this time without the risk of it setting off
a chain reaction throughout the southern part of the continent.

The oil crisis further stressed the growing importance of oil-
producing countries such as Venezuela, Ecuador and Mexico, especially
in the near future. Paradoxically, the expected wealth for those countries from their oil resources undoubtedly increases their power
position, but at the same time makes them more vulnerable and dependent on the United States since they have to be more careful about
transgressing the margins of political security imposed on them by the
superpower. Two of those countries, Venezuela and Mexico, undertook
the initiative of developing a Latin American Economic System (SELA).
In a meeting that took place in Panama in August 1975,[74] delegates
from 25 countries met and decided to create a permanent consultation
system, by the co-ordination of already existing economic subregional
groupings, to mobilise financial resources and promote scientific-
technical exchange. This trend towards economic co-operation was also
accompanied by the organisation of producer groups — less fortunate
than the vital OPEC oil suppliers — such as the Union of Banana Exporting Countries (UPEB), with Panama, Colombia, Costa Rica, Guatemala
and Honduras (and with the notable absence of Ecuador), the group of
Latin American Sugar Exporting Countries, the *Cafes Suaves Centrales
SA* made up of four countries for the defence of coffee prices on the
world market and the Caribbean Fleet which includes capital from the
Caribbean, Cuba and other South American states. A trade policy
oriented to the diversification of trade and better marketing without
serious political deviations might still fall within the area of freedom of
action left by the margin of political security of the second option. The
greatest acceptable departure from the average regimes — Cuba
excluded — would be moderate regimes of the 'democratic left' such as
Presidents Carlos Andres Perez and Daniel Oduber in Venezuela and
Costa Rica respectively.

The long expected trip of Secretary of State Kissinger in February
1976 did not produce any spectacular change in the existing political
restrictions. His 'Amity Plan' consisted mostly of economic benefits for
Latin America. Although when referring to the Panama Canal issue he
promised that the United States would negotiate 'on the basis of parity
and dignity', at the same time the secretary re-asserted the US commitment to hemispherial security and against 'those who would seek to
undermine solidarity, threaten independence or export violence',[75]

NOTES

1. These alternatives coincide with the model utilised by Campbell for the analysis of the United States' policy in Eastern Europe. John Campbell, *The American Policy Towards Communist Eastern Europe: Choices Ahead* (The University of Minnesota Press, Minneapolis, 1965).

2. For a further development of the subject see E. Kaufman, 'La Politique de l'Union Sovietique en Amerique Latine: echec ou reussite?', *Res Publica*, vol. XIV, no. 3, Brussels, 1971), pp. 567-90.

3. Stephen Clissold, (ed.), *Soviet Relations with Latin America 1918-1968 – A Documentary Survey*, p. 157. Account of an interview in *Pravda* with Stalin, who accused Latin American countries of furthering US aggressive policies at the UN, February 1951.

4. K. Khachaturov, 'Anti-Communism in Latin American Policy of the USA', *International Affairs*, no. 6 (Moscow, 1970), p. 54.

5. S. Clissold, (ed.), ibid., interview given by N.A. Bulganin, Chairman of the Council of Ministers, to a correspondent of 'Vision', *Pravda*, 12 January 1956.

6. Statistics published by the Banco do Brasil, *La Opinion*, Buenos Aires, 31 December 1972.

7. Herbert S. Dinerstein, op. cit., p. 88.

8. 'U.S. Ideological Expansion in Latin America', in *International Affairs* (Moscow, July 1972), p. 39.

9. (Tansky's revised estimates) Mr Tansky indicates that much of this information is drawn from numerous official and nonofficial publications available to the public. A primary source of information is the annual reviews of the Communist aid programmes published by the Bureau of Intelligence and Research of the US Department of State. The last of the series, 'Communist Governments and Developing Nations: Aid and Trade in 1967', was published in August 1968. The figures for 1966 and 1967 were made available since publication of Mr Tansky's original study in *New Directions in the Soviet Economy*. By the end of 1967 total Soviet military aid to developing countries amounted to about $5 billion.

10. According to a paradoxical version by Jack Anderson, 'President Nixon would have been ready to re-establish commercial links with Cuba in exchange, for instance, for a more moderate Soviet line on Vietnam.' *Washington Post*, 14 September 1972.

11. The Soviets find that 'serious changes within the OAS which have resulted from the Latin American countries' resolve to pursue an independent foreign policy line'. N.Chigir, 'USA-Latin American Tense Dialogue', *International Affairs* (Moscow, July 1972), p. 87.

12. *La Opinion*, Buenos Aires, 23 February 1972.

13. S. Clissold, op. cit., p. 240. Press report of *La Mañana*, Montevideo, 5 October 1966.

14. *Amerique Latine*, no. 10, Paris, May 1967, p. 7.

15. Luis Corvalan, 'The Peaceful Way, A form of Revolution', *World Marxist Review*, vol. VI, no. 12, (Moscow, December 1963).

16. Although on several occasion mention is made of clandestine subversive operations carried out under KGB instructions and aimed at creating turmoil and internal unrest, none of these possible actions have produced a significant effect. John Barron, *KGB, the Secret Work of Soviet Secret Agents* (Corgi Books, Buffalo, 1975), provides us with some sensational information about the KGB involvement in guerilla operations in Mexico

(pp. 298-334), but even in such case it was attributed to North Korea, the network itself was promptly dismantled, and five Soviet diplomats were suddenly expelled from Mexico.

17. Wayne S. Smith, op. cit., pp. 1122-3. 'Its breaking of diplomatic relations with Chile following the military coup there in September 1973 must be regarded as falling outside the norms of Soviet behaviour of recent years.'

18. F. Parkinson, *Latin America, the Cold War and the World Powers, 1945-1973*, p. 248.

19. Ibid., p. 21.

20. 'These three interests serve the most elemental of the national interests of the United States: the security of the United States in the Western Hemisphere through the preservation of its unique position as a hegemonial power without rival.' Hans Morgenthau, *A New Foreign Policy for the United States* third printing, (Prager, New York, 1969), p. 157.

21. D.C. Watt, Frank Spencer and Neville Brown, *A History of the World in the Twentieth Century* (Hodder & Stoughton, London, 1967), Part II, by F. Spencer, p. 603. Rapoport remarks that there were two incompatible opinons about Poland's lot at Yalta: 'One was that Roosevelt sold the Poles down the river and with them the American national interests in Europe. The other was that Stalin doublecrossed the West and reneged on his promise to allow a "democratic" Poland.' Rapoport, Anatol, *The Big Two, Soviet-American Perceptions of Foreign Policy* (Pegasus, Bobbs-Merrill Co., New York), p. 81.

22. Ghita Ionescu, *The Break-up of the Soviet Empire in Eastern Europe* (Penguin Books, Harmondsworth, England, 1965), p. 18.

23. Anatole Snub, 'Lessons of Czechoslovakia', *Foreign Affairs*, vol. 47, no. 2 (January 1969), p. 277.

24. John Campbell, op. cit., p. 102.

25. A report on CIA activities gained wide publicity after a congressional debate, and stressed the policy of refraining from any subversive activity in Eastern Europe, while admitting recurrent involvement elsewhere. *TIME* Magazine, 30 September 1974.

26. This text is mentioned in an article by Jerzy Lukaszewski, 'Western Integration and the Peoples' Democracies', *Foreign Affairs*, vol. 46, no. 2 (January 1968), p. 368.

27. 'We are aware that the Soviet Union sees its own security as directly affected by developments in this region. Several times, over the centuries, Russia has been invaded through Central Europe; so this sensitivity is not novel, or purely the product of Communist dogma. It is not the intention of the United States to undermine the legitimate security interests of the Soviet Union. The time is certainly past, with the development of modern technology, when any power would seek to exploit Eastern Europe to obtain strategic advantage against the Soviet Union. It is clearly no part of our policy. Our pursuit of negotiation and detente is meant to reduce existing tensions, not to stir up new ones.' R. Nixon, *op. cit.*, p. 106.

28. Ibid.

29. Declaration mentioned in an article by Adam Bromke, 'Poland Under Gierek', *Problems of Communism* (Sept.-Oct. 1972), p. 16.

30. John Pinder, 'European Common Market and COMECON', in Joseph S. Nye, Jr., op. cit., p. 41.

31. *New York Times*, 31 July 1975.

32. *Daily Telegraph*, London, 28 July 1975.

33. *Le Monde*, 5 February 1976, p. 5.

34. *Guardian*, 31 March 1976. See the condensed official State Department

version of Sonnefeldts' speech in *Le Monde*, 14 April 1976.

35. Pierre Renouvin, *Le XIXe Siecle, Histoire des Relations Internationales* vol. 16 (Hachette, Paris, 1955), pp. 172-4.

36. 'The first set . . . amounted to a camouflaged incorporation of Eastern Europe by the Soviet Union. The main difference between a Socialist Soviet Republic and an Eastern European People's Democracy was that the the latter remained formally independent and sovereign, with separate armies, bureaucracies and parties of their own. Theoretically, the 1952 system of linkages could have served indefinitely as a substitute for annexation.' R.V. Burks, 'The Communist Policies of Eastern Europe', in James Rosenau, *Linkage Politics*, p. 303.

37. J.F. Brown, 'Detente and Soviet Policy in Eastern Europe', *Survey*, vol. 20, no. 2/3 (91/92) (Spring-Summer 1974), p. 46.

38. An analysis of the differences in Soviet policy toward Central Europe and the Balkans is discussed by John C. Campbell in 'Soviet Strategy in the Balkans', *Problems of Communism*, vol. XXIII, 4 (Jul-Aug 1974), pp. 1-16.

39. Harlan Cleveland, 'NATO after the Invasion', *Foreign Affairs*, vol. 47, no. 2 (Jan. 1969), p. 253.

40. William E. Griffith and Walt W. Rostow, *East-West Relations: Is Detente Possible?* (American Enterprise Institute for Public Policy, Washington D.C., 1969), Rostow's expose, p. 49.

41. 'Certainly, events in Eastern Europe that many people now remember as little more than minor episodes of intra-Communist politics have had far-reaching consequences in and for the USSR.' Adam B. Ulam, op. cit., p. 2.

42. 'Foreign policy was never a major concern of the reform movement.' Galia Golan, *Reform Rule in Czechoslovakia* (Cambridge University Press, Cambridge, 1973), p. 200. See Chapter 9 dealing with foreign policy, pp. 200-17.

43. James H. Billington, 'Force and Counterforce in Eastern Europe', *Foreign Affairs*, vol. 47, no. 1 (October 1968), p. 29.

44. Thomas W. Wolfe, *Soviet Power and Europe 1945-1970* (John Hopkins Press, Baltimore, 1970), p. 297.

45. J.F. Brown, 'Detente and Soviet Policy in Eastern Europe', op. cit.

46. Anthony Hartley, 'Europe Between the Superpowers', *Foreign Affairs* vol. 49, no. 2 (Jan. 1971), p. 277.

47. 'From the Soviet point of view, the "Finlandization" of Eastern Europe (as opposed to Western Europe) is inadmissible and the preservation of Communist regimes remains an absolute imperative in Moscow's eyes.' Adam Ulam, op. cit., p. 6.

48. Anthony Hartley, op. cit., p.277.

49. Alexander Bregman, in Z. Brzezinski (ed.) *Dilemmas of Change in Soviet Policy*, p. 187.

50. Anthony Lukaszewski, op. cit., p. 385.

51. *Time* Magazine, 18 August 1975. 'To some extent both fret about their continuing dependence on the Soviet Union as supplier of raw materials and a market for their manufactured goods. And both have good reason to be fearful of Soviet-inspired political unrest, knowing that Soviet intelligence organizations have been active within their countries.'

52. *Observer*, London, 27 July 1975.

53. H. Seton Watson, *Eastern European Revolution*, p. 86.

54. The texts and commentaries of the different declarations have been selected from the following books: Carlos Machado, (ed.), op. cit.; Earl T. Glauert and Lester D. Langley, *The United States and Latin America* (Addison-Wesley, Reading, Massachusetts, 1971); Federico Gil,

Latin America – United States Relations (Harcourt, Brace and Jovanovich, New York, 1971).

55. 'The domination or control of the political institutions of any American State by the international Communist movement . . . would constitute a threat to the sovereignty and political independence of the American States, endangering the peace of America.' Secretary of State John Foster Dulles justified this step by the fact that Communist 'agitators' trained in Moscow had been infiltrating 'public and private organizations' in Guatemala, adding that 'the intrusion of Soviet despotism was, of course, a direct challenge to our Monroe Doctrine, the first and most fundamental of our foreign policies' and warning that 'if World Communism captures any American State, however small, a new and perilous front is established which will increase the danger of the entire free world and require even greater sacrifices from the American people.' E. Glauert and L. Langley, op. cit., pp. 140-1.

56. Address by President Kennedy, 22 October 1962, quoted in Robert Kennedy, *Thirteen Days* (W.W. Norton, New York, 1969), p. 168.

57. Helio Jaguaribe, op. cit.

58. Anatol Rapoport, op. cit., p. 189.

59. See Richard J. Walton, *Cold War and Counter-Revolution* (Penguin Books, Baltimore, 1973), chapters on Cuba, pp. 34-60, 103-42.

60. Professor Pablo Gonzalez Casanova, former rector of the national autonomous university of Mexico (UNAM) has listed 784 interventions by the United States between 1800 and 1969, out of which 270 were perpetrated in Mexico, 92 in Cuba, and 79 in Nicaragua. 'The United States President who ordered most interventions in the period was Woodrow Wilson, with 89, followed by Lyndon Johnson, with 65 . . . many of these were planned under the assassinated John Kennedy, whom he accused of responsibility for the "interventionist strategy" of the 1960s.' *Latin American Newsletter,* London, 21 November 1975.

61. The CIA involvement in subversive activities in Latin America came out into the open in 1973, but previous references are made in Gregorio Selser, *Espionage en America Latina* (El Pentagono y las Technicas Sociologicas), Iguazu, Buenos Aires, 1966).

62. See part II in NACLA Handbook, *The U.S. Military Apparatus* (Berkeley and New York, 1972).

63. In a series of articles published in *La Opinion,* Buenos Aires, an important Latin American military general in dymos (incognito) reports on the Latin American-USA military relations. Referring to the Tenth CEA meeting that took place in Caracas in 1973, while the most pro-American elite elements were favouring a 'collective military defence system' (in other words, the legal possibility of military intervention in other countries) more independent military leaders such as Commander General Carcagno from Argentina, expressed disagreement with such a proposal. (21, 22, 23, and 24 November 1974).

64. *El Cronista Comercial,* Buenos Aires, 5 June 1974.

65. Richard Walton, op. cit., p. 113. Fulbright, partisan of the third option, clearly states the alternatives in a memorandum to President Kennedy, one month before the Bay of Pigs invasion (Karl Meyer, (ed.), *Fulbright of Arkansas* (Lice Inc., Washington, 1963), p. 195) : The question of United States policy toward Cuba involves a choice of two practical possibilities: 1. Overthrow of the Castro regime. 2. Toleration of the Castro regime, combined with efforts to isolate it and to insulate the rest of Latin America from it. To these might be added a third possibility – reformation of the Castro regime. But Castro has had so many opportunities to

reform and has rebuffed all of them that this course seems more theoretical than real. Perhaps, however, it should not be rejected out of hand until the President has consciously satisfied himself, through whatever private channels are available, that it is a futile course to pursue.'

66. J. William Fulbright, op. cit., p. 105. But at the same time the Senator stresses that this policy was never carried out because of the fear of Communism which makes the American leadership hesitate to face the possibilities of social reform, and often it prefers to be the 'friend of military dictators and reactionary oligarchies'.

67. *Clarin*, Buenos Aires, 3 January 1975.

68. *Le Monde,* 18 October 1969.

69. Jose Luis De Imaz, op. cit., p. 9.

70. *La Opinion,* Buenos Aires, 20 December 1972.

71. Richard R. Fagen, "The 'New Dialogue' on Latin America", *Society,* vol. II, no. 6, September 1974, p. 30.

72. In an article welcoming 'one of those infrequent and brief periods in which Henry Kissinger looks south', the author recognises that 'The United States can hardly give Latins everything they want. But it can pay them close attention. That would make up for a lot.' (Stephen S. Rosenfeld 'The Shift in U.S.-Latin Relations', *International Herald Tribune,* 16 April 1975).

73. *La Opinion,* Buenos Aires, 17 July 1973.

74. Elsy Fors, 'Sela: in Defense of Latin America', *Direct from Cuba,* (Prensa Latina), no. 131, 15 October 1975.

75. *International Herald Tribune,* 19 February 1976, pp. 1-2.

6 CONCLUSIONS

The comparative analysis of the superpowers' behaviour in the spheres of direct influence underlines the importance of the external variables for a better understanding of the position of the countries of the two regions in the international system.[1] For such penetrated societies any attempt to provide explanations about social and political change based on the analysis of the country as a closed or quasi-closed system might lead to erroneous conclusions.

From the international system variables, the most significant are the superpowers' policies underlying the direct relationship between the bipolar character of the world community and the existence of two regions of absolute dominance. In fact, the decisive presence of the Soviet Union in Eastern Europe and of the United States in Latin America can be considered as a 'normal state of affairs',[2] irrrespective of the present type of regime. However, the standing aspirations of Russian and North American leaders for control of the adjacent areas are better legitimised in an international system where their status of primacy is universally recognised. It is worth stressing again that the comparison between the superpowers' behaviour in the spheres of direct influences has shown the existence of similarities and differences, and no automatic equalisation should be inferred. A major explanation accounting for the differences is to be found in the distinctive internal political structure and ideology of each of the superpowers. State control economy and totalitarianism, private transnational enterprises in a oligopolitic market, respect for civil rights and opposition are important aspects for determining the type of dominance relationship.

In both cases, it has been shown that the superpowers' attitude towards a country in their sphere of direct influence tends to be more rigid than towards countries outside this region. Different modalities of control characterise each dependency link, but the small impact of multipolarity in Eastern Europe and Latin America stresses even more the actual control of the superpowers over these regions. While economic recession and the oil crisis have recently shown the importance of states not considered to be individual powers (such as the Arab bloc), their ascendancy over the superpowers' 'satellites' was felt less than in other subsystems.

Another interesting observation departing from the analysis of the superpowers' influence in their sphere is that intraregional conflict has decreased; i.e. tight control has in most cases avoided a confrontation among member states in the subsystem. On the other hand nearly all situations of extreme stalemate or conflict have taken the character of a 'client' rebellion or attempted emancipation from the paramount superpower.

The regional context is not to be overlooked since the cohesiveness of the subsystem has direct implications for the possiblity of firmer resistance to the superpower domination. In the case of Latin America, strong and deep-rooted ties have facilitated the development of institutions that exclude the United States and a great deal of regional interaction takes place without the intervention of this superpower. Without disregarding the Soviet Union's inspired type of dominance relationship one could argue that a more extreme intervention is facilitated by the lack of unity and the diversity of historical developments in East European countries. It should be stressed, however, that the regional variables can provide only a partial explanation for the condition of dependency. Spiegel and Cantori's attempt to rank subsystems according to the four regional variables, risks creating a false interpretation of causation, in which the degree of cohesiveness and development determine the higher indpendence of the region in the international system. It is not surprising to find no particular elaboration of the Eastern European subsystem presented in their book, since that analysis could prove to contradict this assumption. The omission of the influence of the international system on the subsystems' ranking fails to explain the role of the spheres of direct influence of the superpowers. Latin America, better placed in the ranking than Asian and African subsystems, is nevertheless less independent in the international system. Eastern Europe, only slightly behind Western Europe in the four pattern variables, has played a much less significant part in world politics. Cantori and Spiegel's framework alone is insufficient as a tool for an explanatory analysis of subsystems in which the intrusive subsystem is partially or totally integrated, as in our case, and therefore additional elements have been introduced into this work.

The same line of reasoning could be extended to the analysis of the individual countries in the spheres of influence thereby raising the question whether the more developed and cohesive states have a better chance of obtaining greater autonomy from the superpower. Without ignoring the relative importance of these elements it should be pointed out that the deviant cases (Yugoslavia, Romania, Albania, Cuba and

Peru), did not appear to show a direct relationship. Other characteristics seemed to have played a more relevant role: out of the six introduced as working hypotheses when treating the peripheral or deviant
cases, one could find that all were relevant in the majority of cases.
More specifically, the first proposition about the 'maximalisation of
intrinsic military potential up to, but not beyond the divide between
conventional and nuclear weapons' is well identified in the cases of
Yugoslavia and Cuba but not in the other three cases. The fourth one,
considering the essential role played by the rival superpower in reinforcing the deviationist regime, is not met in the case of Albania where
China playes such a protective role.

The macro-approach to the subject should not lead to an extremist
deterministic perception; that the countries find themselves in an
inescapable prisoner status. The fact that it was possible to have
mentioned the cases of five varying exceptions of peripheral or semi-
peripheral states in the spheres of influence is *per se* an eloquent argument for proving that when domestic forces proceed in a cautious way,
or when internal unity is strong – and when the international and
regional condition might facilitate it – a different or more independent
relationships toward the superpower is obtainable. All the same, reservations should be expressed as to the possible chances of other
countries successfully following the paths of Yugoslavia, Cuba, Peru or
Romania. The superpowers' alertness to the danger of deviationist tendencies among states in their sphere of influence is to a certain extent a
direct function of the quantity of existing exceptions, with the curve at
the moment indicating that the chances for further states achieving any
independence have been drastically reduced by the mere existence of
the present exceptions.

Although some of the deviant cases have already been well established – i.e. Yugoslavia, Cuba – there is still a feeling that exceptions
are more temporary than superpower rule. As they are usually created
by a miscalculation or mistake on the side of the dominant superpower policy-makers, the option of intervening in order to bring back
the rebel to the submissive line is still open. The question relates rather
to the *cost* of such a possible action than to the actual *capability* of
carrying it out. Romania, Yugoslavia and even Albania are well aware
of such a possibility and in the case of Latin America, plans for the
physical extermination of Fidel Castro and the change of leadership in
the Peruvian military elite clearly demonstrate the extreme fragility of
the exceptional cases. To return to a final comment on the widely dis-
cusssed case of the missile crisis, one could conclude that the 'adven-

turist' strategy of Khrushchev finally led only to the re-affirmation of the principle of supremacy of the United States in Latin America. While President Kennedy had considered on his own initiative the possibility of withdrawing the Jupiter missiles from Turkey even *before* the crisis, when presented by the Soviet Union as a precondition of their with-drawal from Cuba, such a reciprocal claim was rejected by Washington. Though in both cases geographical proximity to the superpowers posed a similar threat, Cuba was considered by the United States as *inside* the sphere of their influence and the Soviets' miscalculated attempt as somewhat similar to an American decision to install nuclear missiles in a deviant East European country. This case, then, further illustrates the limitations imposed by the superpowers even on those cases considered as flagrant exceptions to the rule.

Finally, another proposition that seems to bear close proximity to the possibility of a 'satellite' country gaining a more independent status relates to the character of the regime, or, in other words, the extent to which the leadership can count on popular support. In such penetrated societies one could enunciate the hypothesis that 'the more popular the leadership the greater the possibilities of gaining independence from the superpower'. It is sometimes the process of emancipation itself that contributes considerably to making the rulers more accepted by the people, a fact that serves — to a limited extent — to dissuade the superpower from a persistent interventionist action. The other side of the problem is very typical of the spheres of influence, by which dic-tators in Latin America and *apparatchniks* in Eastern Europe tend to rely heavily on their respective superpowers, sometimes even more than expected by their 'masters'.[3]

The second part of the book dealt with the evaluation of the policies of the superpowers in both eastern Europe and Latin America. As regards the *first* set of options, out of the three alternative policy out-comes of the superpowers towards the states in their *own* sphere of influence one could say broadly that throughout the different admini-strations since 1948 the 'communal' (third) one based on a principle of free will co-operation has never been pursued. Since 'peaceful coexis-tence' both the Soviet Union and the United States have attempted to follow the second alternative of restricting the freedom of action of the states in their sphere of direct influence to a middle position. Resorting repeatedly to the first interventionist option, they preferred usually to grant some degree of autonomy which would create a more positive type of relationship.

When considering the *second* set of options it is not to be doubted

that the choice of an insurrectional strategy was never seriously considered by either the Soviet Union or the United States in Latin America
and Eastern Europe respectively. It was rather between the second and
third options that their attitudes have varied. Basically following the
third alternative, Washington has recognised on diverse occasions the
fact that any possible opening of Eastern European countries to the
West has to be related to the favourable disposition of the Soviet
Union and therefore Moscow appeared to be the key for any change in
this area. The Soviet Union has repeatedly attempted to approach
Latin American governments irrespective of their political orientation.
This second option, for the United States, when compared with the
Soviet opportunities in Latin America, is much more restricted;
basically due to the tight political control exercised by the Kremlin
within its sphere of influence. In both cases, the relations that have
developed between the countries of both spheres of influence with the
rival superpowers are basically 'non-political' in nature. This is shown
by the fact that on the surface at least, neither superpower has
attempted to challenge the basic political orientation or loyalty of the
subsystems to the respective leaderships. Furthermore, until recently,
the intensity of the efforts shown by the United States in Eastern
Europe has been of a lesser strength than that displayed by Soviet
policy in Latin America.

Recent developments in world politics can be considered in this
general framework. The results of the Helsinki European Conference
seem to indicate that the United States has openly legitimised the
existence of the *status quo* in Eastern Europe. On the other hand,
specific clauses guaranteeing a wider respect for human rights have been
signed by the Soviet Union and the satellite regimes. This exchange
does not necessarily mean a rapid application of these principles. On
the contrary, there is some fear, expressed particularly by Yugoslavia
that since these 'liberal' clauses could create exaggerated expectations
in Eastern Europe, that the immediate Soviet reaction would be to
increase controls even more, so that no false illusions could be developed. In the long run, though, it is believed that since the Soviet Union
can now see herself even less threatened in her quest for hegemony in
Eastern Europe, this could lead to some gradual relaxation.

In Latin America, the idea of a better economic integration, spon-
sored by the important Mexican and Venezuelan regimes has been formalised in SELA. To what extent this proposed new system is going to
work remains to be seen. But this initiative falls, no doubt, within the
framework of freedom of action generally tolerated by the United

States. This is especially so after they have received a round of public
criticism of the covert actions planned or executed by the CIA in Latin
America, and also because of a low level of interest manifested by
Washington *vis-á-vis* Latin America: it could therefore be conceived that
such a move would not meet obstinate opposition from the 'big
brother'.

In both areas, such processes provoke an interesting question: what
will be the impact of the present atmosphere of *detente* and the trend
to wider fields of understanding between the superpowers, on the
spheres of influence? While this process may produce, on a global scale,
a slightly more liberal or tolerant attitude towards smaller states, it
can have the opposite effect of dissuading the superpowers from jeo-
pardising their achievements at the international level by challenging
the *status quo* existing in the rival's sphere of influence, and as a result
submitting those countries to further dependency.

Indeed it is a sad conclusion for the left-wing forces in the Latin
American continent to draw that for the time being it is quite evident
that neither the option of revolution or of electoral success has a realistic possibility of achieving power and, what is more difficult, of
maintaining it. The margins of security of the United States reduced
freedom of action to moderate changes in the social structure and in
the dependence relationship. The cases of the 'populist' regimes of
Costa Rica and Venezuela, representing a sort of midway type of social
democratic alternative, are perhaps the furthest a regime can allow
itself to reform while being quite secure in its moves. Independent attitudes in the regional framework, nationalisation of US interest with
due compensation, timid attempts at redistribution of wealth, full
maintenance of human rights, etc. are policy elements tolerated by the
superpower. At the same time, a basic allegiance to Western democracy,
the respect of private initiative and restraint in foreign policy remain a
required precondition of other changes.

In Eastern Europe the need for a gradualistic strategy should be
emphasised even more. In a study of Romania's foreign policy, three
possible lines of action are suggested:[4] co-operative submission to the
superpower; direct confrontation leading to war and conflict; or a
varying policy of both co-operation and confrontation. Only the third
way could present any possiblity of success for a country situated in a
superpower sphere of influence. While a miscalculation by the superpowers, or a specific international situation may provide the chance for
a 'satellite' country to emancipate itself using means of direct confrontation, but without reaching the stage of war (or a limited version,

as with the case of the Bay of Pigs invasion of Cuba), this in itself is an exception.

There are still many questions about the spheres of direct influence that remain unanswered and others that require more systematic elaboration, among them the following:

(a) The preparation of indicators that may permit the measurement, or at least the comparison with more exact instruments, of the dependence relationship of the different countries in the sphere of direct influence *vis-à-vis* the dominating superpower.

(b) On a subsystem level, to analyse how unique the spheres of direct influence are when compared with other regions adding to the four pattern variables of Spiegel and Cantori other external determinants.

(c) It is important to provide further explanations as to the relationship of the existence of two spheres to the present bipolarised structure of the international system; a deeper examination of this aspect could lead to interesting perspectives as to how the incorporation of more superpowers (i.e. China) in the international system, if recognised as such, could carry along with it the formation of a corresponding new sphere of influence, and how such multiplication could reduce the present level of dependency on the existing spheres of influence.

(d) A deeper investigation of the deviationist cases in both spheres of influence may reveal additional propositions as to the causes of their greater independence. In this particular context it could be most fascinating to study the types of relationship maintained among the deviationist countries themselves and how their awareness of their particular status is increasingly linking them.

(e) Another interesting aspect of the superpowers' policy in their spheres of influence is what was termed the 'margins of political security'. The extent of freedom granted to the countries in a subsystem varies in relation to several variables, as mentioned briefly in this work. Further analysis of this phenomenon is required with correlations of them more accurately established and recorded.

I would like to conclude by referring again to the highly sensitive nature of the comparative exercise that has been undertaken. In attempting to compare the foreign policies of the USSR and the US in the adjacent spheres of influence, one is faced with certain problems of a normative nature. Earlier published work of mine dealing with this question produced, paradoxically, two diametrically opposed reactions;

one positive and the other negative, but both wrongly assuming that in my text I considered the superpowers' policies as identical, as in an equation.[5] Therefore I consider it necessary, once again, to stress that in using the term 'comparative', in this case or in any other, one is concerned with the exposure of significant regularities, and patterns of behaviour. Everything is comparable on principle and for any two objects at least one common feature can always be discerned. If both David and Goliath fell under the category of 'human beings' we can well accept the fact that any two states — regardless of size, ideology or degree of development — are comparable: this statement is significant in our case, especially when comparing the existing differences between Soviet and American policy, as they are often accompanied by levels of power which are remarkably similar.

To a great part of the industrialised Western society, the suffering of East Europeans seems more acute than Latin American hardships. Maybe the knowledge of the glorious past of some of the East European countries, the close ties that have been maintained with some of them in recent times, the greater understanding of the meaning of totalitarianism by citizens of representative democratic regimes, and the fear of communism, makes a Western audience more sensitive to their plight. Latin America is easily forgotten. It is geographically distant, there is a more generalised perception that the people of Latin America are not yet politically mature and are economically backward; that dictatorships and violence are inherent in the Latin American continent, existing before and without North American intervention.

In the same way, if one was requested to pass a judgement about which type of dependence is more painful, for many of us it is quite obvious that deprivation of human rights and totalitarian control over our private lives appear immensely more horrifying. However, the alternative presented in Latin America, where a greater extent of freedom is allowed, should be viewed against a background of economic inequality, misery and poverty that makes the majority of the population unable to enjoy the full exercise of those rights. To mention only one aspect, freedom of press means little when the majority of the population is illiterate. The dichotomic argument of economic equality (Eastern Europe), *vis-à-vis* political democracy (Latin America), is largely a fallacy. Very few regimes in Latin America maintain a functioning democracy while inequality among and within the popular democracies is more profound than in many Western societies. Whatever the personal opinion might be as to the extent of injustice involved in *each* sphere of direct influence, it is my hope that this book has contributed to the formation of a deeper understanding of the issue of super-power domination in both regions.

NOTES

1. Chalmers has insisted that with reference to Latin America 'any theories of comparative politics must pay more attention to external factors than has usually been the case'. While Latin American economists have somewhat exaggerated the uni-causation of their countries' economic situation to the dependence on a foreign power, political scientists have usually adopted the other extreme attitude. Douglas A. Chalmers, 'Developing on the Periphery: External Factors in Latin American Politics', James N. Rozenau (ed.), *Linkage Politics,* The Free Press, N.Y., 1969, p.90.
2. 'In a normal state of European equilibrium, Russia would naturally have the principal influence in Eastern Europe.' H. Seton-Watson, *Eastern Europe between the Two Wars,* op. cit., p. 268.
3. In the words of the Chilean President General Pinochet: 'We are better friends of the United States than the United States is to us' (*Sunday Times,* 1 December 1975).
4. Stephen F. Larrabee, 'The Rumanian Challenge to Soviet Hegemony', *Orbis,* Vol. XVII (Spring 1973), p. 227.
5. *Le Monde,* Paris, article by Charles Vanhecke, 'Amerique Latine: Les Caribes restent le seul point chaud', 23 May 1972, and *La Opinion,* Buenos Aires, an article by Sergio Barrocal, (AFP), 'La Politica de Estados Unidos para Latinoamerica es Igual a la que Moscu aplica en Europa Oriental', 4 March 1972.

INDEX